ENCLAVES OF AMERICA

ENCLAVES OF AMERICA

THE RHETORIC OF AMERICAN
POLITICAL ARCHITECTURE
ABROAD, 1900–1965

Ron Robin

PRINCETON UNIVERSITY PRESS   PRINCETON, NEW JERSEY

Copyright © 1992 by Princeton University Press
Published by Princeton University Press, 41 William Street,
Princeton, New Jersey 08540
In the United Kingdom: Princeton University Press, Oxford
All Rights Reserved

Library of Congress Cataloging-in-Publication Data
Robin, Ron Theodore.
Enclaves of America : the rhetoric of American political
architecture abroad, 1900–1965 / Ron Robin.
p.   cm.
Includes bibliographical references and index.
ISBN 0-691-04805-3
1. Embassy buildings—United States.   2. National cemeteries,
American.   3. Architecture and state—United States.
4. Architecture, American.   I. Title.
NA4441.R63   1992
725'.17—dc20   92-8520

This book has been composed in Linotron Sabon

Princeton University Press books are printed
on acid-free paper and meet the guidelines
for permanence and durability of the Committee
on Production Guidelines for Book Longevity
of the Council on Library Resources

Printed in the United States of America

10 9 8 7 6 5 4 3 2 1

Contents

List of Illustrations	vii
Preface	xi
Abbreviations	2
Introduction	3
PART ONE	13
1. Prologue: Hesitant Beginnings	15
2. Incident at Sivry-sur-Meuse: Great War Monuments and Cemeteries in Western Europe	30
3. From Palace to Plantation House: The Political Architecture of American Embassies, 1926–1932	63
PART TWO	89
4. Interlude: Marking Time, 1933–1945	91
5. "Our Own Land on Foreign Soil": The Overseas Military Cemeteries of World War II	109
6. Foreign Bodies: American Imperial Architecture, 1945–1965	136
7. Epilogue: Retreat	167
Notes	179
Bibliographical Essay	197
Index	203

List of Illustrations

1. Plan for Manila, 1905 (Daniel H. Burnham, architect). From *Proceedings of the Thirty-ninth Annual Convention of the American Institute of Architects* (Washington, D.C., 1906) 27
2. Montfaucon Monument (John Russell Pope, sculptor). Courtesy of the American Battle Monuments Commission 51
3. St. Mihiel Monument (Egerton Swartwout, architect). Courtesy of the American Battle Monuments Commission 52
4. Chateau-Thierry Monument (Paul Cret, architect). Courtesy of the American Battle Monuments Commission 53
5. Chapel, Aisne-Marne Cemetery (Cram and Ferguson, architects). Courtesy of the American Battle Monuments Commission 56
6. Chapel, Somme Military Cemetery (George Howe, architect). Courtesy of the American Battle Monuments Commission 58
7. Oise-Aisne Military Cemetery (Jacques Greber, landscape architect). Courtesy of the American Battle Monuments Commission 59
8. American Embassy, Rio de Janeiro, Brazil, ca. 1923 (Frank Packard, architect). Courtesy of the National Archives 68
9. American Embassy, Mexico City, 1925 (J. E. Campbell, architect). Courtesy of the National Archives 69
10. Two views of the American Embassy, Beijing, China, ca. 1920 (supervising architect of the Treasury Department) 72
11. United States Post Office, Newport, Kentucky, 1898 (supervising architect of the Treasury Department). From *Annual Report of the Supervising Architect of the Treasury, 1898* (Washington, D.C., 1898) 73
12. British Embassy and Chancery, Washington, D.C., 1927–1930 (Sir Edwin Lutyens, architect). From *National Republic* 18 (December 1931) 77
13. Model for American Legation, Managua, Nicaragua, 1927 (Aldrich and Chase, architects). From Foreign Service Buildings Commission, *Report of the Progress on the Purchase of Sites and Construction of Buildings for the Foreign Service* (Washington, D.C., 1929) 81
14. American Consulate, Amoy, China, 1931 (Elliot Hazzard, architect). Courtesy of *Foreign Service Journal* 82
15. Artist's impression of American Embassy, Lima, Peru, 1931 (architect unknown). Courtesy of *Foreign Service Journal* 83
16. American Consulate, Yokohama, Japan, 1932 (Jay Morgan, architect). Courtesy of *Foreign Service Journal* 87
17. American Embassy, Tokyo, Japan, 1932 (Harold Van Buren Magonigle, architect). Courtesy of the Department of State 87

LIST OF ILLUSTRATIONS

18. Artist's impression of American Legation, Monrovia, Liberia, 1938 (supervising architect of the Treasury Department). Courtesy of *Foreign Service Journal* — 95
19. Remodeled, present-day version of original Monrovian building. Courtesy of the Department of State — 95
20. American Legation, Baghdad, Iraq, 1938 (architect unknown). Photograph by W. Robert Moore, © National Geographic Society. Courtesy of the National Archives — 97
21. American Embassy, Chungking, China, 1943 (architect unknown). Courtesy of *Foreign Service Journal* — 98
22. American Embassy, Lima, Peru, 1944 (Leland King and Franz Jaquet, architects). Courtesy of the Department of State — 100
23. Artist's impression of American Legation, Managua, Nicaragua, 1940 (Harrie T. Lindeberg, architect). Courtesy of *Foreign Service Journal* — 103
24. Memorial chapel and hemicycle at Manila Cemetery (Gardner A. Dailey, architect). Courtesy of the American Battle Monuments Commission — 118
25. Memorial chapel at Ardennes Military Cemetery (Reinhard, Hofmeister, and Walquist, architects). Courtesy of the American Battle Monuments Commission — 119
26. Artist's impression of proposed chapel at Luxembourg Cemetery (Ralph Walker, architect). From Ralph Walker, *Ralph Walker, Architect* (New York, 1957); sketch by E. P. Chrystie — 121
27. Memorial sculpture. Courtesy of the American Battle Monuments Commission — 123
28. Lorraine Military Cemetery (Allyn R. Jennings, landscape architect). Courtesy of the American Battle Monuments Commission — 125
29. Margraten Cemetery (M. Rapuano, landscape architect). Courtesy of the American Battle Monuments Commission — 125
30. Donald DeLue, *The Spirit of American Youth*. Courtesy of the American Battle Monuments Commission — 129
31. Paul Manship, *Brothers in Arms*. Courtesy of the American Battle Monuments Commission — 130
32. Side panels, Ardennes Military Cemetery (Dean Cornwell, designer). Courtesy of the American Battle Monuments Commission — 131
33. American Embassy, Rio de Janeiro, Brazil, 1953 (Harrison and Abramovitz, architects). Courtesy of the Department of State — 144
34. American Embassy, London, Great Britain, 1956 (Eero Saarinen, architect). Courtesy of the Department of State — 154
35. American Embassy, Dublin, Ireland, 1959 (John Johansen, architect). Courtesy of the Department of State — 156
36. American Embassy, Athens, Greece, 1962 (Walter Gropius, architect). Courtesy of the Department of State — 158
37. American Consulate, Fukuoka, Japan, 1961 (Clark, Beuttler, and Rockrise, architects). Courtesy of the Department of State — 159

LIST OF ILLUSTRATIONS ix

38. American ambassador's residence, Baghdad, Iraq, 1961 (José Luis Sert, architect). Courtesy of the Department of State 159
39. American Embassy, Accra, Ghana, 1959 (Harry Weese, architect). Courtesy of the Department of State 161
40. Model for American Embassy, Rabat, Morocco, 1961 (Ketchum, Gina, and Sharp, architects). Courtesy of the Department of State 163
41. American Embassy, New Delhi, India, 1959 (Edward Stone, architect). Courtesy of the Department of State 164
42. Frederick Hart, *Three American Soldiers*. Photograph by the author 170
43. Model for American Embassy, Bangkok, Thailand, 1959 (John Carl Warnecke, architect). Courtesy of the Department of State 171

Preface

IN GEORGE ORWELL'S "Shooting an Elephant," a young colonial official is called upon by the natives to subdue a rampaging elephant—he being the only one in the village who is permitted to use a firearm. By the time he finds the animal, it has passed through its temporary rage and therefore does not need to be killed. Orwell discovers, however, that he has no choice. The villagers expect him to use his weapon; they demand that he behave in accordance with the etiquette of the sahib. As a ruler he must follow conventions of power, or lose face. This book is about the American people's own observance of the etiquette of empire, a hesitant and sometimes self-contradictory effort to produce their own imperial symbols, lest they lose face.

Throughout the first sixty-five years of the twentieth century the United States planted impressive architectural statements of its power in its burgeoning sphere of influence. On the surface, these exercises in political architecture resembled those of French and British predecessors. Some crucial differences in both style and content, however, suggest a different agenda behind the American projects.

To begin with, American monuments were rarely accompanied by significant and enduring changes in the internal arrangement of the host countries. Although they often behaved to the contrary, Americans apparently believed that they could rule by example and through symbols of power instead of relying on despotic colonial bureaucracies and permanent military garrisons.

But perhaps the most intriguing feature of American political architecture was its somewhat enigmatic political significance. The United States erected a wide range of symbolic monuments and edifices throughout the world; but these architectural projects elicited very little debate. Government files, professional periodicals, and the memoirs of protagonists are replete with grand technical details. There is, however, no theoretical discourse. Unlike the British and French, the Americans did not develop an imperial school of architecture.

The lack of theory, as well as the frequent shifts in style, suggests an uncertain concept of empire. These artifacts of poorly defined and constantly changing political content reveal a lack of consensus over the desired dimensions of America's global role. My analysis of American political symbolism abroad conforms to the conventional historiographical divisions of American foreign policy, from the rise to power at the turn of the century through the relative decline in the 1960s and after. However,

I have not discovered the imprint of an overriding vision on the making of this country's foreign relations, such as the constant presence of variations of the missionary impulse, or the unrelenting pursuit of well-defined economic goals.

At its most fundamental level, the architecture of American diplomacy indicates a fitful approach to the mission of foreign policy. Neither tenacious bureaucrats nor ambitious politicians, nor for that matter their constituents, controlled national symbolism abroad. American foreign policy, as represented through its monuments, appears to have been characterized by jostling, infighting, and the ephemeral triumphs of a variety of groups espousing different and sometimes competing agendas, be they civil servants seeking continuity, politicians aspiring to leave their mark on history, or experts attempting to ignore the counsel of laymen. The ultimate result was, of course, an architecture of compromise, which never satisfied entirely the objectives of any of the parties, and did not reflect a monolithic approach to world affairs. Under the facade of a single-minded pursuit of a Pax Americana lies an uneasy and continually shifting compromise between competing interests within the American body politic.

Many colleagues and friends have aided me in my attempts to understand this nexus of architecture and politics. I owe a deep intellectual debt to Gunther Barth, who taught me to pay attention to visual artifacts. Akira Iriye, Walter LaFeber, Collin Jones, Edward Linenthal, and Peter Bacon Hales took time out from their busy schedules to comment on the manuscript. I am grateful for the encouragement and goodwill of Paula Fass, Paul Boyer, and Andy Heinze.

Researching and writing American history from abroad is an expensive and difficult feat. The Council for the Exchange of Foreign Scholars, the United States–Israel Educational Foundation, and the American Council of Learned Scholars (ACLS) offered much-needed financial support. A year as an ACLS Visiting Scholar at the University of California, Berkeley, provided constant intellectual stimulation.

I owe special thanks to the many librarians and archivists who have aided me in this project, in particular, Susan Snyder and Elizabeth Grossman at the environmental design library at Berkeley, as well as Hank Griffith and Susan Wilkerson at the National Building Museum in Washington, D.C. Lore Mika at the State Department and the staff of the American Battle Monuments Commission researched and supplied me with most of the illustrations in this book. *National Geographic* and *Foreign Service Journal* have graciously permitted me to reproduce illustrations from their respective publications.

I have had the good fortune to enjoy the moral support of friends and family, in particular, my in-laws Shlomo and Hanna Wolff, my mother Shani, and my father Eli, whose love of architecture and engineering I share. I am deeply grateful for the good humor and hospitality of Jim and Jean Collin, and the moral support of Lyda Beardsley, Peter Barta, and Daniel Krauskopf. At Princeton University Press, Edward Tenner, Lauren Osborne, and Annette Theuring have shown uncommon civility and professionalism in preparing the manuscript for publication.

I dedicate this book to Livi Wolff Robin and our children, Gal, Sivan, Noa, and Matan, my constant companions and frequent fliers during our 1990–1991 wanderings between Israel and the United States.

ENCLAVES OF AMERICA

Abbreviations

AAP	Architectural Advisory Panel, Office of Foreign Buildings Operations, Department of State
ABMC	American Battle Monuments Commission
AEF	American Expeditionary Forces
AIA	American Institute of Architects
CFA	Commission of Fine Arts
DEMO	British Directorate of Estate Management Overseas, Department of the Environment
FBO	Office of Foreign Buildings Operations, Department of State
FSBC	Foreign Service Buildings Commission
IWGC	Imperial War Graves Commission
NBM	National Building Museum, Embassy Files, Washington, D.C.
RG 59	Files of the Department of State, Record Group 59, National Archives, Washington, D.C.
RG 66	Files of the Commission of Fine Arts, Record Group 66, National Archives, Washington, D.C.
RG 117	Files of the American Battle Monuments Commission, Record Group 117, National Archives, Suitland, Maryland
RG 353	Interdepartmental government correspondence, Record Group 353, National Archives, Washington, D.C.
USIS	United States Information Service

Introduction

AN ALUMINUM EAGLE with a thirty-five-foot wingspan and a golden sheen unleashed a storm of controversy in 1960. Perched over the entrance to the new American Embassy in London, this heroic-sized emblem heightened an ongoing debate about American symbolism in foreign lands. Critics, led by Columbia University historian Richard B. Morris, questioned the use of a symbol of "naked power" to represent American ambitions abroad. Morris invoked Thomas Jefferson, who had never cared much for the bird, and cited examples of callous emperors from forgotten times who had adopted the eagle as a metaphor for oppressive power. Europeans had a better knowledge of history than Americans, he warned; they were liable to interpret the statue as a sign of American rapacity and imperialism. "An eagle screams," Morris wrote, "but a powerful and confident nation can afford to communicate with others with greater composure."[1] Supporters led by the embassy's architect, Eero Saarinen, responded that the eagle was a traditional American symbol. Its image was acceptable because in the modern mind the bird represented "courage, strength, heroism and keenness of vision."[2]

The controversy, then, was between defenders who perceived the eagle as a suitable symbol and critics who longed for a more subtle iconographical artifact, such as a representation of Columbia or Lady Liberty. No one questioned the appropriateness of heroic-sized American motifs. By now, some sixty-odd years into the twentieth century, high-profile symbols of America in foreign lands were quite commonplace. During the course of the twentieth century, and as part of its efforts to consolidate its international standing, the United States had systematically constructed a wide array of federally owned edifices and monuments abroad. Under the guidance of specialized federal agencies, an official image of the United States had been etched in stone throughout the world.

The advent of the World Wars and their most meaningful result for the United States, the emergence of the country as the main beneficiary of a new world order, functioned as a catalyst for this exercise in propaganda through architecture. In the aftermath of the Great War, a network of eight American cemeteries and numerous monuments speckled the landscape of western Europe. The American Battle Monuments Commission (ABMC), a newly formed federal bureaucracy whose task it was to supervise the form and content of these memorials, added fourteen cemeteries to this arsenal after World War II. These artifacts of Americana, according to the ABMC, were not planned solely to commemorate individuals who had lost their lives in the service of their country. They were, in the words of their architects, explicit artifacts of "American patriotism and culture" expressed through the evocative medium of "architecture and sculpture"; moreover, they were deliberately planned for foreign display.[3]

The monuments of war were not the only official icons of America on foreign soil. They were complemented by ambitious designs for new legations and embassies. Working under the assumption that the country's diplomatic structures often offered the only glimpse of the American way of life for the vast majority of foreigners, the State Department created an infrastructure to maintain and design these buildings. This Office of Foreign Buildings Operations (FBO) built about thirty buildings in the 1920s and the early 1930s. Following World War II, hundreds of additional diplomatic structures were constructed as symbols of America, rather than simply as functional abodes to house the government's representatives. These buildings, according to official policy, needed to look like "oases of American soil" in alien surroundings.[4]

On the surface, these two separate projects seem unrelated. The commemoration of sacrifice in battle appears to have little in common with the routine business of foreign relations. However, neither the construction of battle monuments nor that of the legations was approached as a narrow, functional project. Both schemes were designed to enhance foreign policy objectives through architectural symbolism. As symbolic rather than functional structures, the cemeteries and legations harbored a range of meanings beyond their nominal roles. As symbols of the American entity abroad they conspicuously portrayed the foreign policy objectives of the United States. Both the cemeteries and the embassies were means to broad global aspirations. As instruments of public diplomacy, they strove to win the sympathies of, or induce awe among, foreign beholders.

The projects were interrelated technically as well. From the very beginning, the symbolism of the various structures was subject to the scrutiny of the Commission of Fine Arts (CFA), the federal body whose task it was to create and monitor a formula of national symbolism. In the case of the ABMC the ultimate authority of the CFA had been written into law. The relationship between the CFA and the FBO was more informal. Even though the State Department was not required to obtain prior approval for its designs from the CFA, routine consultations were the norm.

The architects and artists involved in these affairs constituted an additional common denominator. Both the FBO and the ABMC relied primarily on the services of the private sector rather than the talents of government-employed artists and architects. The architects were prominent members of the American Institute of Architects (AIA); they belonged to a select group of professionals who had been involved in federally ordained architectural enterprises within the United States. The sculptors and muralists were invariably members of the National Sculpture Society, a conservative body of artists finely attuned to the objectives of its federal clients and somewhat hostile to the avant-garde. Moreover, the actual form of symbolism employed by these individuals relied on a shared prescription for translating ideas into images. Their works of art were designed to distinguish the United States from other national entities by the transposition of its principles and goals into a supposedly universal language of visual form.

This extensive use of political architecture was not a mere aesthetic sideshow of American design. Rather, these symbols of America abroad functioned as substitutes for the use of military might. To be sure, the United States had shown little reluctance to enhance its international strategy through the use of force. American military intervention abroad increased simultaneously with the growing perception of a symbiotic relationship between the nation's well-being and the affairs of others. Yet, in a departure from traditional imperial practices, the United States avoided the trappings of conventional colonialism. The sustained presence of troops on foreign soil and the direct rule of the affairs of others by means of a colonial bureaucracy had been the exception rather than the rule. Instead, the United States consistently sought to display surrogate representations of its power. Political architecture, a symbolic illustration of American power and willingness to intervene forcefully in the theater of international relations, played a significant role in the complex mission of orchestrating world affairs while refraining from an enduring and large physical presence abroad. Thus an analysis of the symbolism of American architecture abroad reveals the crystallization of fundamental American goals in the international arena.

Foreign policy objectives, as reflected through these architectural endeavors abroad, divide neatly into two periods. The first phase, which began with the construction of Great War battle memorials and ended roughly during the first years of the Depression, represented a stage of experimentation in which nothing more than an incoherent American presence abroad was announced. The battle monuments boasted heroic proportions but very little originality. For the most part, they echoed the styles and symbolism of Allied sister projects: pseudo-classical structures promoted a sense of commonality with other western nations, monotonous landscaping functioned as a symbol of national cohesion, and sculptured gestures of fraternity represented affinity with a fin de siècle European world order (which for all intents and purposes no longer existed).

During this same period, the United States also articulated a strategy of embassy architecture that complemented the political implications of the battle monuments and cemeteries. Under the guidance of the Foreign Service Buildings Commission (FSBC)—the antecedent of the FBO—the United States developed a two-pronged strategy. In most regions of the world, the State Department built palaces according to the regional styles of local elites. These symbols of an American presence were weakened by a nagging incoherence of long-term geopolitical objectives; the palatial embassies were impressive, yet without a trace of American uniqueness. By contrast, the United States employed a different architectural strategy within the confines of its traditional sphere of influence. In Central America and China, the State Department planned replicas of southern plantation manors. These curious structures clashed deliberately with the architecture of the host surroundings. They were icons of paternalism, physical representations of a master-subject relationship that the United States aspired to maintain in these regions.

In many ways, this uniquely American style of "plantation" embassies paved the way for the second generation of political architectural projects. Following the Depression and the further trial of world war, the United States renewed efforts to express its foreign policy through architecture. The new generation of cemeteries and embassies reflected a maturation of objectives, a less self-conscious attitude toward the goal of global preeminence. Accordingly, the monuments of World War II were distinctly American; they paid no tribute to traditional values and were abruptly future-oriented. The symbolism stated unequivocally that the war had been won because of superior American technology and management skills. The iconography implicitly demanded a preferred status for the American political entity in the international arena.

The exact contours of this new American role were articulated forcefully in a new generation of embassies. These innovative structures ostensibly sought to blend uniquely American modern building techniques with local customs. In actual fact, however, the embassies trivialized the traditions of host countries by transforming local functional building techniques into abstract decorations for uniquely American structures. As monuments to American prestige, the embassies demanded deference by demeaning competing ideologies. Redemption of stagnant cultures, the architecture of American embassies implicitly stated, required subordination to innovative, future-oriented American goals.

Foreign policy objectives are of course symbiotically related to internal transitions. They are mirrors of any given society's innermost concerns. Thus, these monuments unwittingly provide a biography of a culture in transition. The passage from a laissez-faire mentality to one befitting a regimented, urban-industrial society affected the style of the monuments and embassies of the pre-Depression era. A process of hyperindustrialization, hastened by the advent of the Great War, produced an American society that espoused technology, but was emotionally committed to preindustrial values. The vast number of war casualties in the cemeteries abroad was itself evidence of an efficient manner of killing that only a regimented industrial society could produce. Nevertheless, these mass cemeteries were replete with symbols of heroic individualism, images of a crusade of volunteer warriors who had matched their particular skills against those of their adversaries. Images of a "war machine," in which the individual was no more than a cog, were attenuated. An illusory, romantic ethos of voluntarism overshadowed the role of government as orchestrator of the war effort.

The architecture of embassies conveyed a preindustrial ethos as well. By the late 1920s, when the majority of Americans resided in cities and worked in factories, the embassies reflected a nostalgia for that antithesis of modern life, the gentrified southern plantation. Contemporary American culture expressed its dissatisfaction with modernity by conjuring up a mythic agrarian utopia in which democracy thrived alongside paternalism. The embassy as plantation house was an integral element of the southern nostalgia that swept through the United States during the first two decades of the twentieth century.

The new generation of post–World War II political architecture in foreign lands revealed changes in America's social and cultural concerns. In the second batch of American military cemeteries abroad, the increasingly important role of an activist government was expressed. A complex government-run battle machine replaced the individual American soldier as the ultimate hero of the war. The voluntarism and individualism played up by the previous batch of cemeteries were gone. Victory, according to the new iconography, was the result of a sophisticated machinery and intricate coordination that only an activist government could accomplish. Above all, these artifacts of an official American image illustrated the centralizing pressures that had eclipsed traditional conceptions of laissez-faire government and unfettered individualism.

The hundreds of diplomatic construction projects of the postwar years highlighted another important transformation of the American social texture. Here, the search for legitimacy by tracing roots to the past was conspicuously absent, as was the celebration of rural democracy. The architecture of embassies suggested that America gained its strength from its future-orientation. Modernization, not the tracing of footsteps to a previous age, functioned as the guiding light of society.

These overseas political architectural projects of the twentieth century are extremely rich sources of information. As historical documents, the federal architectural activities transcend the somewhat narrow field of foreign affairs. They denote significant foreign policy transitions and important internal transformations in the nation's character. Yet, curiously, historians have ignored these very bold articulations of global objectives and their social and cultural foundations. This neglect derives in part from the interdisciplinary nature of the subject matter. American political architecture in foreign lands does not fit into any narrowly defined discipline. It falls in between the cracks of diplomatic history and cultural history; it touches upon the history of art and demands a rudimentary familiarity with the principles of architecture.

An additional obstacle is related to the nature of the sources. Most of the project material is filed in the National Archives in Washington, D.C. However, the voluminous files of the ABMC, the CFA, and the State Department present a frustrating series of problems. The files of the CFA do indeed discuss, albeit briefly, the ideological underpinnings of symbolism. However, the two major file groups, that of the ABMC and the State Department's FBO files, contain mostly technical information. There is much material on engineering problems and financial concerns, but only occasional, mostly vague, references to ideological issues.

One possible explanation for this silence might be that board meetings were mere formal occasions for ratifying policies that had been decided upon elsewhere. Crucial decisions regarding the style and content of the country's symbolic architecture were registered laconically and without debate in the minutes of the ABMC and the FBO. These documents suggest that the recommendations of architects and the occasional opinionated board member were accepted without comment because most committee members were quite confused by their country's sudden rise to global preeminence. They had not formulated strong opinions on the appropriate dimensions of an American presence in foreign fields; they chose silence rather than disclose their bewilderment. Fortunately, this lack of interpretive material in the official records is compensated for somewhat by write-ups in the contemporary press and professional journals. Thus, a composite picture can be pieced together by reading the fragments of information in official files and press comments.

An additional reason for the sparse attention paid by historians to these ambitious projects derives from the fact that these architectural artifacts failed to accomplish their objectives. Failure has led to disinterest. The reasons for this failure are varied. At the most concrete level, failure came about through a faulty relationship between the architects and their client, the federal government. At times, as the following pages will reveal, the final form of the monuments was the result of internal skirmishes within the architectural profession, with only incidental attention being paid to the specifications of the federal client.

Failure resulted also from unfamiliarity with the concept of political architecture. Indeed, the first generation of projects ignored cardinal principles of political symbolism. In emulating the styles of other nations, the first batch of cemeteries and palace embassies failed to produce a unique image of America, one that would set it apart from the pack. As for the plantation embassies, their styles were too introspective, too uniquely American. They were, for the most part, unreadable, totally incomprehensible in foreign surroundings. A different set of problems, but similar results, beset the second generation of political architectural projects abroad. An aggressive architecture, which praised American control of technology while trivializing the accomplishments of other nations, backfired. Rather than arousing awe or admiration, America's symbolic representations triggered animosity. The new nations of the world, in particular, viewed these symbols of a foreign power as an attempt to reshackle them with colonial chains of the past.

All efforts to produce an effective form of political architecture abroad were undermined by a fundamental problem. Politicians and architects consistently produced inappropriate architectural symbols because they entertained unclear and often conflicting concepts of their mission. An inherently conservative and sometimes confused establishment, both political and architectural, coped poorly with the many transitions, crises, and rethinking of values that characterized American society in the sixty-five years studied here. Consequently, American architecture abroad reacted belatedly to the changing times. All too frequently, it vacillated between conflicting values, thereby producing jumbled messages. Under these circumstances failure was inevitable. Political architecture was an unwieldy tool for a democratic society, in which compromise and diversity, rather than a single-minded mission, were the norm.

And yet the ultimate failure of these architectural ambitions should not have led to the banishment of these projects to a historical purgatory. America's political architecture in foreign lands is a good source for tracing national ambitions above and beyond the eccentricities of specific administrations or individual power-wielders. In a society that has always been captivated by the visual arts, this mobilization of art is also a fine indicator of the changing perception of government and national identity during the first sixty-five years of the twentieth century. Thus, the following pages will reveal the ideological underpinnings as well as the iconographical significance of these artifacts of America on foreign soil.

Given the interdisciplinary nature of this study, a few words concerning its theoretical framework may help to clarify my intentions. The work is designed to illuminate the process of harnessing architecture for political purposes. I have defined political architecture as a mode of monumental construction that openly demands some form of privilege for its patrons by distinguishing the particular dimensions of their power from those of rival political entities. The ultimate objective of American political architecture abroad during this period was two-pronged: to extract prerogatives from the host nations, and to offer an alliance with the United States as an alternative to competing demands from other expansionist powers. For the most part this form of national symbolism abroad attempted to fulfill its mission through direct appeal to those ordinary citizens who were exposed to the artifact. America's national architectural artifacts abroad represented an alternative to normal diplomatic channels and conventional forms of international relations. My attempt to decipher the meaning of these artifacts has been constrained, in part, by unforeseen technical difficulties. In return for the cooperation of the State Department—in particular, their granting me permission to use pictures of various embassies—I have agreed not to use blueprints or large overviews of contemporary embassy compounds. Thus, I have limited my discussion of diplomatic architecture to sculptural facades and exteriors, where, indeed, most of the inherent symbolism appeared.

Two basic theoretical assumptions underlie my investigation. To begin with, I have adopted Jules Prown's interpretation of artistic style as a valid form of historical evidence. In any age there are "assumptions, attitudes, values" that are so deeply ingrained in the minds of human beings that they remain unstated. "As such," Prown suggests, "they are most clearly perceivable, not in what a society says . . . but rather in the way in which something is done, produced, or expressed in its style."[5] Certain aspects of society are more clearly expressed through the subtleties of style than through conscious articulation. Generally speaking, the less coherent the verbal statements available, the more likely we are to find evidence of values in stylistic expression. Under these circumstances, it is the task of the cultural historian to "factor out" the function of the artifact, be it a building, chair, or teapot, thus leaving its style as an expression of the fundamental values of its creators. Once we remove from consideration the function of the embassy building as a manipulation of space to supply offices for American governmental activity abroad, or of the military cemetery's provision of burial space, we are left with form and style as evidence of ulterior motives and intentions. By focusing on form rather than function, it is possible to ferret out concepts that receive only veiled references in verbal statements. In fact, given the laconic nature of my sources, I have had little alternative but to work as an archeologist seeking meaning and motivation in style.

The other central assumption of this investigation is what the geographer Peirce Lewis has called a fundamental axiom for deciphering the cultural significance of landscape. Human beings, Lewis has asserted, are quite conservative in the construction of their edifices, whether they are for ceremonial or mundane functions. Societies as well as individuals tend to change styles and adopt different architectural strategies only when confronted with markedly strong cultural, social, or political pressure.[6] I have accepted this assumption, most often used by cultural geographers, as a challenge to seek significant social and cultural change in the background of all stylistic change in both the embassy and cemetery projects. My criteria for differentiating between the trivial and the important, the significant and the peripheral, has been repetition. The recurrence of certain motifs, and the ultimate scuttling of previously prominent architectural forms of symbolism, serves as the basis for the discovery of the impact of culture on the relationship between architects and federal clients during the first sixty-five years of the twentieth century.

"Landscape shifts and adjusts according to the rhythms of our days, the intervention of clients, designers, and users, the forces of an impatient future," Spiro Kostof reminds us.[7] The following pages will document the contributions of a variety of influencing factors—the overbearing architect, the demands of the federal client, and the sometimes elusive impact of routine political pressures. This, then, is not an architectural history, but an attempt to discover how America's concepts of the global arena were etched in stone. The architects mentioned in the following pages were actors in a drama written and directed by State Department officials and other advocates of an active American foreign policy. At times, when the inexperienced directors and scriptwriters appeared confused, these actors fleshed out their roles with personal interpretations. Nevertheless, this study is not an examination of individual talent and virtuosity, but an analysis of the text and stage directions. My goal has been to reconstruct the rhetoric of these monuments and their organization of American political objectives on foreign soil into a coherent statement. I have included mention of many of the diplomatic buildings and military cemeteries. However, my overriding concern has been to discover recurrent themes that demonstrate the evolution of representative symbols of the nation, as well as the transition from restrained concepts of the American dominion to more grandiose designs.

PART ONE

1

Prologue

HESITANT BEGINNINGS

A DISTINGUISHED-LOOKING American wandering through the streets of London during a typically dark and wet evening attracted the attention of a passing policeman. "What are you doing walking about in this beastly weather?" the officer queried. "Better go home." "I have no home," Joseph H. Choate replied, "I am the American ambassador."[1]

This anecdote surfaced frequently during the course of an extensive campaign for expanded diplomatic representation in the early twentieth century. The virtues of the story lay in its disclosure of the quest for a meaningful American presence in other lands. The ambassador's aimless meandering suggested that although the United States had become a force in world politics, it had not developed a clear global sense of purpose. Lacking an official abode—an opportunity to etch in stone its distinguishing qualities—the country could not translate clearly its cardinal principles into a readable and attractive formula. The vignette underscored a new sensitivity to "appearances" in foreign lands, a growing awareness of the need to devise an official American image abroad. Twentieth-century American diplomacy could no longer rely on the uncoordinated good works of private citizens. A forceful policy required sustained guidelines from the government and permanent representation on foreign soil.

Parables of the nation as "home" were not unusual. American public language invariably invoked familial and domestic terms to describe the country's political agenda. Historian George B. Forgie has observed that "in a society that valued progress and equality and in which authority of any kind, no matter how mild, was on the defensive," the concept of family, hearth, and home was the one "hierarchical institution compatible with modernity and democracy."[2] Conversely, metaphors such as "rocky foundations," a "house divided," and "homelessness" were conventional analogies for political crisis, and calls for action.

The curious aspect of the tale of the homeless ambassador is the use of the metaphor to describe political aspirations outside of a familiar geographical setting. In contrast to the traditional image of the home located within firm perimeters, this tale of "home" and "homelessness" beyond the national borders reflected a crucial transition in the American frame of mind.[3] The story suggests that twentieth-century American society, aided by new communication technologies that had expanded horizons and conquered geographical barriers, had discarded traditional divisions of space and distance.[4] The political metaphor of "home" had lost the restrictive connotations of the previous century, when most citizens still clung to the belief that the government had no business involving the nation in foreign affairs outside of its direct sphere of influence.

Indeed, only once prior to the turn of the century did Congress appropriate large funds for an overseas activity, the occasion being relief for victims of the Venezuela earthquake of 1812. Legislators defeated similar measures for overseas famine aid packages introduced in 1847 and 1892 on the grounds that the use of public funds for foreign aid was unconstitutional.[5] A nineteenth-century Victorian mentality, with its emphasis on a proper place for everything and its ordering of the world into distinct and mutually exclusive categories of familiar and foreign, would have found the removal of the metaphor of home from restricted surroundings quite confusing. Nineteenth-century Americans still believed that their continent had been conquered, a rebellion crushed, and unprecedented economic gains acquired in a relatively independent and isolated fashion. Moreover, American cultural mores consistently discouraged the presentation of national interests within a global context. A strong agrarian tradition, according to historian Henry Nash Smith, "made it difficult for Americans to think of themselves as members of a world community because it . . . affirmed that the destiny of this country leads her away from Europe toward the agricultural interior of the continent."[6]

The absence of broadly based and acceptable national interests in overseas foreign affairs prior to the turn of the century had endowed special interest groups with undue influence in shaping the country's international image. As foreign affairs assumed a small place among national priorities, private groups influenced quite heavily the course of America's foreign policy. Commercial organizations, humanitarian foundations, religious missionary movements, and the occasional wealthy individual exerted an influence disproportionate to their numbers. America's status and image abroad was the sum of the cumulative and ostensibly uncoordinated efforts of its businessmen, its philanthropists, and its missionaries.[7]

The peculiar story of the creation of official ties between the United States and Persia serves as a good example of the haphazard development of official American interests abroad.[8] The establishment of a diplomatic mission and numerous consulates in present-day Iran was the result of a massive influx of American missionaries to that part of the world. The first American missionaries had reached Persia as early as 1835; forty years later there were twenty-four American missionary stations, and twenty-five churches, most of which supported some form of educational facility. Congress consistently rejected attempts to establish diplomatic ties to the region. Not even a direct plea from President Buchanan in 1857 could persuade Congress to send permanent emissaries to Persia. In this "house divided," North and South united momentarily in their deep suspicion of the executive branch's involvement in the affairs of the world. Given the overwhelming preoccupation with an internal political crisis, Congress found no validity in Buchanan's visions of economic benefits that could be reaped through the appointment of official American representatives.

Finally, and quite abruptly, the United States established diplomatic ties in 1882. Congressman Rufus B. Dawes of Ohio accomplished the feat by single-handedly persuading his fellow legislators to approve the presence of American representatives in Persia. Dawes pushed through legislation to establish a legation in Teheran, as well as consulates in provincial cities where American religious foundations were most active. Within weeks, Persia was transformed from a country with no official American representation to one with the most elaborate, expensive, and widespread operations of the State Department. The indefatigable congressman's efforts and successful crusade sprang from a personal crisis that had nothing to do with the management of foreign affairs. He had a personal stake in the Kurdish uprising in Azerbaijan—then part of the Persian empire—where his sister was serving as a missionary. Dawes's colleagues had been moved to establish ties with a far-removed empire as a favor for a fellow legislator rather than out of some sudden interest in global affairs. Indeed, the primary function of the country's diplomatic outposts in Persia up until the Great War was the provision of diplomatic protection for American missionaries.

As the case of Persia suggests, the United States never formulated firm grand designs for its foreign dealings before the turn of the century. Consequently, unusual and ambiguous testimonials to national power accompanied the erratic development of America's diplomatic presence abroad. The typical sign of an outsider's interest in the affairs of any given nation usually took the form of an ostentatious embassy, the gift of a statue of a national hero, or, in extreme cases, a military garrison. Americans, by contrast, marked their presence on foreign soil with urban sewage plants, rural rehabilitation projects, or civil service reform initiatives. As practical persons, those private American citizens who initiated most of the country's global activities apparently felt that the nation's international interests were best served by good deeds rather than naked symbols of power.

Even in countries in which the United States had clear-cut vested interests, Americans translated their ambitions into practical projects. The United States initiated numerous civic reforms throughout Latin America, the intent being the establishment of model, albeit hazily defined, democratic infrastructures based loosely on the U.S. prototype. The common denominator of these hemispheric designs, according to historian Merle Curti, was the lack of a clear-cut political objective. "The motives were so mixed that American aims were never clearly defined beyond a vague desire to maintain a series of reasonably stable republics free from non-American domination."[9]

This failure to establish a formal foreign presence was aggravated by the poor quality of the Foreign Service, perhaps the final residual of the nineteenth-century spoils system. Appointments to the service were based not on merit but on political favoritism. Consequently, each new presidential administration in the late nineteenth century carried out wholesale firings of diplomatic and consular officials. Between March 1897 and November 1898, the incoming administration of William McKinley removed 238 of the 272 principal consular officers. Four years earlier, the Democratic administration of Grover Cleveland had effected a turnover of about 90 percent in the consular service. The secretary of state had little control over the Foreign Service, Richard Werking observes in his study of the makings of the modern State Department, because all major appointments to the consular and diplomatic service were subject to congressional approval. The civil service reform act of 1883, which had not affected the Foreign Service, increased the pressure for political appointments in this final bastion of favoritism. Owing to shrinking opportunities to use federal appointments as political payoffs, the exploitation of the Foreign Service reached absurd levels. In 1898, when the consul general at Berlin died, politicians from nearly every state in the union suggested replacements even before the funeral.[10]

The state of affairs in the diplomatic branch of the Foreign Service was particularly bad. As late as 1892, the United States had no ambassadors abroad, and only a handful of ministers, most in the important capitals of Europe. The home staff of the State Department amounted to a mere seventy-seven employees, including messengers; the department's annual budget was $131,500.[11] Because the duties of a diplomat precluded collection of consular fees or other types of graft to supplement the low salaries, only well-to-do gentlemen could afford to hold the position. Consequently, the fulfillment of their duties was linked, in part, to their investment of personal funds.

The most glaring weakness of American diplomacy was its neglect of decorum and protocol. Power and prestige in the diplomatic world were traditionally conveyed by expressive embassy buildings as symbols of the nation. But as far as the United States was concerned, the location and form of the embassy edifice depended mostly on the whims and financial resources of individual appointees. The affluent and free-spending emissaries rented lavish palaces; their more parsimonious colleagues lived in modest abodes.

This uneven representation of America abroad aroused only sparse concern in the United States. The predominantly business culture of the nineteenth century could appreciate the necessity of consular functions such as certifying invoices and other commercial duties. But the responsibility of a permanent diplomatic mission based on an elaborate ceremonial representation of the government was hard to grasp.

Change in public attitudes toward explicit representation of the American government abroad occurred during the dramatic overhauling of the country's international objectives at the turn of the century. Economic realities dictated modifications in the United States' approach to foreign affairs. In the 1880s, American exporting underwent a transition. The country, which had hitherto been a predominantly agricultural exporter, now assumed the role of the world's leading producer and exporter of manufactured goods. Agricultural exports were seasonal and directly related demands for staples, but the selling of finished goods required promotion to sustain a steady market for an equally unwavering level of production. Businessmen, who had previously relied on their own resources in capturing foreign markets, now turned to the government for help in promoting their goods. They demanded an expansion of consular and diplomatic presence abroad as leverage in the ongoing battle to capture markets. The systematic market intelligence and the business propaganda that the government could provide through its legations appeared crucial. The wrenching depression of the 1890s heightened pressures for a methodical approach to analyzing foreign countries and their markets. The unprecedented economic slump rocked the foundations of American society. A debilitated economy produced specters of social cleavage and the breakdown of the free enterprise system. Continuing economic expansion and political and social stability hinged on the expansion of the country's horizons beyond its immediate borders.[12]

The call for diplomacy as an effective political tool coincided with significant reforms in the Foreign Service. By the early twentieth century, the State Department had been effectively purged of the spoils system. Like the rest of the civil service, the Foreign Service was transformed into a relatively apolitical, formal bureaucracy. Beginning in the 1890s, a series of congressional initiatives and executive bills produced a government infrastructure based on merit and talent rather than political favoritism. Initial reforms began at the consular level during the Cleveland administration. Based on the authority of the 1871 Civil Service Act, new consular appointments were offered only to the existing staff of the State Department or to outside applicants who had passed a civil service exam. In 1906, President Theodore Roosevelt issued a crucial executive order mandating promotions on the basis of demonstrated excellence. By mid-1906, the crucial elements of a nonpartisan, professional consular service were in place.[13]

Reform of the diplomatic branch of the Foreign Service quickly followed the consular overhaul when Congress authorized the appointments of the country's first ambassadors in 1893.[14] Salaries rose to realistic levels, merit exams were instituted, and the State Department developed a new organizational structure of specialized sectors based on geographical divisions. Bolstered by an esprit de corps and buoyed by heightened prestige, this new body of ambitious bureaucrats sought clarification of its mission, for the functions of American diplomacy were still amorphous.

The new breed of professional diplomat found willing allies among businessmen who, by the turn of the century, accepted the need for the visible hand of government in negotiating favorable international trade agreements and sustaining access to foreign markets. This meeting of the minds between the diplomatic corps and businessmen culminated with the creation of the American Embassy Association, a lobbying group advocating the expansion of diplomatic representation and the erection of embassy edifices abroad. The hundreds of members of the association's national advisory committee included the presidents of chambers of commerce from practically all large and medium-sized American cities, at least fifty bank presidents and directors, numerous state governors and ex-governors, members of Congress and the Senate, and chairmen and chief executive officers from scores of American corporations who stood to gain from an expanding American profile abroad.[15]

Previous public campaigns for the reform of the Foreign Service focused on improvement of the human element in the State Department. The unique aspect of the American Embassy Association's strategy was its almost exclusive concern with formal symbolic appearances abroad. This new interest in the style and number of diplomatic structures represented a compromise that was quite typical of contemporary American politics. A forceful symbolic appearance promised to serve the interest of American businessmen by promoting "product awareness." By the same token, the limiting of American expansionism to diplomatic representation addressed the pervasive fear that American involvement in international affairs would suck the country into divisive colonial adventures and unnerving global conflicts. Given new developments in communications, advocates of embassies declared, there were alternatives to European-style empires as safeguards of the nation's legitimate concerns in other lands. A well-crafted and expressive building as a symbol of the United States' prowess could fulfill the role of a permanent colonial presence. A nation "is not only the more respected and feared in foreign lands from the appearance it presents," noted a supporter of embassies over armies. "The resulting prestige makes not only for material gain along commercial lines, but goes far towards the conservation of peace."[16]

The purpose of the American Embassy Association, according to its president, E. Clarence Jones, was the promotion of a symbolic American presence in foreign lands:

> Foreigners necessarily judge us by what they see of us in their own country. . . . Their opinion of our country and its resources is formed largely by the character of our embassies, the manner in which our representatives are housed. . . . The conditions of our embassies has lowered their estimation. That was proved just prior to the Spanish American war, when the majority of Europeans believed that Spain was greater and more powerful than the United States. . . . We feel ashamed at appearing poverty-stricken in the eyes of the inhabitants of other countries and of placing ourselves commercially below third or even fourth rate powers. Even some of the South American republics, through their stately embassies, present a better front than does the United States. . . . The nation that lives within itself cannot hope to influence international opinion any more than the individual who leads a life of recluse can aspire to shape public opinion.[17]

Jones's speech summed up much of what would eventually become the formal rationale for American political architecture abroad: First, the association identified the inevitable connection between economic expansion and international relations. Sustained economic fortitude depended on a powerful and eloquent American presence abroad. Second, a symbolic presence appeared politically more expedient than a physical presence. The implication behind this lobbying for embassies was that governments could achieve their global objectives through symbolic acts as well as through actual coercion. Finally, much like the goods they were attempting to sell, these monumental structures needed to be standardized and uniform. Standardized goods were easier to produce and promote. In other words, in addition to the traditional function of providing economic leverage through treaty negotiations and intelligence-gathering for an expanding economy, the diplomatic outpost would serve as a modern-day billboard. Impressive symbols of the United States would heighten an awareness of American goods through imposing and aesthetically pleasing political symbols.

Despite these growing demands for explicit and impressive diplomatic representation, a reluctant Congress dragged its feet. Legislators avoided enhancing the power of the executive branch in any facet of public policy, especially in the area of foreign relations, where Congress had no direct constitutional authority. Eventually, Congress was cajoled into action by the ever-active J. P. Morgan, who offered a huge palatial expanse for a permanent embassy in London. Spurred on by this gesture as well as an unrelenting lobbying campaign, Congress passed a bill for embassy construction and building in 1911. The bill, known as the Lowden Act, appropriated the sum of $500,000 per fiscal year to the State Department for either the purchase or construction of new embassies abroad. At the time of the passage of the Lowden Act the United States owned embassy and legation buildings in only four foreign capitals: Constantinople, Beijing, Tokyo, and Bangkok. The government also owned four dilapidated consular premises in Tahiti, Amoy, Seoul, and Yokohama. Most of these buildings had not been purchased or constructed by the government, but had been acquired haphazardly or through gift.[18]

The Lowden Act, however, produced few tangible results. Some of the bill's provisions—in particular, the need to acquire congressional approval for each purchase or construction plan—severely hampered its effectiveness. Many members of Congress frowned upon governmental spending in general and viewed the bill as an unnecessary waste of public funds. A strong isolationist lobby was instrumental, too, in deflecting funds from overseas activities to internal construction projects, such as rural and small-town post offices.

Unprecedented federal construction at home further impeded architectural expansion abroad because all federal architectural projects, domestic and international, were handled by an understaffed supervising architect of the Treasury Department. In 1899 the office had responsibility for construction and management of about four hundred buildings within the United States. By 1912, the same staff confronted the difficult task of handling a workload in excess of 1,100 federal buildings. This new federal presence, according to historian Robert Wiebe, was a by-product of the country's transition from a mentality of isolated island communities to a more uniform national consciousness.[19] Under the auspices of the supervising architect of the Treasury Department, and as part of its "search for order," the federal government scattered hundreds of neoclassical post offices, courthouses, and other federal buildings throughout the nation.[20]

Given the domestic priorities of the supervising architect of the Treasury, and in lieu of any alternative apparatus, all plans for construction abroad languished in forgotten drawers. To make matters worse, Congress also repealed the supposedly wasteful and expensive Tarnsey Act, which had provided for the assignment of government architectural projects to private architects. With little or no change in the size of its staff, the office of the supervising architect struggled with an almost impossible workload. The solution offered to the problem of small staff and heavy workload—the Treasury Standardization Act of 1915—hurt the cause of foreign construction projects even further.[21] A standardized, bland, pseudo-classical building was quite adequate for a regional federal building. However, such designs did not suffice to represent something uniquely American in a foreign land.

The Lowden Act remained ineffective because it failed to provide a mechanism for transforming ideas into reality; moreover, the dry legal wording of the act ignored the issue of the form and shape of a uniquely American style of political architecture in foreign lands. In all fairness, it should be noted that neither lawmakers nor the Treasury architects received any guidance or inspiration from the State Department. Diplomat John Bassett Moore, writing in 1905 for *Harper's* magazine, lamented the lack of an American brand of diplomacy and "the visible tendency towards conformity to customs elsewhere established."[22] Numerous magazine articles called for the construction of respectable-looking embassies that would compare favorably with those of other powers, but no intrinsically American style of embassy building emerged from this public debate.[23] Deeply entrenched suspicions of diplomacy and diplomats further impeded the bolstering of America's physical presence abroad. The association of diplomacy with antirepublican intrigue and duplicity was quite widespread. In addition, the elitism of America's first generation of professional diplomats whittled away even further at congressional support for ambitious projects such as the Lowden initiative.[24]

By 1924, the State Department had acquired only nine additional embassies; none had been built from scratch. The total appropriations of funds for embassy buildings from 1911 to 1924 amounted to only $1,669,123.[25] The Lowden Act laid the basis for a systematic program for the extension of American political architecture abroad. But, lacking a crucial philosophical framework for diplomatic architecture, and hampered by the delaying tactics of a recalcitrant Congress, the bill had meager results.

Where, then, should we seek the seeds of the monumental projects that would burst onto the scene following America's involvement in the Great War? Where should we delve for the genesis of centrally directed architectural assignments in foreign lands, those plans and images initiated by the federal government rather than private individuals? Gestation occurred in the fertile soil of the Philippines, where for the first time the U.S. government sponsored an elaborate articulation of its political image for foreign display. Despite serious public misgivings concerning the moral, political, and economic virtues of empire, the federal government enthusiastically endorsed the refashioning of the archipelago as a facsimile of American society. In what might be interpreted as a precursor of the Peace Corps, an army of American teachers, social workers, and administrators fanned out through the Philippines to spread the gospel of the American way. The captains of America's policies in the Philippines invested immense human and material resources in a modern school system, the spread of the English language, and the establishment of American-style government practices, their assumption being that such efforts would deepen allegiances and re-create the archipelago "in our own image."[26]

This strategy of Americanization called for a conducive physical setting. Turn-of-the-century Americans were great believers in environmental determinism, the idea that carefully planned surroundings could reshape the political and social creed of a region's inhabitants. Consequently, one of the most enthusiastic supporters of the Americanization movement, William Howard Taft, used his influence as governor of the archipelago, secretary of war, and, finally, president of the United States to encourage the exporting of the physical as well as ideological facets of the American way. With Taft's blessing, the Chicago-based architect and city planner Daniel Burnham presented plans for a refashioning of Manila and the construction of a summer capital in Baguio, a village in the mountains of Luzon.

Daniel Burnham, as his biographer has noted, brought to the Philippines project some very impressive credentials.[27] He had been the mastermind behind the architecture of Chicago's White City, the Columbian Exposition of 1893. On the swampy shores of Lake Michigan, Burnham had fashioned a lavish demonstration of the tenets of the "City Beautiful" movement, of which he was an enthusiastic exponent. Two fundamental principles of this movement to reform America's cityscape dominated the exposition plan. First, his buildings were monumental, uniform in style, and basically neoclassical. Second, their arrangement was harmonious and formal. Style and arrangement provided an uplifting lesson in civics, especially for the masses, whose ever-growing presence raised fears of impending chaos among America's elite. In Burnham's own words, "the beauty of [the fair's] arrangement and of its building made a profound impression not merely upon the highly educated part of the community, but still more perhaps upon the masses."[28]

Burnham was not a city planner in the modern sense of the term. He cared little for the residential periphery of a city other than the laying out of arteries leading to the monumental city center. His singular concern was with a formal urban core, characterized by vigorous public architecture and vast, carefully planned recreational areas as visible lessons on the virtues of order. His widely acclaimed triumph at Chicago provided great impetus for the City Beautiful movement. Favorable reactions led to a series of prestigious city planning commissions in Washington, D.C., and Cleveland as well as the much-coveted appointment to resurrect San Francisco in the aftermath of the 1906 earthquake. He was, then, an obvious choice for the remaking of Manila, as well as the planning of a completely new town in Baguio.

Burnham envisioned Baguio as an American version of Simla, summer capital of the British Raj.[29] The master plan called for a garden city, somewhat like an upstate New York resort town magically transplanted to this oasis of almost familiar weather and terrain. Of course, the plans for Baguio never had the ponderous moral overtones of the City Beautiful, as it was designed specifically to serve the needs of local American masters who had no need to be reeducated. Burnham and his associates aspired to re-create the atmosphere of small-town America, a place where fatigued colonial officials would find spiritual replenishment in familiar ways of life. Baguio's planners ignored the issue of monumentalism. They concerned themselves primarily with the placement of recreational facilities and the provision of functional office space for the islands' government work during the hot summer months. They gave little or no consideration to the uplifting of the indigenous population. As Paul Wheatley has observed, the city "was an island of European metropolitan values and symbols . . . whose primary purpose was to enable residents from temperate latitudes to preserve the personal, domestic, and civic practices to which they were accustomed."[30]

For our purposes, the case of Manila is much more revealing. The new Manila boasted the same central motifs of order, efficiency, and power of the City Beautiful in the United States. The design was a product of what Paul Boyer has called positive environmentalism, the attempt to transform the behavior and values of the masses through environmental reform.[31] Of course, the environmental setting of an overseas territory had connotations that outstripped the objectives of the City Beautiful movement in American cities. Superimposing an American plan on a distinctly foreign city distinguished foreign ruler from local subjects. Both layout and architecture revealed the imperial designs of the interloper. The Manila plan echoed the urge of urban uplifters in the United States to manipulate space in order to propagate the system of beliefs of an empowered elite. In addition, this exportation of American civic forms to a foreign country implied a negative perception of local culture and the urge to subdue, refashion, and tame the native environment.

Rather than striving for the same ponderous neoclassicism of the City Beautiful, both Burnham and the executor of his plans, William Parsons, forged a new form of expressive political architecture by introducing selective local design elements into their creations. Tiled roofs, shaded porches, and broad, deep archways of a Spanish type characterized the monumental structures of Manila. Aesthetically, these modifications represented a recognition of the elegance and utility of local styles. Politically, they signified a translation of the political messages of American imperial architecture into the local vernacular, in an attempt to convey an instructive sense of order that Filipinos could understand. Burnham stated quite explicitly that the ceremonial sector of his Manila design represented an attempt to produce the same imperial effect "put to the test in notable examples from the days of Old Rome to the Louvre and Versailles of modern times."

The significance of the American presence in the Philippines appeared in the clustering of the Filipino-imperial–style government buildings in a familiar American pattern. While the architecture of these edifices had distinct local features, their layout was explicitly imported. Basically, the Manila plan echoed the American capital's distribution of power (Fig. 1). The master plan demonstrated the concept of the separation of powers in government. The ceremonial axis of the city—the mall leading up from the seashore to a complex of government offices—was capped by the capitol. This implanting of the capitol at the pinnacle of the hollow square of government buildings clearly underscored the supremacy of the legislature. All major thoroughfares fanned out from the eastern facade of the capitol, highlighting the preeminence of the legislative branch, "an arrangement entirely fitting for both practical and sentimental reasons," Burnham noted. The ceremonial convergence of major arteries was "practical because the center of governmental activity should be accessible from all sides [and] sentimental because every section of the Capitol [sic] City should look with deference toward the symbol of the Nation's power."[32] The hall of justice received an appropriate separate location south of the main governmental group as if to demonstrate its independence; the governor's mansion, the local equivalent of the White House, was placed even further south.

Quite deliberately, this blueprint conceded nothing to local political practices and institutions. The overall image of the imperial buildings—boasting readable symbolism, and organized in a didactic pattern—registered the primary impulse of making over the Filipino population in the image of its American masters.

Americans never repeated an ambitious project of such dimensions; thus we need to use caution before interpreting the Philippine case as a model for future projects of political architecture. The Philippine experience of architectural proselytization was an exercise in imperialism, inspired in part by a desire to impress other well-established international powers. Britain's widely acclaimed monumental architecture in India during the early part of the twentieth century obviously informed these grandiose representations of an American spirit. American officials in the Philippines deliberately planned Baguio in the image of Simla, and there is little doubt as to the influence of the building of New Delhi on the Manila plans.[33]

The architectural schemes of the Philippines, then, might conceivably be seen as an exception rather than an archetype. Moreover, America's

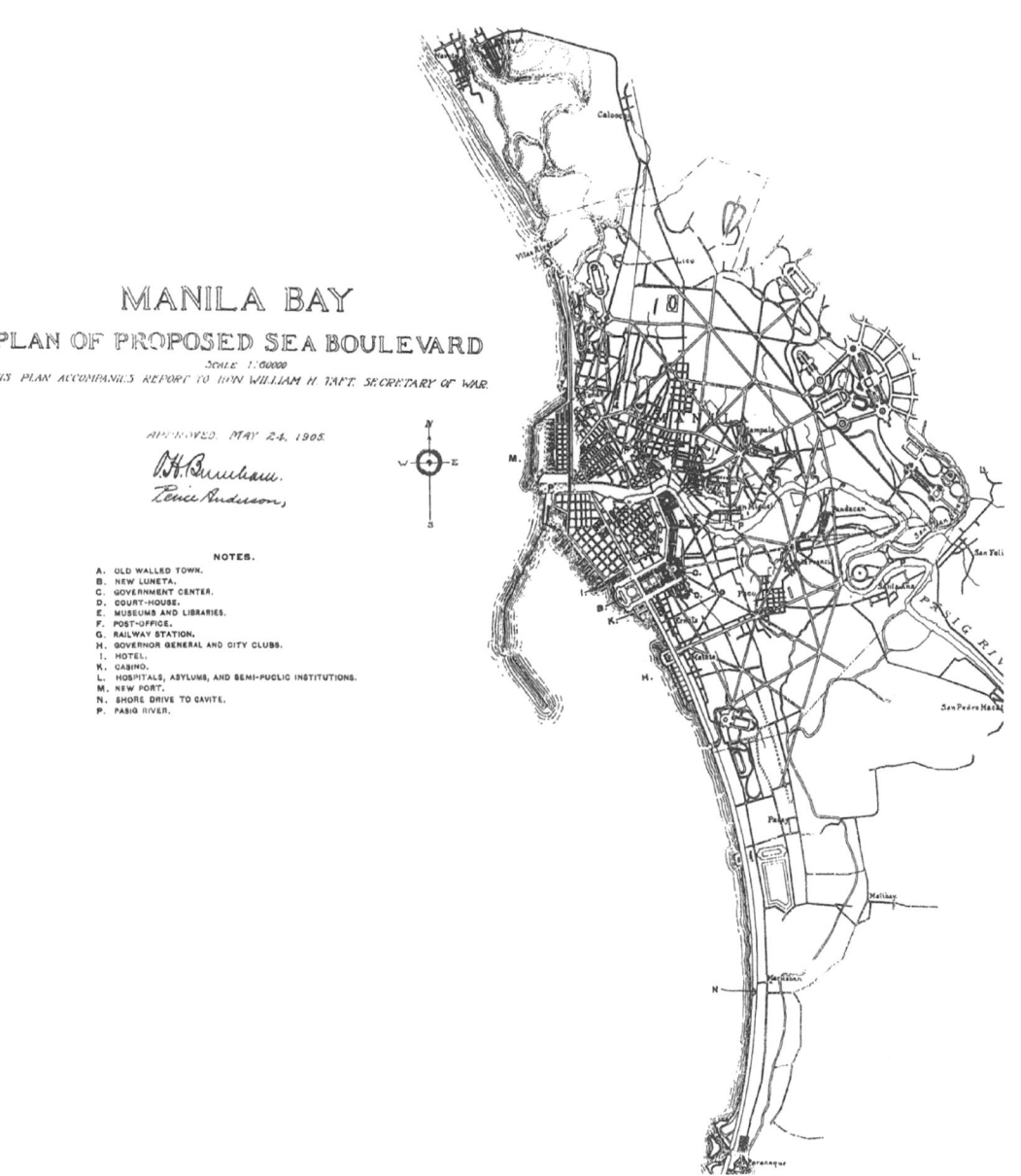

1. Proposed plan for Manila, 1905 (Daniel H. Burnham, architect)

colonial designs in the Philippines were never as clear as the architecture suggests. The United States' imitation of European colonialism produced uneven results and much political dissension, blunting enthusiasm for the economic benefits associated with newly acquired insular territories. Indeed, internal dissension suggests that the United States never advanced much beyond a haphazard colonial policy. In the Philippines, the United States committed itself almost by default to a form of colonialism that it had never clearly envisioned and that would have been difficult to defend beforehand.[34]

Despite these peculiar circumstances, the Philippine venture does offer an opportunity to chart the pattern of harnessing architecture in the service of foreign policy—in particular, the technical process of translating political objectives into artistic form. To begin with, this enterprise exposed the massive faith and self-esteem that American policymakers brought with them to the twentieth century. On a technical level, the most obvious lesson here came from the role played by the central government. Such political exercises could be translated into larger-than-life metaphors only when unhampered by political objections on the home front. The architects had implemented their ideas with little interference from conflicting interest groups in the United States. The fiscal autonomy of the Philippines' military government allowed for considerable discretion and little public scrutiny.

And yet, even under these circumstances of relative freedom in conveying political messages through architecture, the Philippine experience exposed the apparent limits of America's global plans for the twentieth century. Policymakers and architects experienced "linguistic" difficulties in translating paradigms of American power into another cultural idiom. Irrespective of the architectural adaptations of specific buildings to the local architectural patois, their American sense of order was distinctly foreign, perhaps even incomprehensible, to the target audience. No matter how hard Burnham and his associates tried to immerse themselves in "the Orient," their ultimate models for Manila were Rome and Versailles, and the contemporary equivalent, Washington, D.C. As for Baguio, they could not rid themselves of the aesthetic references to the "hill towns of Italy and France" or, at best, the Adirondacks. In both cases, architects and administrators were obsessed with an impulse to recycle American ideals on foreign soil. The mentality that lay behind the Philippine designs—and ultimately the driving force behind all meaningful American symbolism in foreign surroundings—was the idea of the enclave, a foreign presence isolated by its own peculiar conventions, prejudices, and sense of duty.

America's colonial architecture in the Philippines suggests, too, that the motivating forces behind America's global designs derived neither from abstract concepts nor from the detached concerns of foreign policy strategists. As would often be the case with the future construction of more modest feats of political architecture, the policies were variations of domestic issues. The remaking of Manila and the construction of Baguio were versions of the crusade to uplift the masses at home. Burnham's plans for the Philippines suggest that foreign designs reflected many of the nation's internal preoccupations, with only secondary attention, if any, being paid to the systems and conventions of the host people.

Finally, these intimate ties between the City Beautiful movement and American foreign policy demonstrated an unrelenting faith in the power of symbols as well as an urge to manipulate space and form as political tools. Indeed, as we shall see, the fundamental principle underlying all future architectural abstractions of an American spirit abroad was that careful design could change societies.

As fate would have it, a great and disruptive world war halted whatever immediate ramifications of the Philippine policy there might have been. Global conflict, rather than a brief colonial foray, provided the first set of pertinent metaphors for America's postcolonial architectural symbolism abroad. Initial impetus for defining a meaningful, shared concept of national character originated with the armed forces, the one national entity whose very existence depended on enduring, uniform paradigms of nationhood. As is often the case in young nations, the military had traditionally fulfilled the function of a melting pot, where East met West and rural and urban sets of mores were forged into one. During the course of a bloody civil war, innovative military technology as well as new modern systems of command and control hastened the rise of a modern industrial nation out of the ruins of a rural, sectional country. Indeed, the nation's Civil War cemeteries represented the first cohesive attempt to define a binding concept of nationhood since the early national period. These shrines to the nation's dead would provide both precedent and substance for the first global articulation of the nation in foreign fields.

2

Incident at Sivry-sur-Meuse

GREAT WAR MONUMENTS AND CEMETERIES
IN WESTERN EUROPE

GENERAL JOHN J. PERSHING, former commander of the American Expeditionary Forces (AEF) in France and American hero, found himself in the uncomfortable position of being attacked by his own troops. The battle arena was a small town near Verdun, Sivry-sur-Meuse, where, in 1931, veterans of the 316th Infantry of the Seventy-ninth Division had erected a monument to their fallen comrades-in-arms. In order to circumvent a Franco-American agreement prohibiting the erection of private memorials without prior approval of the U.S. government, the monument had been constructed on private property and under the auspices of a French veterans' organization. Pershing, the U.S. government's supreme coordinator for American battle monuments abroad, urged French premier André Tardieu to destroy the monument. The prime minister refused; instead he offered to change the memorial plaque. In accordance with Pershing's instructions, the original bilingual plaque commemorating the fallen comrades-in-arms of the unit was removed; a new, officially approved inscription read, "In Memory of the High Achievements of the American Troops Who Fought in This Region During the World War." Angry veterans and their families called Pershing's action "desecration." The General replied that he was merely enforcing government regulations that prohibited private monuments and stipulated that "no memorials shall be erected to any unit of the American Army in France of lesser size than a division."[1]

Pershing's actions, and his laconic statement, implied that American battle monuments and cemeteries abroad were not meant merely to commemorate individual victims or personal tragedies and could not be left in the hands of private citizens. Rather, the cemeteries and monuments served primarily to represent the American political creed abroad. They were indicators of the most enduring result of the global conflict: a forceful American presence in the cultural and political landscapes of other countries. The disputed private monument and its plaque commemorating the individual soldiers had bypassed the national issue, thereby attracting the attention of Pershing and his colleagues. Establishing elaborate military cemeteries for foreign display was a way of demanding certain privileges for the United States in other lands. The articulation of an "American sacrifice" in extremely dramatic tones was a tool for consolidating America's newly adopted international agenda in the postwar period.

The employment of military cemeteries for political purposes was, of course, nothing new. The technique was developed during the course of the Civil War.[2] Driven by a desire to create a positive legacy from the war casualties, the United States had consecrated the Union effort by segregating military and civilian graves, separating loyal Union tombs from those of Confederates, and by converting crucial battleground into cemeteries–cum–national monuments of unity. James Curl notes that the Civil War was the first war of modern times in which the graves of the fallen of all ranks were laid out in formal patterns to achieve national designs. Appropriate, didactic forms of burial rationalized the mass carnage of the Civil War through the transformation of tombstones into symbols of national unity.[3] Arlington National Cemetery served as the central repository of the military dead, and it swiftly acquired the status of a national monument. Crucial battles, such as Gettysburg, became national shrines through the interment of the fallen on the battlefield.[4]

Military men had apprised the nation's civilian leadership of the political potential of military cemeteries. During a pause in the Battle of Chattanooga, Major General George H. Thomas buried his dead in ceremonial fashion on a commanding hill situated within a natural amphitheater and overlooking the battle site. Quartermaster General Russell Meigs, who commanded a provisional division defending Washington, D.C., against the threat of a Confederate attack in July 1964, decided against evacuating the bodies of casualties to nearby concentrations, preferring instead to bury them in the middle of the battlefield. "It is hoped," he mentioned in his annual report as Quartermaster General, "that Congress will see fit to cause a monument to be erected to the memory of these patriots who fell in defense of the Capital itself."[5] His request was granted, and this burial site became the Battleground National Cemetery.

The intellectual inspiration for these deeds was the Athenian custom of erecting "trophies" on the sites of victorious battles and the establishment of state burial grounds on the outskirts of the polis "for purposes similar to those now served by Arlington on the Potomac and by 97 other national cemeteries."[6] In a typical analogy, a *New York Times* correspondent who had lost his son at Gettysburg likened the struggle to Thermopylae. In the years that followed, historian John Patterson notes, such comparisons appeared quite frequently, as the classic paradigm contributed to national self-importance and offered a welcome rationalization of the carnage.[7] It was the Greeks who had first devised a meaningful commemoration of citizen sacrifice in battle through funerary rites. Logistical problems had prevented repatriation of all Athenian casualties, but selective remains were brought home as symbols of the desire to repatriate all the war dead. The Athenians buried the remaining war casualties on the battlefield and marked their individual resting places with a mound crowned with an inscribed star.[8]

The Greek paradigm was particularly attractive because of its sublime interpretation of death in battle. In the *Iliad*, as Sharon Scholl points out, Achilles had the choice of living a full life and dying unremembered or, conversely, "living a brief life and being immortalized in story and song."[9] The example of the *Iliad* was all the more compelling for a nation stricken by a vicious civil war, because the death of the warrior did not appear as some earthly folly but was in accordance with some vast, cosmic scheme. The Greek tradition, then, provided a much-needed explanation by removing death in the service of the community from a terrestrial sphere and placing it instead within a quasi-religious, national context. Inspired by the classical analogy, and in response to broad public pressure to commemorate the dead, President Lincoln delivered his version of Pericles' funeral oration in the shadow of the graves of the union's fallen at Gettysburg. The graphic display of sacrifice allowed Lincoln to present his personal vision of the nation's future as the unfinished work of those whose bodies were interred on the battlefield.

The major political significance of the Civil War cemetery, and, thus, its compelling attractiveness for those charged with commemorating the Great War, was its glorification of principles rather than persons. Ever since the planning of the Capitol in Washington, D.C., national representations of the spirit of federalism had all but disappeared. In the divided nation of the antebellum period, the country had developed a cult of local heroes rather than national causes. Rival interpreters of the national spirit advanced their causes through the erection of monuments and statues to local leaders and partisan heroes; the celebration of elusive national bonds in public art had all but ceased.[10] With the Civil War having resolved the question of the supreme sovereignty of the federal government, the new, more abstract symbolism of military cemeteries offered alternatives for the personification of political causes. Federal officials consistently discouraged the public erection of statues of generals and other Union heroes within these national shrines. The eclectic statuary at Gettysburg and other sites bore witness to the limited success of this effort. The Quartermaster General did, however, succeed in preserving the rows of tombstones as the central motif of this celebration of nationhood. These grave markers provided the building blocks for an abstract monument celebrating ideals rather than valiant leadership.

This same urge for sublime interpretation of the country's political bonds informed the guidelines for new twentieth-century interpretations of death in the service of the nation. No personification of the crisis could do justice to the profound international and national implications of this first instance of global war. As had been the case after the Civil War, the United States found itself in a position of demanding new clarification of government's political powers and its sphere of influence. Civil War commemoration had testified to the national prerogatives of the federal government. The Great War demanded further expansion of federal authority, since the restriction of government activities to the continental United States no longer mirrored reality.

Despite consistent calls from isolationists to withdraw from international security arrangements, the United States was inextricably involved in global affairs. By 1918 the U.S. government no longer limited its role in international commerce to the task of aiding the foreign trade of particular industries or individual businessmen, but was firmly entrenched in the world economy as a creditor nation. In 1914, the United States had been a debtor nation. Yet a mere five years later, private American individuals had loaned out almost $3 million, while the government had extended to foreign governments over $10 million. This shift from being a debtor nation to being the largest lending nation in the world represented, according to William Leuchtenberg, "one of those great shifts in power that occur but rarely in the history of nations."[11] The U.S. government now needed a significant foreign presence not only to protect the economic interests of private citizens but also to secure and monitor its own investments. "Our business abroad has expanded in an enormous degree in the past few years," observed Secretary of Commerce Herbert Hoover in 1926, "and it has expanded not only because of the larger problems of international relations grown from the war, but because of the great expansion of our trade, our foreign investments and our travellers and tourists. Our trade has more than doubled in ten years. . . . Our overseas shipping has increased from 750,000 to 7,000,000 tons since 1913. . . . In that time our tourists have increased from about 200,000 to 600,000."[12]

Given these irrefutable facts, the United States could not allow the dynamics of international affairs to evolve spontaneously. Barring blunt interventionism, a tactic frowned upon by many Americans, other more subtle reminders of the new American global presence appeared on the scene. It is indeed within this context that government pushed forward its program to dramatize America's altruistic sacrifices as a way of demanding extraordinary privileges in the postwar era. Lest the political significance of these cemeteries be confused with any narrow glorification of the technical ability of the armed forces, the president removed the project from the jurisdiction of the War Department and the office of the Quartermaster General, which had hitherto managed all military cemetery projects. Instead, these memorials and cemeteries were managed by a prestigious civilian board that reported directly to the president. The fundamental idea, according to General Pershing, was to construct large monumental complexes that dominated the landscape as everlasting testimony to the American contention that the country's "blood sacrifice" had been the "decisive" factor in the Allied victory.[13] The unspoken logic was that America's unselfish sacrifices called for some form of retribution.

The ambitious cemetery-abroad project also underscored a crucial transition in the relationship between government and its citizens in the arena of international affairs. If before the war America's foreign image had been shaped by private initiative, the postwar government now sought to impose a more controlled, standardized image, one that reflected the search for order that characterized the federal government's domestic objectives as well. The cemeteries and battle monuments illuminated transitions that the Great War had induced in American society as well as the expression of these cultural shifts in its foreign policy. The insistence on controlled form and content indicated that the American government intended to use the war to impress upon its citizens that organized collective behavior was not anathema, nor did it contradict American political principles. A successful war effort, which was due in no small part to the industrial might of the United States, rendered the regimented life of an industrial society coherent and beneficial. In fact, the very act of leaving American remains on foreign soil was a convincing testimony to the new power of government over its citizens. The government took control of its image at home and abroad and directed the activities of its citizens even after their demise. Within this milieu of changing relations between individuals and establishment, as well as the new symbiotic relationship between domestic and foreign affairs, the federal government launched its American battle monuments project abroad.

Limited and qualified precedents for erecting overseas monuments to casualties of the nation's foreign wars had been established during the Spanish-American War and in the wake of the United States' involvement in the Boxer Revolt in China. In the early twentieth century the private and pro-expansionist Cuba-China Battlefield Commission and the American Historic and Scenic Society received charters from Congress to mark the sites of important battles with modest tablets.[14] Yet prior to the Great War the only instance of interring American soldiers on foreign soil occurred in Mexico, which for all practical purposes was viewed as the country's backyard rather than another sovereign nation. This first national cemetery on foreign soil was established in Mexico City in 1851. The site contained the remains of some 750 unknown soldiers whose bodies were not repatriated after the cessation of hostilities.[15]

All of these locations, Mexico, Cuba, and China, were areas where the United States assumed it had special rights and political prerogatives, and the battle markers underscored this assumption. But only at Mexico City did the United States inter the bodies of its servicemen in a manner that might be interpreted as a politically laden gesture of a permanent American interest outside of its national borders. Such an interpretation should be qualified, however. To begin with, the remains in Mexico were all unidentified, thereby making it somewhat easier to avoid repatriation; there were no grieving families demanding the return of the remains of their loved ones. Moreover, the Mexican cemetery, rather than being a radical innovation, followed a standard pattern of military burials.

Traditionally, and almost exclusively during the antebellum era, the military had fulfilled the function of a frontier police force rather than a national army. Spread out in isolated forts and far removed from major population centers, local garrison commanders had no choice but to bury their dead at the sites of battle or within the perimeters of a nearby post. The commanders of the Mexican expedition, then, merely followed precedent. If anything, the Mexican cemetery served as a memorial to the thousands of bodies that were never recovered, having being buried on the trail during the swift and often disorderly campaigns of Generals Kearny, Taylor, and Scott. It was, then, primarily a gesture to those whose final resting places remained unknown, an acknowledgment of the inability of the armed forces to provide an accurate account of its casualties, rather than a singular effort to retain a symbolic presence on foreign soil. Prior to the Great War, Americans never repeated this experiment of burying the nation's dead abroad.

Indeed, in the aftermath of the Spanish-American War and the Boxer Revolt, the War Department took great pride in its new, efficient grave registration service, which minimized the number of unidentified bodies, and boasted of its ability to return all remains to the United States. According to Edward Steere, the historian of the military's grave registration operations, the number of bodies returned to the United States during the apex of America's early foreign escapades, from 1899 to 1902, was 5,931. Of these, 1,336 were interred at Arlington, and another 1,922 were laid to rest at the Presidio in San Francisco. All other bodies were returned to relatives for private burials or for interment at regional national cemeteries that had been established after the Civil War. Eighty-nine percent of all remains were identified, owing to introduction of the "dog tag," the aluminum identification tag that was now standard military issue.[16] No bodies were deliberately left abroad. Reflecting on the return of these remains, the Quartermaster General, Marshall I. Ludington, noted with a certain degree of pride, "'It seems proper to remark here that this is probably the first attempt in history where a country at war with a foreign power has undertaken to disinter the remains of its soldiers who . . . had given up their lives on a distant foreign shore, and bring them by a long sea voyage to their native land for return to their relatives and friends, or their reinterment in the beautiful cemeteries which have been provided by our government for its brave defenders.'"[17] This variation of the Athenian tradition of returning battle victims to the homeland reflected the limited objectives of foreign wars in the American mind at the turn of the nineteenth century. Whatever other conflicting ambitions might have lurked behind America's experimentation with colonialism before the Great War, the single-minded repatriation of military remains suggests the vindication of powerful inward-looking political traditions.

Given this tradition of repatriation, the decision to establish American enclaves in Europe in the aftermath of World War I represented an important cultural and political watershed. Europe, unlike Mexico, could not be categorized as part of America's traditional sphere of influence, nor was the Quartermaster General ever seriously troubled by logistical obstacles in repatriating casualties. In contrast to previous overseas operations, participants in the Great War were not career personnel whose destiny in life and death was tied to the armed forces. They were for the most part civilians who had been removed temporarily from the familiar world of family and community. It was commonly assumed that, one way or another, they would return to their homeland, either to pick up their lives where they had left off or, if they had been killed, as mute testimonials to the price of nationhood.

Prior to the cessation of hostilities, neither the government nor the military offered any indication of plans to sway from the tradition of repatriating military casualties. The swift surfacing of radically different designs for the nation's war dead suggests, however, that this was no spontaneous reaction but a much more deliberate turn of events. The very proposal for a new policy of interment sparked an acrimonious public debate. The controversy reflected fundamental rifts in American society—in particular, the clash between powerful isolationist sentiment and equally forceful internationalist trends. The sometimes vicious exchange of views was stoked as well by a related dispute between supporters of an activist national government, on the one hand, and, on the other, those who viewed with suspicion any attempt to impose uniform norms and practices on a diverse society.

Immediately after the war, various national organizations formed to urge that the dead be left in France or, conversely, to insist upon their repatriation. Those who advocated repatriation attempted to garner support by invoking tradition as well as appealing to the fundamental isolationist streak in American public opinion. "If American dead are left in France," they asserted, "the necessity for preserving the inviolability of our burial places will be more likely to involve the United States in future

European wars." Advocates of stateside burials argued that "our traditional policy—as exemplified in the Philippines, [and] in Cuba . . .—has been to bring back our own." While the bereaved parents of French and Allied war dead were sufficiently close to the war zone to allow them to visit the resting place of their sons, advocates of repatriation pointed out that Americans were separated from their loved ones by a huge expanse of ocean, necessitating a prohibitively expensive transatlantic voyage.[18]

The countereffort to keep the remains overseas benefited from the emphatic patronage of the military establishment and veterans' groups, as well as the support of the federal government, which hoped to use the cemeteries as a tool for consolidating a new agenda of American political objectives at home and abroad. Reasons in favor of leaving the bodies in France were varied, ranging from the supposed unethicality of disturbing the dead, to the political wonders that these symbols of sacrifice would do for America's image.[19] Supporters of burial abroad reminded the American public that, historically, the government had been consistently more responsible than many of the bereaved families in honoring the fallen. Following the Spanish-American War, they argued, countless bodies were left unclaimed by their families on the wharves of San Francisco.[20] These tales of neglect were counterposed against hallowed stories about the close relationship between European villagers and American grave sites strewn throughout the battle arena of the Great War. The typical narrative described how individual French citizens had "adopted" individual tombs, bestowing love and care on American military cemeteries adjacent to their villages. These tales implied that any disruption of this sacred bond might be interpreted as a national affront to the host country. Campaigners against repatriation also appealed to the emotions. Raising the specter of an unholy conspiracy against the American people, supporters spread rumors that the lobby for the return of bodies was financed clandestinely by "undertakers and coffin makers" who hoped to reap great profits from this boom in their trade.[21]

The public campaign in favor of overseas burial was complemented by the actions of the military. In a clear departure from previous tradition, the military did not automatically repatriate the bodies of its casualties. Officially, and somewhat disingenuously, the military establishment harped on the logistical problems that this would entail. Only explicit requests for repatriation were processed. Families who did not reply to the form letters or who could not be reached owing to changes in address or other circumstances were automatically numbered among the families who preferred overseas interment. Out of the 75,000 inquiries sent to the next-of-kin of the Great War dead, about 14 percent did not reply and an additional 26 percent requested interment in the overseas cemeteries.[22]

The military, in turn, received important support for the cemeteries-abroad program from its former troops. Much like their counterparts in uniform, the country's major veterans' organizations demonstrated solid support for the overseas cemeteries. The marking of battlefields and the enshrining of the dead constituted symbolic rallying points for these organizations. Conspicuous "pilgrimages" to these highly visible shrines abroad became integral features of lobbying campaigns to obtain package deals of extraordinary social and political benefits for veterans.[23]

Yet by far the most crucial support for establishing military shrines in Europe came from the federal government, which seized the opportunity to establish powerful and uniform symbols of the national spirit abroad. Despite changing administrations, the government consistently bolstered the campaign for retaining the remains in Europe. With little public fanfare, the federal government reached a series of agreements with its European allies that gave the United States full title and extraterritorial rights to the cemetery sites. In addition, the governments of France, Belgium, and the United Kingdom granted Washington the right of veto over all private American monuments; all Great War monuments had to receive official approval from federal authorities.

In order to avoid antagonizing those sectors of the public that looked suspiciously upon government intervention in private affairs, federal authorities refrained from public comment on the issue of overseas cemeteries. Instead, they encouraged the establishment of lobbying groups, the most conspicuous of which were the various national organizations of bereaved parents. The members of these groups apparently came to terms with their personal tragedies by seeing them as possessing an overarching universal significance. "The cemeteries [need] to depict the ideals for which American heroes have fallen and to inspire thereby the people of Europe," the chairman of the Gold Star Fathers' Association stated. "We gave their ashes to make a part of a great monument in Europe to the cause of America."[24]

The federal government "sold" the project by implying that it did not represent a major departure from previous tradition. The Athenian custom of honoring the dead still lay behind the burial project, the public was assured, but even the Athenians had adjusted their ways when confronted with extraordinary circumstances. Casualties at Marathon, the most crucial victory of the Athenian republic against its antidemocratic Persian enemies, were deliberately buried on the battlefield as a tribute to the supreme sacrifice that these soldiers had made for a sacred cause. The Great War, then, was marketed as a modern-day Marathon, a fight of a freedom-loving people against a powerful despotic coalition. Such an extraordinary event demanded modification of—not departure from—

tradition, the intellectual basis of which was provided by the Marathon analogy.

In fact, at its inception, the overseas military program appeared to be a deceptively modest departure from tradition. Initial federal support for overseas monuments and cemeteries seemed to derive from a desire to behave prudently. All other Allies had interred their dead on the battlefields, and, in an era during which the United States was accused of reneging on many of its global commitments, the federal government had no wish to aggravate its former allies further by breaching what seemed to be an issue of international etiquette.

But the most important motivating factor for the federal government was the veritable invasion of symbolic representations of America in foreign lands, which, in the absence of a firm federal policy, had created an eclectic appearance in the immediate aftermath of the Great War. European Allies were besieged by private individuals, state governments, and veterans' organizations requesting permission to erect a wide variety of statues, markers, and tombstones throughout the former battlefields. This onslaught of private monuments commemorating a national event raised two crucial issues. The immediate problem, government officials informed Congress, was that Allies were liable to be "offended by too great a number of American monuments" that threatened to turn the entire continent into a sprawling and architecturally eclectic "second Gettysburg."[25]

This basically technical reason for intervening in the rush to erect battle monuments raised other, more political concerns. Given the fact that popular pressure rendered the erection of monuments unavoidable, the government attempted to control the content of these symbolic messages. Because the affairs of the United States abroad were no longer a mere collection of private interests, the government could not afford to project eclectic, uneven, conflicting images of itself. The political content of the United States' image abroad could not be controlled in an atmosphere of uncoordinated private monument building. An urgent need to "control" and "censor" battle monuments and cemeteries as "proper" representations of the United States abroad soon became an overriding preoccupation.[26]

To achieve this ambitious goal, the government established the American Battle Monuments Commission (ABMC). This organization, which was officially chartered in 1923 but had actually been functioning under various other names since 1919, was a presidential committee for monitoring and establishing an official style for America's cemeteries and battle monuments abroad. The committee's function was primarily political; the mandate exceeded the mere provision of burial space for America's war dead. Consequently, the care of America's military graves abroad was removed by legislation from the jurisdiction of the War Department and the Quartermaster General corps. Congress acknowledged the request of the executive branch to establish the ABMC as an independent civilian body that reported solely and directly to the president. Warren Harding appointed the first seven-member commission, which included General Pershing as chairman, three representatives of veterans' organizations, a representative of the Gold Star Mothers, a senator, and a congressman.

Because the commission's official meetings were few and far between and its members were engaged in a variety of other activities, the ABMC's permanent staff—in particular, its active chairman, its secretary, and its supervising architect—independently charted much of the commission's routine policies.[27] As active chairman, Pershing was engaged primarily in removing bureaucratic obstacles and in cutting red tape in order to allow his professional staff to work unhindered. In his appearances before Congress, veterans' organizations, and foreign governments, Pershing worked to counteract reservations—fiscal, artistic, and political. Moreover, he appears to have been single-handedly responsible for acquiring both approval and funding for the cemeteries' monumental memorial chapels.

Given his frequent absences from the country, Pershing delegated much of his authority to the committee's secretary, who had the appropriately classical name of Major Xenophon H. Price. A career army engineer who had supervised much of the interment prior to the creation of the commission, Price saw himself as representing the views of the military establishment. In accordance with the opinions of his superiors, he suggested that America's casualties in France should fulfill the function of markers of American military and political accomplishments. Much to the horror of commission member Senator David A. Reed, Price routinely ordered the "re-arranging" of graves—by which he meant the removal of bodies buried in irregular patterns that destroyed the aesthetic contours of the cemeteries-as-monuments. "From this I heartily dissent," Reed protested. "These graves 'not yet re-arranged' are graves made in war time, many of them made immediately after battle, and their irregularity is readily pardoned by everyone who understands this fact. . . . It is possible to have cemeteries altogether beautiful without re-arranging the graves. . . . Surely after seven years the bodies of the men are entitled to be left in peace."[28]

Reed's plea fell on deaf ears. Price's objection to the "effect of the unarranged graves upon the cemeteries concerned" carried the day.[29] This crucial decision underscored the unquestioned acceptance of the primacy of national goals over personal tragedies as regards these war monuments.

Price worked closely with the commission's supervising architect, Paul Cret, a French immigrant who had arrived in the United States at the age of twenty-seven and was professor of design at the University of Pennsylvania from 1903—the date of his arrival—to 1937. During this period, according to the American Institute of Architects' official history of architecture in the United States, Cret became one of the most influential purveyors of monumental architecture in the United States.[30]

Cret was a typical product of the French Ecole de Beaux Arts, which associated monumentality with classical architectural symbols. By the time Cret reached the United States, the Beaux Arts rage had already made the transatlantic crossing. Ever since the White City—Chicago's monumental World's Columbian Exposition of 1893—the Beaux Arts had monopolized the field of monumental and government architecture in the United States. As the most important international exposition ever to take place in the United States, the Chicago fair had turned into a battlefield between different schools among the country's architectural elite. The battle was won by traditionalists who endorsed a neoclassical architecture derived from the Beaux Arts approach. Supervising architect Daniel Burnham, whom we have already met in his capacity as city planner for the Philippines, espoused this basically conservative philosophy of design as part of a new order in American society. The tenets of classical architecture, according to Burnham, counteracted the excesses of the previous Gilded Age. The reintroduction of time-honored symbols of order promised to remedy the mayhem of what Burnham called an "inventive period" during which tradition had been erroneously discarded. In fact, in accepting classicism as the norm, the White City acknowledged the architectural preferences of big business, finance, and monopoly. The neoclassical citadels of America's bastion of conservatism—Wall Street—were sanctioned at the White City as the new public norm. The Beaux Arts form—monumental, uniform, and inherently paternalistic—now became the standard for federal, state, and municipal architecture.[31]

Cret's talent and professional sympathy with the neoclassicism of the country's architectural establishment proved, then, to be fortuitous. His ties to the motherland of Beaux Arts as well as his impeccable education provided him with the necessary springboard to further his career as an interpreter of the national image of the United States. He was an obvious choice for nomination to the federal Commission of Fine Arts (CFA), which was established in 1910 by President Taft. Much like the president, the architectural establishment, which had lobbied hard for the founding of the CFA, hoped to use the commission as a tool for employing neoclassicism as the basis for federal symbolism in Washington, D.C. The commission members accomplished their goal by funneling contracts for a budding federal buildings project toward their allies.

Cret was one of the most adamant neoclassical activists on the CFA. But his influence was destined to transcend the confines of the District of Columbia. As most of the cemeteries were slated for his native France, he also appeared to be the perfect person to guide official styles of American government architecture for foreign display.[32] As such, Cret's nomination ensured the imposition of the aesthetics and symbolism of contemporary government architecture in Washington, D.C., on the overseas cemeteries.[33]

These, then, were the hard facts behind Cret's rise to the position of primary interpreter of the national spirit abroad. The details do not, however, explain how a newcomer to the country, with no prior experience in the field of funerary design, achieved such an august position. Americans were great innovators in the celebration of death. From Frederick Law Olmsted's creation of the rural cemetery to the development of the park cemetery in the early twentieth century, American designers blazed new paths in this sensitive field.[34] But innovation apparently had no place in the designs of the ABMC and CFA as they opted for a conservative and cautious approach to their political mission.

Perhaps Cret's nomination sprang from the same sense of cultural inferiority that had driven the Founding Fathers of the American nation to appoint another Frenchman as visionary planner of the capital. A more likely explanation was the fact that the American political establishment hesitated and vacillated in establishing a clear policy for the country's new global status. Cret's nomination, then, was a compromise. He could produce a project as impressive as that of any other nation; at the same time, his style was innocuous. Pedestrian, well-worn, ecumenical designs promised to avoid any new enunciations and ensuing controversies, aesthetic or political.

Paul Cret's greatest asset as architectural director was his persuasiveness. He was a skilled negotiator, as his handling of the first crisis facing the ABMC demonstrated. After accepting the position of supervising architect, Cret faced the difficult task of convincing Congress to support the concept of pure memorial architecture. Various segments of American society, in particular, civic leaders, preferred the idea of "useful" monuments, such as memorial hospitals, and the dedication of community buildings to the memory of the fallen, both at home and in Europe. The idea of investing money in an architectural project lacking daily use conflicted with a basic pragmatic streak in American society. Critics of pure memorialism believed that memorial community buildings, "even those also in which monumental form is but slight and the arrest of attention less instant may, in the long run, serve a higher purpose as actual memorials, perpetuating in a social service of peace the heroic sacrifices made in war."[35]

Widespread support for useful monuments threatened to undermine the entire master plan for erecting officially ordained monuments to America in foreign countries. Motivated by public backing for the useful memorial, Congress considered commemorating American deeds in Europe by underwriting a memorial highway project that entailed the construction of a network of American-built roads throughout the former battlefields. Much like useful memorials at home, advocates of the highway bill envisioned their project as fulfilling a dual purpose. On a practical level it would provide much-needed relief for the devastated transportational infrastructure in areas hard-hit by the Great War. On a more sublime level, the roads not only would furnish physical linkage, but would also nurture spiritual bonds between gracious American benefactors and grateful European beneficiaries.[36]

Supporters of pure memorial architecture both at home and abroad tried to counteract such popular sentiments by claiming that functional memorials represented a contradiction in terms. One of pure architecture's most articulate spokesmen was the architect Egerton Swartwout, a disciple and ultimately a beneficiary of the ABMC's quest for pure monuments. Utilitarian memorials, according to Swartwout, suffered from two basic problems. First and foremost, useful memorials were usually associated with the philanthropic endeavors of robber barons. The commemoration of a national event and a communal tragedy demanded a medium sufficiently different from the self-aggrandizing legacies of the rich and famous.

> If it is the intention or the testamentary obligation to commemorate the industrial capacity and business acumen of a highly successful manufacturer, say of Chiclets or Esquimo Pie [sic], I can imagine that there might be built, in close proximity to the factory of the deceased, a neat Pompeian swimming pool or an early English billiard parlor, or an entirely modernesque hall for movies and a place of meeting for the social activities of the local Rotary Club ... but I cannot imagine the erection as a memorial, whether by a state or municipality, of a strictly utilitarian building which should properly be paid for by taxation.[37]

Useful artifacts as memorials, he continued, had a tendency to lose their memorial connotations "not because of any lack of feeling or of patriotism, but because we as a people are likely to forget quickly unless we have some visible and beautiful object to awaken our remembrance." In hammering this point home, Paul Cret added that the fundamental problem of utilitarian architecture was the lack of spiritual endurance, the litmus test of a successful memorial: "Does our belief in 'utility,'—however temporary that utility may be,—denote a spirit superior to that which inspired the ... Egyptian and Roman builders, who, intent upon conquering time, were willing to pay the price required, or does it bear witness only to a mean and short-sighted parsimony? . . . Suffice it to say that a work of commemorative architecture which has little chance of enduring is hardly worthy of the name."[38]

But the ultimate argument in favor of sheer monumentalism was political in nature. "Suppose, for example," Egerton Swartwout argued, "those in charge of the Washington Monument had decided to build a new wing to the capitol instead of the majestic shaft which is now the center of the mall treatment. It would have been a practical thing, to be sure, but who in 50 years, or in five either . . . would know that the new wing was a memorial?" Modern war monuments were intended to serve well-defined political goals. Overseas, they galvanized support for a forceful American presence in foreign lands; at home, they reiterated the preeminence of the national state. Any attempt to accomplish additional functions threatened to dilute the political effectiveness of the monument. "No structure can serve two purposes. It is either a memorial of some great act or sacrifice . . . or else it is merely a school or a town hall."[39]

In the case of the proposal for an American memorial highway project in Europe, the concept of useful monuments appeared to have an additional drawback. A widespread network of American-built roads—dotted with innumerable plaques and monuments, maintained by an American agency, and bearing a typically American name, such as the proposed Lincoln or Roosevelt Memorial Highway—could conceivably irritate host countries. It reached far beyond the envisioned aim of maintaining a symbolic American presence in foreign lands, and might, under certain circumstances, induce fears of American imperialist ambitions. The cemetery project, by contrast, appeared in a much more favorable light. It had the monumental qualities that a highway lacked, and it was conducive to the ultimate objective of achieving a coordinated symbolic presence on foreign soil. Given the growing preoccupation with fashioning a standardized national image, and while occasionally agreeing to the construction of modest and privately funded memorial bridges and community centers in the war-torn villages of France and Belgium, the ABMC successfully killed the highway bill and received approval for a program of pure monumental memorial architecture.[40]

Under the supervision and close guidance of supervising architect Paul Cret and commission secretary Xenophon Price, eight American military cemeteries, containing the bodies of 31,000 casualties, were superimposed upon the pastoral countryside of western Europe. All cemeteries employed the same fundamental elements: rigid rectangular designs and rows of immaculate grave markers placed upon tidy lawns. From afar, this combination of white markers on a green background appeared as furrows in a field. Upon closer inspection, the overpowering presence of innumerable crosses and the harsh gleam of marble erased much of this bucolic impression. The unrelenting uniformity of the sites, their standardized styles, laconic epitaphs, and the removal of the graves from the sphere of family and community obscured much of the sense of individual tragedy. Instead, these "silent cities" and the adjacent monuments were fashioned as symbols of a national event, in which citizens were called to exchange individual self-interest for communal goals. Death in battle was not a personal sacrifice but participation in an American mission that in modern times acknowledged no geographical boundaries.

The model, then, was the Civil War cemetery and its invocation of an all-encompassing common cause. But the growing scope of national goals in the early twentieth century induced some fundamental changes in design policy and symbolism. Austere, standardized World War cemeteries replaced the haphazard appearance of Civil War cemeteries, with their large number of private monuments and tombstones. The national significance of some Civil War cemeteries had been obscured by the eclectic grave markers and private statues. In the cemeteries of the Great War there would be no such opportunity for "ostentatious" personal expression.

The ABMC's policy of controlling and censoring the erection of monuments within or in the vicinity of the cemeteries produced a standardized procedure for marking important combat sites and honoring equally the contributions of all participating troops in the Great War. These tight regulations differed quite significantly from Civil War customs. At the Gettysburg battlefield, for example, the absence of a uniform system of marking led to a potpourri of monuments divergent in size, shape, and cost. A casual visitor who perceived the magnitude of monuments as an indicator of actual participation was liable to receive an erroneous impression of the impact of specific units. Troops from New Jersey and Wisconsin, for example, had suffered similar casualties, about six hundred men each. But New Jersey had invested $44,000 for monuments and markers while Wisconsin had spent about $3,000. Even Arlington National Cemetery, supporters of government censorship declared before a House committee, "was marred beyond repair . . . by the permission which had been given to private individuals to erect monuments" in the officers' section.[41]

By contrast, the ABMC hoped to erase any sense of individuality from its European cemeteries, thereby elevating the event of death in national service to a purely abstract level. All features were to be of the same size and shape. The commission disqualified all markers, statues, and other devices intended to celebrate the personal accomplishments of individual soldiers and commanders. Even the epitaphs were uniform. Only name, rank, and serial number appeared on each tombstone. The prevalent British custom of allowing families to engrave short eulogies from an approved list was disallowed, too, so as not to mar the uniformity of the graves. The monuments were there to represent the United States rather than to commemorate the fallen.

These American Great War cemeteries departed in another crucial aspect from previous customs and traditions: they were situated neither on national soil nor within the United States' traditional sphere of influence. Lacking any meaningful precedent, Americans relied on the British experience in adjusting its Civil War concept of the war cemetery to foreign surroundings.

The British had been seeking for some time an appropriate mode of interment of soldiers on foreign soil, one that would underline the implications of multinational warfare for their nation's well-being. As veterans of far-reaching colonial escapades and multinational military campaigns, the British had tinkered with various strategies for employing their military dead in foreign lands as secular monuments of national worship from as early as the Battle of Waterloo. But they formulated a firm policy on this issue only during the Great War. Thus, even before the cessation of hostilities, the recently established British Imperial War Graves Commission (IWGC) devised a plan for uniform tombstones placed upon a neat lawn and capped by a centrally placed monumental design.[42]

The most important decision of the IWGC was its unrelenting resistance to the repatriation of any of the war dead. The sheer number of casualties obviously influenced this policy; the British had suffered over a million fatalities. Repatriation would have been an impossible task. Consequently, British authorities turned their attention to translating a technical obstacle into an ideologically didactic project. A million military graves, then, were transformed from simple burial sites to symbolic representations of the positive qualities of empire. Their designs and symbolism reiterated in one form or another the message that "men of the British Empire took their lives in their hands" in order to "preserve the idea and the reality of freedom not only for the British Empire and its Allies, but for all the world."[43] In less abstract terms, the overseas cemeteries were designed to reassert the primacy of Great Britain in international affairs. Primarily, the British used their overseas cemeteries to strengthen their grip on their rapidly fading empire. By imposing a common burial plan on all nations of the empire, Prime Minister Stanley Baldwin announced, the nation hoped to sustain a Victorian concept of empire in modern times:

> The War itself helped to consolidate the Empire by the bond of united effort and equal sacrifice in a common cause. It is of good augury that in peace the whole Empire has acted in like unison, without any shadow of question or difference, in paying tribute to all those who gave their lives for that cause.

These cemeteries themselves—the thousand habitations of our dead—testify, and will testify to coming generations, to the quickened sense of Imperial unity which has grown out of our great trial.[44]

Accordingly, British authorities placed great emphasis on the architecture and aesthetics of cemeteries in crucial corners of the empire. In newly acquired and highly prized Palestine, for example, the graves of British subjects signaled in no uncertain terms "that a nation which has made such sacrifices for another country has the prescriptive right to control the destinies of that country so that these sacrifices shall not be in vain."[45] The decision to rely exclusively on tombstones "made in Great Britain by British labour and of British material" was an unambiguous and forceful symbol of British power in the global arena. Indeed, the British government argued that the cemeteries represented a test of British will and long-term commitment to its mission. The cemeteries "will be supported and sustained by the wealth of this great nation and Empire as long as we remain a great nation and Empire," vowed the British secretary of state for war.[46]

Within this context, the choice of a lawn cemetery replete with flowers and trees served multiple purposes. The idyllic natural setting allayed the pain evoked by the staggering death toll by suggesting transfiguration rather than the finality of death; the spirit of the dead lived on in the trees and flowers ensconcing the final resting place. Symbolically, the perpetual care of these overseas shrines stressed British commitment to empire. "The strenuous effort to make cemeteries" in foreign lands "more beautiful year by year" indicated "that for the members of a British administration the aim and object will always be to improve year by year the conditions of life of the people."[47] Furthermore, immaculate, parklike garden cemeteries deflected misgivings of next-of-kin concerning the unyielding ban on repatriation. Well-kept gardens were intended to persuade relatives that the graves of their loved ones "were being tended as they would have cared for them themselves."[48]

Another important visual aspect of the overseas British cemeteries was their unrelenting uniformity: evenly spaced graves capped by identically shaped tombstones, with a large stone monument in the forefront as a symbol of the durability of empire. This device, repeated in the hundreds of cemeteries abroad, underscored an even more complex quest than that of maintaining the empire intact. Uniformity implied the prime importance of obedience and unquestioning acceptance of national goals even within a climate of democratization and rapidly expanding personal freedom. Uniform contours represented the unquestioning loyalty of all subjects, the "discipline and obedience to authority" that supposedly characterized all facets of British society.[49] Perhaps there was no better example of the unwavering loyalty demanded by the state in modern times than the actions of a Canadian unit in France that, on the eve of a crucial battle, "had marked out the land, dug trenches, and made all arrangements" for their own burials "in the forthcoming action" in accordance with a burial plan supplied by the IWGC. "Within twenty-four hours of that brilliant and successful feat of arms the graves were each marked and recorded, and the organization did not break down even in that sector where a Canadian Burial Officer was killed."[50]

The most outstanding quality of the imperial cemeteries, however, was their departure from a cardinal principle of imperial rule and a time-honored tradition of a class-conscious British society. In one of its most important decisions, the IWGC had decided to bury its dead without distinction of rank, creed, color, or nationality. Ostensibly, the eradication of social, racial, political, and military distinctions signified the idea of equality in death. On a more practical level, the egalitarian burial ground also elevated the national policies that had led to the war from the level of partisan politics to the heights of class-transcending, sacred national goals.[51]

For the most part, the United States adopted this same strategy for dealing with its war casualties. Britain's designs, after all, accepted many of the guidelines that had informed the Civil War cemeteries project. One should note, however, that some of the adopted British customs conflicted with hallowed American mores, while other important aspects of the British model were modified extensively. Both the modifications and the acceptance of those British designs that clashed with previous American customs demand special attention if we are to seek some uniquely American significance in these national monuments on foreign soil.

Perhaps the most surprising decision of the American authorities was the adoption of the egalitarian mode of burial. In this sense the United States' cemeteries in Europe deviated from well-entrenched domestic traditions—in particular, the imposition of the country's class and racial distinctions on its military cemeteries. At Gettysburg, where the graves and monuments were used to reconstruct the battle lines and actual deployment of troops, there had been no distinctions on the basis of rank or color. But this was not the case in other Civil War cemeteries. The model was Arlington National Cemetery, where officers were interred in separate sections, their graves often adorned with ostentatious private tombstones. Moreover, the repatriated bodies of Great War casualties at Arlington were segregated according to race; ironically, the graves of black casualties of the Great War lay in the immediate vicinity of the Confederate plot.[52] On foreign soil, then, the United States hid its internal conflicts and presented, through its overseas cemeteries, a united front that belied the social and economic schisms of the country.

The employment of America's war dead as political monuments deviated from the British scheme because of technical problems as well. Relative to its partners-in-arms, American casualties had been modest. The loss of life among Allied powers was staggering. The British Empire had lost 1,104,890 men; France lost 1 in 28 of her entire population. By contrast, Americans suffered losses of 1 in 2,000. The American dead for the entire war numbered about 74,000; the number of British missing just at the Battle of the Somme was over 73,000. The high rate of repatriation of American war dead left only a handful of graves in each of the more than eight-hundred temporary burial grounds that were established immediately after armistice. These scattered remains in sparsely populated cemeteries were poor material for the building of monuments.

The solution offered was to remove the bodies from their temporary burial grounds and concentrate them in a small number of large cemeteries where the implications of America's war effort could be articulated in more potent tones. Accordingly, the largest cemetery at Meuse-Argonne received about 14,000 bodies. Five other cemeteries in France varied in size from 1,900 graves at Somme to the 6,000 tombs at Oise-Aisne. Two small cemeteries in Flanders Field, Belgium, and Brookwood, England, contained only a few hundred graves each as token symbols of the American war effort outside of France. In contrast to the British plan of establishing hundreds of small military cemeteries in order to emphasize their quantitative impact on the war, a limited number of large American cemeteries underscored the magnitude of America's sufferings. Concentration of a large number of graves at each site suggested that even though America suffered comparatively few casualties, the loss was still significant.

The significance of the cemeteries as monuments to an American achievement was further enhanced through the use of a unique grave marker. Rather than the unimposing rectangular tombstone, which was employed by Americans as a standard Civil War marker and by the British in their Great War cemeteries, the ABMC implanted marble crosses. The freestanding cross implied sacrificial death—a symbol of the Passion of Christ—the significance of which would not be lost on the mostly Catholic population of the war zone. Here, once again, the architects of American cemeteries hoped to counteract the impression of relatively modest casualties. Aesthetic, artistic, and technical objections to the use of this new form of marker were brushed aside by the politically motivated members of the ABMC. "Imagine McCrae's poem rewritten like this," Senator David Reed argued: "In Flanders Field the Poppies Grow; Between the squat little headstones, row on row."[53]

These cross-laden fields represented the central but not the only motif of the project. Numerous monuments were strewn throughout France. The most important memorials were three large monuments erected at the sites of the three crucial battles in which the AEF had played a significant role. These monuments, of mostly heroic proportions and positioned on dominating hills, acted as signposts calling attention to the nearby cemeteries. The importance of the American contribution to the war effort was underscored by placing these oversized monuments within a setting of "vestiges de guerre." At Montfaucon, John Russell Pope's towering victory column was surrounded by the relics of a village that had been destroyed during the course of the war. American authorities hastily purchased a newly constructed house in the vicinity of the monument, only to demolish it promptly so as not to spoil the general appearance of an American victory column rising out of a European ruin.[54] In addition to marking the sight of a crucial battle, this American memorial shaft soaring above French ruins signified a new order emerging from the ashes of battle. At the same time, Pope's generic neoclassicism was a wonderful indicator of just how vague the contours of the new order were. The column was a replica of McKim, Mead, and White's memorial column at West Point. The monument deliberately avoided the proclamation of new political and aesthetic parameters. It was big and impressive, but quite light on content (Fig. 2).

Like the Montfaucon Monument, Egerton Swartwout's Doric temple at Montsec, which commemorated the capture of the St. Mihiel Salient, employed predictable classical lines. Swartwout's Propylea perched upon an Acropolis-like hill overlooking the nearby Necropolis, home of America's martyrs for the democratic cause of all western nations (Fig. 3). This gesture to Athenian origins not only followed the tradition of using classical motifs to interpret the significance of national war dead; it also implied that the United States had control of the necessary cultural apparatus to assure continuity of western political and cultural traditions across the rupture of the Great War.[55] The immortality of western values was embodied in this replication of the Athenian Acropolis, for here, an inscription read, "Time will not dim the glory of the deeds."

Swartwout's monument had the advantage of being imposing yet not imperious. The use of a standard classical architecture placed upon an intimidating topographical site suggested importance, but, being a generic form of monumentalism, the American Propylea contained no heavy nationalistic undertones. In fact, all of the American memorials ensured through careful choice of style that their ostentatious contours would impress yet not antagonize. For the most part they avoided aggressive, exclusively American symbolism, relying instead on abstract values or singing the praises of Allied cooperation. Thus, the Montsec monument contained an inscription in French and English that characterized the temple as "a lasting symbol of the friendship and cooperation between the French and American Armies."[56] The United States cautiously

2. American victory column rising out of European ruins: Montfaucon Monument (John Russell Pope, sculptor)

3. Propylea-style monument: St. Mihiel Monument (Egerton Swartwout, architect)

4. The United States and France as co-partners: Chateau-Thierry Monument (Paul Cret, architect)

presented itself as an important participant rather than the unchallenged leader. For example, in the third large memorial, the Chateau-Thierry Monument, representations of the United States and France stood side by side as identical figures of equally heroic proportions, co-partners in war and its aftermath (Fig. 4).

There is little doubt, then, that the august yet polite cemeteries and monuments sought to impress but not annoy foreign hosts. Cautious diplomacy is only part of the story, however. Internal machinations within the United States, and issues not directly related to the project, influenced its final form as well. Intentionally or otherwise, these artifacts also reflected issues that were not necessarily tied to the ulterior motive of furthering the United States' international aims. Much of the symbolism in these projects chronicled internal cultural turmoil in the United States. A preoccupation with the implications of cultural change and continuity in the wake of the Great War permeated the cemeteries.

Indeed, the cemeteries of the First World War clarify the historical debate about the ramifications of global warfare for the American psyche. According to Henry May, the First World War represented a watershed, the "end of American innocence." May's seminal investigation of turn-of-the-century American elites suggests that massive mobilization of the nation's resources, the regimentation of personal lives, and the unprecedented carnage eradicated cherished nineteenth-century notions of individualism and laissez-faire thought in the political, cultural, and economic spheres.[57] David Kennedy argues otherwise. A brief nineteen-month adventure, in which few of the conscripted troops were actually involved in combat, was much too fleeting an experience to challenge entrenched mores and values. The American people, according to Kennedy, went to war imbued with nineteenth-century ideas and images concerning warfare's noble and heroic possibilities, which were derived from the rhetoric of the Civil War. The Great War was too brief and its casualties too few to unsettle fundamental cultural concepts.[58]

At first glance, the overall impression of Great War cemeteries appears to support Kennedy's contention; the shrines evoked traditional values. The historical designs of turn-of-the-century monumental architecture in the United States had inspired much of the architecture of the cemetery chapels and other memorial structures. Given supervising architect Paul Cret's loyalties within the architectural profession, the predominance of ponderous classical designs is not surprising. Cret claimed in his own defense that his designs were more than a mere adaptation of the style of his masters. He stated that neoclassicism in military funerary architecture was also a symbolic affirmation of America's traditional democratic ethos; the mimesis of Greek temples invoked the humanist traditions that Americans had always associated with classical form. The use of "Greek simplicity," Cret wrote, was not a slavish "archeological adaptation," but followed "the American tradition of the past colonial period."[59] By using classical motifs, rather than inventing new symbols to commemorate the tragedy of modern warfare, Cret and his federal client had found an artistic idiom for representing a sense of continuity with the past. Given the many examples of classical funerary architecture that had survived the test of time, Cret stated categorically that the "individuality of the artist," or, for that matter, the aspirations of a nation, had "no need of any brand new theme": "The architect of tomorrow may find in the good old program . . . an opportunity for work just as characteristic of his times as the examples we have cited are vividly characteristic of their own periods. There is no time-worn theme, but only time-worn ways of treating it as well as methods which are fresh and new."[60]

Cret appeared to be saying that his reliance on classical architectural idioms was not motivated by an uncensored admiration of anything specifically Roman or Greek. Instead he found classicism to be a universal motif that transcended the barriers of time and place. On an abstract level, then, Cret expressed what James Early has called a lingering prerelativist belief "in a uniform standard of taste valid for all arts in all ages . . . analogous to Newton's effort to comprehend all the diversity of the physical universe within a single system of mathematical laws."[61]

In addition to the classical designs of most of the funerary architecture, and without sensing any contradiction in terms, the ABMC also approved some medieval-style artifacts (Fig. 5). This particular historical form consecrated the war effort by evoking comparisons between the Great War and the Crusades of a distant medieval age. In the Great War as in the Crusades, according to this unspoken logic, the self-appointed civilized nations had joined hands in a struggle for a holy cause that transcended their differences. Thus, a visit to the Great War cemeteries in the years following the war was considered a "pilgrimage," not unlike the journeys to holy shrines following the Crusades.[62]

The iconography and statues of the Great War cemeteries complemented the Crusades comparison as well as the more general assertion that victory would strengthen traditional order rather than forge novel designs for a brave new world. Sculptures of soldiers of the Great War were juxtaposed with representations of knights, symbols of a personal style of warfare never again to be waged. The depiction of modern-day soldiers as individual fighters—contemporary versions of medieval warriors who were stripped of any meaningful reference to the larger war machine of which they had been part—paid homage to the type of personal war of valor that most Americans apparently thought they had fought.[63]

This cautious and conservative memorialization of the war effort did not go unchallenged, of course. The ABMC confronted a growing resistance to its designs, even within the architectural establishment. In 1919, the American Institute of Architects' Subcommittee on Education lashed out at the reliance "on architectural forms belonging to an aristocratic culture of the past," and castigated the "practice of teaching without any contact whatsoever with the world of reality" and the "dynamic" nature of American society.[64] The ABMC withstood these attacks on its worldview because, irrespective of the many misgivings, modern American society failed to produce suitable symbolic alternatives for articulating the

5. Medieval architecture in American military cemeteries: Romanesque chapel, Aisne-Marne Cemetery (Cram and Ferguson, architects)

impact of the Great War. Consequently, the architectural symbolism of America abroad gravitated toward the point of least resistance: the repetition of well-worn clichés.

This tenuous interpretation of the significance of a momentous contemporary event was not only an architectural issue; it also appeared in written engravings. The cemeteries and their adjacent monuments were accompanied by small medallion-type maps, which described the courses of the major battles in similarly anachronistic terms. These descriptions avoided any meaningful documentation of the mechanics of modern warfare—in particular, the interaction between men and the machines of battle. The rhetorics of the campaigns of the First World War were simplified chronologies of victory resulting from valorous human behavior. "On October 4," a description of the attack on the Hindenberg Line engraved at the Meusse-Argonne Cemetery reads, "a second general attack was launched by the First Army and vigorously pushed, during the course of which many important gains were made." Eventually, "the 32nd Division on October 9 pushed forward part way up the slopes of the Côte Dame Marie . . . where it established itself in a trench of the Hindenberg Line."[65] This typical pedestrian blow-by-blow description of American accomplishments in the Great War did not document how the actual battle was fought and managed. Descriptions of the devices of modern warfare that had brought about the capitulation of German forces were conspicuous by their absence. We are led to believe that mere willpower or fate had induced the turn of events.[66]

The iconography of the actual war effort within the cemeteries did little to dispel this notion of individual effort and personal warfare. The machinery of war, the primary reason for victory and the force behind the United States' obvious international superiority, received scant attention. Soldier-warriors were glorified, machines were not. To the degree that instruments of war appeared in the United States' European cemeteries, the weapon of choice was the cannon, which harked back to the symbolic rhetoric of Civil War monuments. The occasional employment of modern weaponry in the cemeteries' iconography, such as the tank and rifles adorning the exterior of the Somme chapel, were depicted without establishing any relationship between the arms and their operators. The lonely tank and rigid lines of rifles did not imply any connection between their function and the war. They were not depicted in a state of action, but rather as mute reminders of the terrible toll of battle. Silent, immobile weapons were used to enhance classic motifs of death in battle. The lone cannon and the soldierless rifles were traditional symbols mourning the military casualties (Fig. 6).

Indeed, the art and architectural designs of the cemeteries and monuments were mostly commemorative; they were not bearers of tidings. To use the terminology of Erwin Panofsky in his own categorization of funerary monuments, the Great War monuments were retrospective rather than prospective. They evoked tradition. Here, death had no bearing on future developments. The notion of resurrection, the traditional figurative vehicle for describing future designs, was conspicuously absent. The statues evolved around the themes of remembrance, valor, and romance. With the exception of the Pegasus statue at St. Mihiel—a winged horse representing the soul in flight—the statues of the Great War did not address the fate of the fallen warrior as representative of the nation beyond his grave.[67]

6. Chapel at Somme Military Cemetery (George Howe, architect)

The anachronistic concept of voluntary premodern sacrifice was retained through the design of the gateways, the layout of the tombs, and the placement of the official monuments. In seven of the eight Great War shrines, the "pilgrim" entered the site through a sea of individual graves; the initial confrontation of the visitor was with the personal side of death in war (Fig. 7). The obliteration of distinctions according to rank, creed, or color emphasized the theme of voluntarism; a citizens' army drawn from an egalitarian society lay beneath the crosses. Unlike the British tradition of crowding the tombstones, the American graves were laid out spaciously, thereby enhancing the individuality of each plot. The well-spaced Latin crosses and Stars of David perched on thin supports created an optical illusion of ample private space for each individual plot.[68] Only after wading through the sea of markers, the multiple signs of personal sacrifice, did the visitor stumble upon the official version of the war related by the art and architecture of the chapel area. These structures were invariably situated at the point most distant from the entrance. In accordance with the architectural guidelines laid down by the ABMC, the chapels and other official edifices were of a modest character so as not to upstage the grave area.[69]

And yet, this recycling of anachronistic themes—individualism, voluntarism, laissez-faire government—appears to be more the result of uncer-

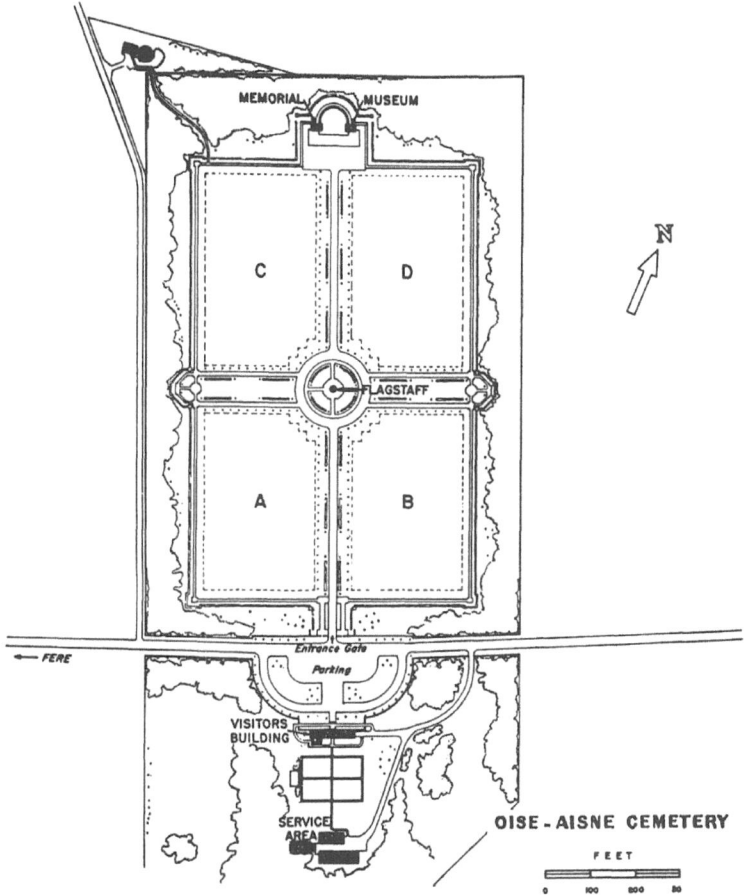

7. Typical layout of American Great War cemetery: Oise-Aisne Military Cemetery (Jacques Greber, landscape architect)

tainty than a reactionary manifestation of latent conservatism. Nothing in this harking back to the themes of a now-defunct political culture could erase the bold decision to erect permanent American political statements on foreign soil. Indeed, a careful look at some of the design elements suggests the ramifications of change. The landscaping of the cemeteries, in particular, acknowledged the passing away of preindustrial voluntarism. This ostensibly technical issue reflected efforts to reconcile tradition, voluntarism, and individualism with an incongruous setting of rapid modernization.

In a somewhat covert fashion the cemeteries' layout recognized that the Great War had been a feat of modern times, the harnessing of individual human beings to the imperatives of machines and anonymous policymakers. Hence, the direction of the walkways was such that all visitors ultimately confronted the buildings, with their official interpretation of the war effort. This steering of visitors toward the official structures assured that due homage would be paid to government for its role of coordinating the will of the people (see Fig. 7). Moreover, much of the sense of anachronistic individuality was overshadowed by the overall standardization of design. Identical tombstones arranged in uniform patterns and rows produced an aesthetic that only a society that had internalized the discipline of urbanization and industrialization could appreciate. The powerful gesture of eradicating distinctions of rank did not affect the constant specter of collectivism; equality in death, like equality in life, could be achieved only by the exercise of the power of the state. Ultimately the repetitive grave sites evoked images of persons as replaceable cogs in the machine of war rather than models of personal valor and individual sacrifice. Tens of thousands of American families had accepted that the most important aspect of their loved ones' lives was their sacrifice for an abstract cause; consequently, they surrendered their sons to a national shrine rather than mourn their death as a personal family tragedy. This communal gesture, which resulted in no small part from strong governmental pressures, was a stark commentary on the anachronism of individualism in a modern setting.

The difficulty in the symbolism of the cemeteries of the Great War lay in using a modern event to celebrate the virtues of the past, and in employing a pathological development of an urban-industrial society as an affirmation of America's allegiance to time-honored values. Thus, the assignment of traditional symbolism to articulate the Great War should not be taken as an indication of the total lack of impact that the event had had on the American psyche. Each element of tradition was balanced by a subtle acknowledgment of its limitations in the new age. The employment of architecture and imagery to define America's attachment to traditional, preindustrial creeds was counterbalanced by the very decision to bury Americans on foreign soil. Paeans of individualism confronted equally forceful indications of regimentation and the suppression of individualism for the common good.

The cemeteries suggest that in the 1920s, when these monuments were being constructed, the perceived benefits of modern times on an American way of life remained undetermined. The fundamentally classical designs of the cemeteries attempted, however unevenly, to assure continuity despite obvious signs of upheaval. At the same time, elements of the landscaping acknowledged the inadequacies of traditional formulas in a world of confusing dilemmas.

If the cemeteries left internal cultural issues unresolved, they also failed to accomplish their designers' goals as tools of foreign policy. By the late 1920s America's European Allies were completely disenchanted with the war. It appeared that the only vestiges of the war were burdensome debts, economic disarray, and social turmoil. Great War monuments and cemeteries failed to evoke sustained admiration for an American way of life. As early as 1926, reports on vandalism of American cemeteries filtered back home. "French hatred of the United States is so intense," observed Senator Thaddeus H. Caraway of Arkansas upon returning from France, "that they do not hesitate to insult the 30,000 American World War dead who rest in French soil. . . . Go into these cemeteries and you will find ribald and insulting remarks chalked or penciled on many of the little white crosses."[70]

By the late 1920s, the image of Americans abroad contrasted sharply with the legends of the cemeteries. At the Grand Parade of the American legion in Paris of late 1927, where Parisians were exposed to the living rather than the dead, an American reporter witnessed an army of "the obviously arrogant, the obviously drunk, giving vent to the opinion that all of Paris is a bar and a brothel—and that the town is ours!" America's demands in the wake of the war effort were symbolized by the inebriated veterans staggering by the Arc de Triomphe in an array of vulgar costumes.[71]

The thwarted goals of the Great War obviously affected the significance of the cemeteries as political monuments, but the primary reason for the project's ineffectiveness was its irresolute symbolism. The private tastes of architects, incoherent specifications of the federal client, and a pervasive uncertainty as to the role of the United States in the postwar years conspired against the creation of a politically impressive project. The choice of historic themes for the war cemeteries was, perhaps, prudent. However, American funerary innovations and the flair for dealing with death in an imaginative manner had no effect on the ABMC. The emulation of others, the selection of a foreign-born, French-educated chief architect, and the lack of any meaningful innovation beyond the ideas crystallized during the American Civil War: all of these factors point toward an ambivalent assessment of the postwar global standing of the United States.

In 1914, Walter Lippmann described Woodrow Wilson as a person who "knows that there is a new world demanding new methods, but he dreams of an older world. He is torn between the two."[72] This inner contradiction between change and continuity that permeated the political culture of the United States accounts for much of the hesitant symbolism of the country's monuments abroad. Change had proceeded too rapidly for either politicians or architects to keep pace, and they retreated toward the symbolism of other cultures and an earlier age.

Discontent with visionary cemeteries even led to sporadic demands for their dismantling and the return of the war dead to the United States. Yet this was not to be. Indeed, disappointment, rather than leading to the abandonment of monument building in foreign lands, spawned another, related project. The solution offered was to expand the number of American monuments abroad and move beyond the narrow context of a historical event of uncertain legacy. The theme of war and sacrifice was now complemented by the more conventional idea of fashioning diplomatic outposts as national monuments. Once absolved of the burden of producing a positive interpretation of a discredited war, the country's political architects set their sights on developing a more coherent and uniquely American symbol for foreign exhibition.

3

From Palace to Plantation House

THE POLITICAL ARCHITECTURE OF
AMERICAN EMBASSIES, 1926–1932

THE FOREIGN POLICY of the United States during the 1920s has often been characterized as unimaginative, bland, and self-defeating. The central figure during these years, Secretary of State Charles Evans Hughes, spent most of his efforts devising schemes for scaling down American involvement in multinational ventures, while his successor, the mediocre Frank Kellogg, is credited with doing nothing significant. "The makers of American Foreign Policy," William Leuchtenberg stated in his study of the interwar years, either marked time or "concentrated on destroying instruments of power."[1]

This uncomplimentary assessment of U.S. foreign policy does injustice to the grand designs of the Republican administrations of this era—in particular, their ambitious plans for expanding the country's diplomatic presence abroad.[2] During the 1920s, the United States methodically developed the framework for its informal empire, the so-called Pax Americana; expanded diplomatic outposts promised to be one of the most tangible aspects of this new foreign policy agenda.

Both the Harding and Coolidge administrations pushed through Congress a series of measures aimed at strengthening the diplomatic corps as a policy tool by constructing a series of monumental diplomatic edifices abroad. The design of these buildings represented an ambitious exercise in political architecture. The embassies were meant to be more than mere abodes for diplomatic activities; they were conceived as symbols of the American political entity on foreign soil. Even though the plans were only partially completed, the infrastructure for devising a strategy of political architecture remained intact, and has influenced the dynamics of American diplomacy to this day.

The formulation of a comprehensive strategy for diplomatic architecture abroad was directly tied to America's unique status in the immediate postwar years. The United States had acquired an empire, which in itself was not an unusual phenomenon; the spoils of war invariably land in the lap of the victor. However, the American understanding of global power was novel. "We are able to dispense with the soldier almost completely," commented the noted theologian and philosopher Reinhold Niehbur.

"We are the first empire of the world to establish our sway without legions."[3] The United States influenced the affairs of others, according to historian Charles Beard, because of its newly acquired economic hegemony, the attractive, leveling forms of its popular culture, and its manifest dynamism.[4] Yet, like any other product, sustained acceptance of the American way demanded constant monitoring of international trends as well as a comprehensive, coordinated advertising campaign. The promotion of a positive image could not be left to chance, nor could it be a private initiative, Secretary of Commerce Hoover implied. International perceptions of American culture and society affected the fortunes of American commerce abroad. Image and the marketing of goods were intertwined in an intricate network of international relations to which only governments were privy. Under these circumstances, Hoover stated, the government needed "adequate" diplomatic and consular quarters abroad to coordinate this complicated matrix of trade.[5]

Immediately after the First World War, the United States found itself in the awkward position of lacking the necessary devices for managing and monitoring its new status of global superpower. The country's diplomatic presence abroad remained negligible. The Foreign Service was still quite suspect in many quarters, and, irrespective of the legislation of 1911, the systematic acquisition of diplomatic property had not materialized. By 1924 the Lowden Act of 1911 had led to the acquisition of only nine buildings. The slow implementation of the bill, according to the official history of the State Department, was due primarily to "the limitations of $150,000 on the amount to be expended at any one place and the requirement that a specific appropriation be made for the purchase of each property."[6] No less important was the fact that the Lowden Act did not establish a bureaucratic apparatus for handling the acquisition, construction, and maintenance of American government property abroad. The procurement of embassies and legations to function as tools for American diplomatic activity remained a haphazard affair.

The first steps toward sharpening the diplomatic profile of the United States in the postwar years came with enactment into law of the Rogers Act of 1924. This crucial piece of legislation provided a new framework for a modern career Foreign Service. The Rogers Act established a unified Foreign Service in place of the previous separate diplomatic and consular branches. All appointments were to be by commission to a class rather than a particular post, and promotions were to be based on an institutionalized merit system. Thus, with the implementation of a more peaceful tone of international relations in which persuasion or economic might rather than gunpowder figured as the main form of dialogue between nations, the American diplomatic corps appeared fit to meet the challenges of a new era. Salaries matched real needs, and talent rather than wealth became the ostensible criterion for diplomatic assignments. The groundwork had been laid for a new approach to foreign policy.

In order to complement the transformation of the Foreign Service into a modern and workable tool of the executive branch, legislation was enacted to provide the tangible means for carrying out the work of diplomacy: the embassy edifice. During the Harding and Coolidge years, the presidents personally cajoled a reluctant Congress into opening its purse strings for the construction of American legations and embassies. In 1926, President Coolidge signed the Porter Act into law. The act established the Foreign Service Buildings Commission (FSBC), a powerful political body comprising the secretaries of state, commerce, and the Treasury as well as ranking members of the House and Senate Foreign Affairs Committees. The task of the commission was to devise the architectural strategies and construction priorities of American legations abroad. An unprecedented Foreign Service Building Fund of $10 million financed the construction programs, and the State Department created the Foreign Service Buildings Office to administer the program. The procedure for expanded embassy construction had become a reality.

By 1932, the United States owned property in forty different overseas locations, and the administration had requested an additional multiyear funding program to construct almost one hundred new diplomatic outposts.[7] Unfortunately, neither the official records of the State Department nor the files of the administrative office illuminate the significance of this swift rise of American symbols throughout the world. With the exception of fragmentary exchanges of correspondence in the files at the National Archives, the laconic minutes of the FSBC, and short communiqués in *American Foreign Service Journal*, there is little official information on the ideological underpinnings of the commission's many decisions. Nevertheless, it is possible to reconstruct much of the logic of the commission by juxtaposing recurring architectural motifs in this first generation of embassy buildings with the social and political climate of the period.

The very concept of implanting artifacts of American power in far-flung corners of the globe represented a compromise between conflicting sentiments in the American body politic. A symbolic diplomatic presence—small in numbers, yet covering almost the entire globe—reconciled simultaneous demands for a return to isolationism on the one hand, and expansionist government aid for capturing foreign markets on the other. A few buildings and a coterie of diplomats were, as far as isolationists were concerned, far easier to swallow than the entanglements they feared would result from binding commitments to collective security agreements or protracted use of the military in foreign lands.

The manner in which the U.S. government eventually devised a systematic approach to international affairs, the transformation of haphazard responses into a political philosophy, was a by-product of the Great War. However reluctantly, the United States accepted its position of global preeminence, and, despite the powerful pull of isolationists, withdrawal from the international scene was not a realistic option. The same government that shunned international entanglement and multinational security agreements had persuaded the families of Great War casualties to surrender the remains of their loved ones for the national cause abroad. Along these same lines, and guided by the same logic, the government sought to bolster its diplomatic efforts with visible and prestigious embassies. "Many people visualize a country through . . . tangible evidence," noted a ranking member of the House Foreign Affairs Committee in calling for a massive campaign of embassy construction. "How can an untravelled Russian or Italian have a very great esteem for a nation whose representatives live from pillar to post, oftentimes in inadequate quarters or in remote portions of his capital?" he asked rhetorically.[8]

Yet defining a respectable American image in foreign lands was not an easy task. To begin with, there were no pertinent role models. Monumental government architecture in the United States had not adapted to the changing times. Beginning in 1926, Congress authorized the construction of nine new government buildings in the Federal Triangle in Washington, D.C. In this most ambitious attempt of the twentieth century to define the character of the American nation, an entire city core of Victorian-style buildings was razed. The replacements, however, blazed no new trails. They were large, unwieldy, unimaginative designs "reminiscent of ancient Rome."[9] Urged on by the conservative Commission of Fine Arts (CFA), Congress avoided the opportunity to define a new national image through its public buildings. Familiar names from the cemeteries-abroad program—John Russell Pope, Egerton Swartwout, and of course the omnipresent Paul Cret—received lucrative commissions in the Federal Triangle project. They had already committed themselves to classical designs of the American spirit. Having carved a comfortable niche for themselves, they were disinclined to toy with success. Their effective cornering of the federal monumental style assured little innovation or path-breaking from Washington.

A further complication arose from the unclear contours of America's ambitions abroad: there was no one pattern to the enterprise. Economically, the United States sought to achieve a variety of goals, ranging from stark colonial exploitation and protectionism in its own hemisphere to the grand ideals of free trade in other parts of the world. Political goals were equally diffuse, moving intermittently from aggressive intervention in Latin America to altruistic and somewhat vague support for freedom and democracy in the world at large. These fluid concepts of empire hindered the search for a pertinent archetype of national symbolism abroad.

The first steps toward establishing a symbolic international presence in the immediate postwar period were, then, predictably hesitant and devoid of a uniquely American context. Unused to their new status, and lacking internal guidelines, Americans tended to measure themselves according to the imperial practices of other powers; their place under the sun acquired meaning only by comparison with the British, French, and German examples, as well as less ambitious models. The federal government set out to acquire and build diplomatic abodes that merely claimed a place for the United States as a power among powers; the architecture did not focus on anything that was specifically American.

This vague sense that national greatness was best expressed through architectural extravagance led to the construction of a series of opulent yet unimaginative structures. The mimesis of well-worn images of grandeur, according to this strategy, would convince skeptical foreigners of the existence of a mature and powerful American nation.[10] In such divergent corners of the globe as Spain and Chile, Mexico and Germany, the United States either acquired or constructed an array of palaces. When purchasing a palace, the government would often highlight the fact that it had housed the potentates of present or defunct regimes.[11] One does not have to search far for an understanding of this love affair with the pedigree palace. After all, America's plutocracy had systematically pillaged the castles of Europe in order to prove to themselves and others that their time had come. The country's diplomatic representatives were the emissaries of this business class. Their palatial abodes suggested that they aspired to greater things than material gain; they craved legitimacy and respect.

The newly constructed palatial embassies were built in accordance with prevailing regional imperial styles. The role model was architect Frank Packard's embassy building in Rio de Janeiro (1923), which was designed in the "Portuguese Colonial style" (Fig. 8). The 1924 World's Fair at Rio provided the incentive for choosing Brazil as the site for this challenging attempt to build a diplomatic monument. Given Brazil's peculiar situation as the leading economic power of Latin America, and an uncommitted political spirit to boot, the United States joined other industrial nations of the world in using the fair as living proof of its postwar viability. On the fair's main thoroughfare, the Avenue of the Nations, the great nations of the postwar period erected opulent structures that were all intended to be converted into embassies after the close of the fair. Most nations built structures that incorporated elements of their national architectural styles. The United States chose otherwise. In a message directed to an audience beyond the confines of the fairground, the United States produced a variation of Latin American colonial architecture. This attempt to emulate "the Brazilian mode of architecture" fused generic

8. American Embassy, Rio de Janeiro, Brazil, ca. 1923 (Frank Packard, architect)

symbols of imperial strength—columns and an august entrance—with what the architect saw as "distinctively Latin American" forms, represented most explicitly by the red tiled roof and the inner courtyard. The building signaled quite clearly to the Brazilian hosts as well as the other embassies along the Avenue of the Nations that the United States saw itself not as a bungling upstart but as a sophisticated power among powers. Indeed, this impressive emulation of elitist architecture had been executed for the American government by an American architect. The building implied a demand for special treatment and respect by demonstrating both understanding and control of local mores.[12]

The State Department executed similar projects in other corners of Latin America as well. One year after the Brazilian project, the United States erected a new embassy in Mexico City. The project was the work of an American architect, J. E. Campbell, who had had twenty-five years of experience in Mexico City and was considered an expert of the "Mexican Beaux Arts." This school of architecture espoused the use of neoclassical design together with Hispanic ornamentation, a conciliatory marriage between two cardinal contributors to the contemporary Mexican

9. American Embassy, Mexico City, 1925 (J. E. Campbell, architect)

heritage. The fusion of European design with indigenous Hispanic ornamentation was very much along the lines of the architectural vogue of Mexico's elite (Fig. 9).[13]

The palatial approach to the diplomatic outposts of the early 1920s aroused much criticism at home. Opponents lashed out at the pretensions embodied in the philosophy of opulent political architecture. "I am simple-minded enough to think that a good case, simply stated, cutting out the fog and mystery of diplomacy and the elegance of surroundings, is more likely to be carried out to a successful conclusion," observed Martin B. Madden, chairman of the powerful House Appropriations Committee.[14] Like other luxuries, grand government architecture appeared superfluous, if not pernicious, for it fulfilled no real need. Ornamental structures, usually the products of a decadent leisure class, had no place in a society that placed dynamic individualism and egalitarianism at a premium. These palaces also had obvious divisive social connotations. Old World aristocracies had been their patrons, and to cultivate their tastes was to encourage the transplantation of foreign class divisions. Moreover, rich architecture, like other luxuries, was the product of aging societies; it implied imminent decay. Indeed, the traumatic events of the Great War suggested that opulence ranked among the achievements immediately preceding national decline. Extravagant edifices aroused associations of corruption, tyranny, and dissolution, not greatness, democracy, and progress.

An alternative strategy, the transfer of commissions for the design of embassies from ambitious private architects to the pedestrian office of the supervising architect of the Treasury Department, proved equally displeasing. The repertoire of the Treasury Department was limited to the run-of-the-mill federal buildings of the period. Thus, when commissioned to construct an embassy in Beijing, and lacking any clear guidelines from the State Department, the Treasury architects constructed an embassy compound of four buildings, all built in the style of a typical "Middle West Post Office," which, according to the understated criticism of the *New York Times*, looked "a bit odd in China" (Fig. 10).[15] Lacking guidelines for monumental government architecture abroad, the architects of the Treasury fell back on the only type of symbolic structure they knew how to design.

Indeed, the buildings in the Chinese embassy compound bore a striking resemblance to the new post office headquarters in Newport, Kentucky, it too the work of the supervising architect of the Treasury (Fig. 11). Like the Newport post office, the Chinese representation of the American way had an inordinately high ceiling and much wasted space on the ground floor. "Oppressively low" ceilings on the second level forced many of the embassy's functions into crowded quarters that were more suitable for the sorting of mail than the performance of regular office procedures. The ordinary post office as embassy was, indeed, a stark reminder of the absence of clear expectations in American foreign policy in the immediate postwar years. Precise aims and intentions beyond the urge to cut an impressive figure had yet to be articulated.

Greater clarification of ambitions and objectives abroad appeared by the mid-1920s. If official attitudes toward embassy buildings are to be seen as a reflection of policy, then 1926 represented a turning point. Under the uncharacteristically watchful eye of President Coolidge—who was not known for his support for extravagant government spending—the Porter Act sailed through Congress and was signed into law. Representatives from farm states mustered an ineffective opposition to the bill. To no avail, they recounted "tearful appeals from the farmers and boys who want post offices, but couldn't get them on account of" the mystifying policy of the administration to slash government spending at home while expanding federal construction projects abroad.[16]

The bill, which had originally called for a five-year, $5-million appropriation for the acquisition and construction of diplomatic outposts, was doubled after energetic lobbying by Secretary of State Kellogg. By far the most important facet of the bill was the creation of the FSBC, consisting of the secretaries of state, commerce, and the Treasury, and ranking members of the Foreign Affairs Committees of Congress. Their task, according to the bill, was to select sites, decide on priorities, and devise an architectural policy for diplomatic edifices.[17] Stephen G. Porter, a Democrat from Pennsylvania and chairman of the House Committee on Foreign Affairs, was the most active committee member. He handled much of the committee's routine work and devised its philosophical framework. Porter had been the principal sponsor of the bill for overseas construction. He achieved bipartisan support for his plan by cooperating with J. Charles Linthicum, the Republican representative from nearby Maryland. Both congressmen were active advocates of increased government involvement in world affairs. Almost by default, Porter and Linthicum were given free rein in deciding where and how to build American legations. Within the span of four years they crisscrossed the globe, presenting both Congress and the executive branch with well-defined plans that were routinely rubber-stamped well into the early Roosevelt years. When asked to explain this somewhat odd concentration of authority in the hands of two congressmen, Secretary of State Henry Stimson pleaded expediency:

> As a practical matter, it is impossible for members of the Cabinet, during their incumbency, to visit any but the posts nearest to Washington. It has been possible, however, for members of Congress, when that body is not in session, to make such journeys as will enable them to appear with a detailed personal knowledge before their fellow commissioners and, on the interchange of ideas at a meeting of the commission, shape a policy of acquisition and construction along the lines of greatest benefit to our government.[18]

Foremost among the tasks undertaken by Porter and Linthicum was the rationalization of haphazard architectural practices for America's diplomatic edifices. A "standardization of appearances" was intended to deflect criticism from palatial embassies and remove the stigma of aristocratic airs. Standardized procedures were the epitome of a "democratic doctrine"; they restricted extravagance and produced a dignified, sober, and creditable image of the nation.[19] Standardization also served a didactic purpose. A repetitious architectural motif was a prerequisite for the more important objective of hammering home a clear and concise political message. A modular political architecture with simple, decipherable motifs and recognizable symbols promised to enhance the political objectives of architectural repetition.[20] "A uniform style . . . of legation buildings in all capitals," a seasoned diplomat observed, "would be distinctive of our country and at once recognized."[21]

Guided by these thoughts on repetition and simplicity, the commission never considered the duplication of the ponderous style of the Federal Triangle. Perhaps sensing the speciousness of this latter-day adherence to L'Enfant's European designs in the southern United States, perhaps aware of how classicism had been thoroughly trivialized over the years, the com-

10. Two views of the American Embassy, Beijing, China, ca. 1920 (supervising architect of the Treasury Department). *Top:* From *Travel* 51 (July 1928); photograph by Underwood and Underwood News Photo Service. *Bottom:* From *Asia* 25 (25 March 1925); photograph by Erwing Galloway

11. United States Post Office, Newport, Kentucky, 1898 (supervising architect of the Treasury Department)

mittee rejected the formalist Beaux Arts monumentality of contemporary government architecture. Instead they sought the implementation of a uniquely American style.

Of course, this search for an original American architecture was all the vogue in the 1920s and was by no means limited to those concerned with American architecture abroad. The entire American architectural profession in the 1920s was preoccupied with defining an American style that would reflect the country's national characteristics. Aside from the stubborn and still influential group of classicists, there were at least two other very vocal schools of thought. One powerful faction advocated a futuristic modernist architecture. "This is the age of the skyscrapers, subways, and telephones," Kem Weber, the German-born champion of modernism, announced. Machine-age modern innovations, he declared, provided the basis for an original American architectural expression, "different from that of any other country."[22]

An equally outspoken faction, whose main support came from the designers of private domestic homes, demanded strict adherence to a supposedly pure American historical style. One of the most prominent figures in this colonial revival was the architect John Taylor Boyd, Jr., a cultural isolationist who advocated an uncompromising colonial renaissance. The early American tradition, according to Boyd and his many supporters, had "driven out whatever foreign importations it could not easily assimilate. . . . The temper of American design is coming to a point where it can hardly accommodate itself to any foreign spirit in form."[23]

The commission's verdict in this fundamental controversy between tradition and innovation as the embodiment of the American spirit was quite predictable; they opted for the colonial-style edifice as an American embassy prototype. The identification of a robust nation with historic roots was very much in accordance with international conventions. Greatness in the international arena was evoked through the use of retrospective architecture. Historical continuity—the transferral of an imperious style from a nation's Golden Age to the present—implied endurance, stability, and strength, qualities in demand during an age of confusing and volatile international relations. Historicism, whether of a sham classical genre of the Allied military cemeteries in France or the arrogant forms of the British Raj, was the norm from which the cautious architects of American foreign policy had no desire to stray.

On a more abstract level, the employment of historical styles and rejection of modernist designs reveals much about concepts of history and progress in the United States of the 1920s. The attraction of historical representation of contemporary society was derived from powerful urges to control interpretations of the nation's past. Here, as Warren Sussman reminds us, was no simple faith that the past determined the present. Instead, this search for pertinent historical events or symbols was motivated by an understanding that "the way one viewed the past had significant consequences for the way one acted in the present." History represented "a key to ideology, a key to the world view that shapes programs and actions in the present and future."[24]

This quest for a "usable past" was all the more compelling among those who lamented the dislocations of modern times. Conservatives did not approach history as an ongoing process. They sought, instead, to distill, discover, or fabricate timeless values from the past "unaffected by the relativities of the historical process itself." This quest for historical instances that could be abstracted "outside of time and circumstances, and detached from the whole process of development—was largely a device to overcome, to halt, to stem the tide of the ongoing process itself."[25] An appeal to selective historical values in the face of what appeared to be an irreversible process of flux represented the last-ditch effort of conservatives to somehow control the pace and direction of change in modern times.

Hence, the committee's embracing of historicism and its rejection of modernistic designs should be seen as a conciliatory gesture toward conservatives concerned about deviations from the traditionally limited activities of government, whether at home or abroad, as well as an attempt to defuse isolationist criticism of a growing formal American presence in other lands. An embassy that duplicated carefully chosen historical symbols paid homage to cautious, conservative, historical attributes as guidelines for the future. Colonial architecture implied that, irrespective of America's international dealings, the country would make every effort to avoid contamination by foreign ways. Indeed, the call for colonial replications of the United States was accompanied by a decision to use only American materials and furniture. "Americans abroad," noted the *New York Times*, in a caustic editorial, "may have the perfect satisfaction of realizing that when they call on our officials they will be led in on a carpet made in 'God's Country' and seated on chairs made in Grand Rapids beside tables made of 100 per cent American wood by 100 per cent American citizens. The embassy and legation buildings will be havens of Americanism, uncontaminated by the taste or workmanship of the decadent civilizations of Europe."[26] It is within this context of the search for a usable past and conciliatory gestures toward isolationists and conservatives that we need to view the decision to use early American designs in the embassies of the United States.

The commission's first attempt to articulate a format for historical embassies called for the planting of "little White Houses all around the world."[27] On a purely practical level, the White House was ideal as a model for a functional embassy. This multipurpose structure included an office wing, living quarters, and a ceremonial section. Moreover, its architecture was considered "a splendid example of that colonial type which is distinctively American."[28] The White House was simple, easily copied, and uniquely American.

Aside from the very pertinent nationalistic overtones inherent in this outstanding example of early American architecture, the White House plan for foreign legations addressed concerns about the apparent affinities between luxury and decadence, opulence and corruption, that had been raised during the era of palatial embassy procurement, prior to the establishment of the FSBC. The neoclassical White House had terse yet monumental proportions; it avoided the visual richness and elaborate ornamentation that supposedly characterized the monumental structures of decadent societies. At the same time, the neoclassicism of the White House was not bound too rigidly to a leveling, indiscriminate democratic ideology. Indeed, its first great occupants had been patricians, even slaveholders.

And yet, despite initial enthusiastic support for the White House as embassy, the FSBC abruptly abandoned plans for White House embassies as symbols of American political virtues. Nothing in the surviving records indicates why the executive mansion lost favor. One can only speculate that perhaps the committee's most dominant figures—Congressmen Porter and Linthicum—became wary of the political implications involved in adopting an archetype that hailed the virtues of the rival executive branch of government. Still, applying the same philosophical reasoning of seeking a historical, uniquely American style, the commission remained loyal to its quest for a uniform, historical embassy prototype. Instead of the White House, they chose a southern plantation mansion. The primary models, according to the commission's press releases, were the Dunleith house in Natchez, Mississippi, the Westover house on the James River, and other exemplars of plantation architecture. All, according to the commission, were outstanding artifacts of "early American design."[29] All, one might add, were American versions of the English country mansion.

This identification of nationhood with landed gentry appears to have been influenced by the actions of Great Britain, the only pertinent role model for American global aspirations at the time. In 1927 Great Britain announced plans to erect a new embassy building in Washington, D.C. The British government signaled its respect for America's new international status by assigning the task to Sir Edwin Lutyens, the foremost interpreter of Britain's national image abroad. With praise for his architectural triumphs in New Delhi still resonating, and basking in the glory of his didactic designs for British Great War cemeteries and monuments in Europe, Lutyens was now charged with the formidable task of defining Anglo-Saxon virtues for the benefit of the United States, as heir-apparent. He produced "the finest and . . . possibly the most expensive embassy or legation building to be found anywhere."[30]

Lutyens chose to visualize Great Britain as a country house. His embassy complex along Massachusetts Avenue was reminiscent of his designs for lavish country estates in Great Britain before the war (Fig. 12). Following the path of his architectural hero, Sir Christopher Wren, Lutyens included such elements as "great roofs," multiple chimneys, and a warm red brick facade in his representation of the national hearth abroad. The influential architectural magazine *Country Life* noted that the embassy not only was of a distinct rustic design; it also was deliberately foreign.

> To the eyes of Washington the impact of the vertical emphasis in this design is all the greater because it is foreign to the local tradition that is being repeated in the houses of the new suburbs and along Massachusetts Avenue. The colonial and early American houses in Georgetown—the old town that precedes and adjoins Washington—are the modest late eighteenth century type with flat roof-lines and, such ornament as they exhibit, of slender detailing. The robust vitality of the Embassy design excited a certain amount of criticism among those familiar with English tradition.[31]

This model, then, represented the nation through the domicile of landed gentry. In addition, the British national spirit was deliberately

12. British Embassy and Chancery, Washington, D.C., 1927–1930 (Sir Edwin Lutyens, architect)

defined through the mansion's contrast with the architecture of the host country. This articulation of the nation as country squire implied stability; the embassy was not an officious symbol of arrogant power, or fortuitous political circumstances, but a sign of a country with permanent yet circumspect ambitions at home and abroad. The embassy edifice was not the palace of a distant, arrogant monarchy or the garrison of an aggressive military power, but the residence of a nation of gentlefolk who had sent their emissaries to share with an upstart nation the secrets of its endurance and international power. Domestic in manner, but monumental in scale, the British Embassy was a well-crafted understatement of British prowess.

There is no written evidence to support the contention that Lutyens' designs for Washington influenced the design of an American diplomatic prototype as plantation house. However, the proximity of the two events suggests that this was indeed the case. The adaptation of the British Embassy to American circumstances indicates the ideological appeal of domesticity—in particular, the rural aristocratic variation—as symbol of the nation. After all, American democracy had been formulated by country gentlemen not unlike their British counterparts.

Irrespective of these compelling analogies, the choice of a southern model rather than a New England manor or a western domicile requires explanation. Southern architecture also represented the spirit of secession and conjured up memories of internal divisions that had brought the nation to the brink of self-destruction. In addition, the southern plantation house had none of the benign connotations of an English country manor; its political symbolism was entirely different.

Once again, the surviving commission minutes are somewhat laconic, and do not elaborate on the arguments in favor of the plantation manor. But, given the prevailing myths of contemporary American society, the plantation house motif appears to make sense. To begin with, a southern representation of the American spirit seemed all the more attractive given the fact that in foreign lands the stereotypical assessment of Americans was often that of the predatory Yankee or the violent, irresponsible cowboy. One of the few positive stereotypes of American history in the early twentieth century was the resurrected southern gentleman. The new century witnessed a massive sentimentalization of the Old South; modern mainstream American society selectively remembered plantation society as the epitome of a noble way of life, rather than a vile setting for human exploitation. The sentimentalization of the plantation milieu, according to historian William Taylor, was an expression of widespread reservations about the restlessness and materialism of contemporary society. Modern Americans developed pronounced longings for the antithesis of their self-image. "They longed for a class of men immune to acquisitiveness, indifferent to social ambition, and hostile to commercial life, cities, and secular progress."[32]

From the very beginning of the new century, American culture showed numerous signs of being enamored with a sentimental version of the South. In literature this tendency was eloquently expressed in the works of Thomas Dixon. In his best-selling novel *The Leopard's Spots* (1902), the southern domicile appeared as a shimmering ivory-painted temple placed in lush surroundings and inhabited by contented, morally upright folk. The edifice symbolized fundamental values of the American way that had supposedly originated in the South: order, permanence, and a stability derived from close contact with the soil. Dixon reiterated this theme once again in *The Clansmen* (1905), a novel of southern values as the epitome of American mores. Dixon's ideas in general, and his portrayal of the nurturing qualities of plantation life in particular, received wide exposure when *The Clansmen* was immortalized by D. W. Griffith in *Birth of a Nation*.

Dixon was followed in the later years of the 1920s by a cast of "agrarian" writers, who discovered redeeming qualities for the entire nation in a southern agrarian tradition of innocence. The epitome of a healthy American society, according to this school of literature, lay in the deep South, with its "fair balance of aristocratic and democratic elements." National acceptance of these "organic" qualities of southern life promised to counteract the pernicious acquisitiveness of modern times. Donald Davidson, literary critic and articulate spokesman of the agrarian movement in literature, stated that nowhere were the redeeming qualities of southerners more evident than in their architecture, which "was in excellent harmony with their milieu." The old plantation houses, "with their pillared porches, their simplicity of design, their sheltered groves, their walks bordered with boxwood shrubs," implied order, simplicity, and unity in contraposition to contemporary complexity, disorder, and fragmentation.[33]

The love affair with the plantation house was by no means restricted to literary circles. During this same period, suave New York moguls were building summer houses in the style of southern plantations, and employing for these purposes America's premier architects. The much-coveted Harrie T. Lindeberg dabbled in a variety of country homes for the rich, ranging from Tudor cottages to plantation manors. Edward Durrell Stone achieved notoriety with the construction of his elegant Mepkin plantation, north of Charleston, South Carolina. Both Lindeberg and Stone would later be commissioned to construct embassy buildings.[34]

The transfer of the plantation ideal to the sphere of the United States' international designs was comparatively smooth, because in addition to being a supposedly uncontaminated example of indigenous American architecture, this early American artifact implied legitimacy for the American empire by evoking images of maturity. Age in itself was a measure of authenticity, and the plantation embassy was well suited to the task of legitimizing American greatness by virtue of its free use of Greek symbols. Classical metaphors allowed the government to establish its authority by identifying itself with the historical roots of western civilization. The trappings of classicism played upon a now-familiar motif from the military cemeteries in France: that the United States was a contemporary version of an ancient culture and a democratic empire. Greek symbols were particularly appropriate because of the wide variety of connotations associated with this aesthetic form in American domestic architecture. Classical forms in American architecture had, on the one hand, always been associated with individual freedom and political democracy. Yet the prevalent use of Greek elements in southern architecture suggested that Americans also assumed that their society could combine ideals of liberty and egalitarianism with a sense of superiority and dominance. In their southern colonial versions, Greek motifs could also be interpreted as symbols of conservatism and a determination to maintain unequal social and political patterns.

The British prototype of a country mansion as embassy, as well as the prevalent southern nostalgia, explains, at least in part, the affection for the abode of the mythic genteel southern gentleman. The plantation house as embassy made particular sense for the countries that were targeted for immediate embassy construction. In Latin America and Asia, where most of the plans for this new style of building were to be implemented, the United States had demonstrated a consistent devotion to hierarchical mores and imperial ambitions. By 1928, the FSBC had approved the construction of ten new diplomatic outposts. Four buildings were slated for Latin America: in Lima, Peru; Managua, Nicaragua; Matanzas, Cuba; and Panama City. Of the remaining six buildings, three were to be built in what are now called "developing countries": present-day Yemen, China, and India. The remaining sites for new construction were in Japan, Canada, and France.

The ostensible reason for focusing on Central America and "the Orient" was that in these parts of the world "health conditions were bad and European amenities nonexistent."[35] Yet this explanation appears spurious; it disguised intentions more than it explained. Irrespective of the differences in weather and sanitary conditions at the Asian and Latin American sites, they were all stigmatized as wilderness areas with vaguely tropical climates, for which plantation architecture was both politically and environmentally appropriate. Using oppressive weather as a metaphor rather than an objective assessment of prevailing climatic conditions, the State Department in effect divided the world into two blocs. In the empires and "civilized" countries of the world the United States did not use the southern colonial style; in the "uncivilized" corners of the globe a stereotypical tropical climate was invented in order to rationalize condescending representations of the American body politic.

The plantation architecture was a particularly accurate reflection of American objectives in Latin America. The region often appears to be an extension of the American South in the sense that its economic structure was dominated by an American planter class. As for the unexploited regions of Asia, these were part of America's new frontier designs; they figured prominently in the economic and cultural expansionism of the period. Therefore, regardless of the climatic, topographical, and cultural divergence of the first batch of legation sites, the American government decided to build replicas of the Old South in these locations (Fig. 13).[36]

Another reason for singling out China and Latin America as high-priority sites for diplomatic construction was related to violent anti-American sentiments in these politically volatile regions. Commenting on a fact-finding mission to Latin America in 1926, a special envoy of Secretary of State Kellogg had this to say:

> The natural and popular tendency in all of them [the South American republics] is anti-Americanism, and this is the great unifying force of the continent.... These conditions make unified, coordinated, and exceptionally efficient diplomatic administration indispensable.... [But] the chief of the mission, however great his ability and efficiency, is seriously handicapped if he does not possess an appropriate residence and chancery.... In every capital of South America our mission's property should be superior to that of other nations. Anything less will be out of keeping with the predominant position of the United States and liable to subject us to unfavorable comment instead of prestige.[37]

13. Model for American Legation, Managua, Nicaragua, as prototype of plantation house embassy, 1927 (Aldrich and Chase, architects)

14. American Consulate, Amoy, China, 1931 (Elliot Hazzard, architect)

The idea of producing plantation manors as embassies and legations—in particular, the obvious associations of these edifices with the concept of a white master class guiding the deeds of natives—was probably meant to inspire political adherence or fear rather than mere aesthetic admiration. As such, those nations where anti-American feelings were simmering, as in many Latin American countries, or where sentiment had actually been translated into acts of violence against Americans, as had been the case in China, were the primary candidates for this first generation of monumental diplomatic structures.

Lima, Peru; the Chinese cities of Amoy and Mukden; Managua, Nicaragua; and Aden, the gateway to the Persian Gulf, were considered the most urgent sites for variations of the plantation manor, although by the early 1930s only the Amoy building was actually completed (Fig. 14). Here, on the banks of a river, a "Georgian colonial" mansion asserted in no uncertain terms that the United States was less concerned with the freedom of the Chinese than with the freedom to exploit the great China market.

While the construction of other plantation sites was never completed, their architectural sketches and plans reveal much about their salient objectives as artifacts of political architecture. The sketch of the embassy in Lima, for example, displayed all the trappings of a Greek revival plantation house (Fig. 15). The sprawling complex stood within a rambling

15. Artist's impression of American Embassy, Lima, Peru, 1931 (architect unknown)

parklike environment. Like its prototype in Natchez, Mississippi, the monumental columnar porch at its entrance suggested that "the house was more than a man's castle; it was indeed a temple, a shrine encased in classic harmony."[38] Aside from its awe-inspiring scale and temple-like appearance, the plantation embassy had the distinct advantage of being uncontaminated by the taste of those decadent civilizations that had once ruled this part of the world. It was a pure example of New World architecture.

Given the preindustrial state of most Latin American and Asian economies, the pastoral embassy was a most appropriate prototype. Back home, Americans were experimenting with a variety of modern architectural styles that sang the praises of progress and technology as the secret of American success. In America's foreign sphere of influence such a style would have been inappropriate. The agrarian embassy mansion revealed American aspirations to retain a plantation economy in these various corners of the globe. There was no machine in this garden, because American dominance hinged on the preservation of a stagnant, feudal-like state of affairs.

Indeed, the garden surrounding the sketch for a plantation embassy in Lima further revealed the political agenda of an American presence in underdeveloped areas of the world. The grounds consisted of two basic elements: a close-cropped lawn and scattered palm trees. This fusion of divergent cultural symbols—the western lawn and the "tropical" palm tree—implied that the United States owed its preeminence to the blending of a variety of cultures into a hierarchical and workable combination. The cropped lawn, lush yet orderly, was a typical western representation of control of nature. The palm trees were mere clichés of the unexploited abundance of the New World. The cool, arid, perpetually cloudy coastal region of Peru never produced an indigenous vegetation of palm trees or other tropical plants. The orderly layout of the palms, quite distinct from the stereotypical tangle of dense tropical vegetation, signaled the triumph of the visiting civilization over the supposedly unstructured abundance of sumptuous yet primitive surroundings. The subordination of natural abundance to the rational designs of western cultures, the gardens implied, was the secret of American success.

Judging by the various sketches of these plantation embassies as well as the correspondence of the FSBC, these symbolic structures deliberately ignored the environment and architecture of the host countries (see Figs. 13 and 15). The diplomatic edifices were meant to be sharply differentiated from the cities in which they were placed so that their beholders would sense the irrelevance of all but the distinct contours of the American structure. All misgivings concerning the construction of "purely American designs" in foreign countries were brushed aside.[39]

Moreover, the selective implementation of these southern colonial prototypes illustrated the manner in which the State Department had sorted the world into two distinct diplomatic territories: countries where the United States merely intended to show the flag in a dignified fashion; and unexploited regions of the world in which the United States had economic or territorial designs. In those countries where the United States limited its objectives to a dignified display of the flag, the State Department continued its policy of either purchasing or building palaces. In Argentina, where the United States had defined a policy of presenting itself not as the leading power but merely one among many, the palatial structure of 1931 merely announced to the Argentinean audience that Americans were at least as powerful as the British.[40]

Elsewhere, the American palatial embassies adhered strictly to local mores and customs, too. In fact, the federal government went out of its way to avoid offending host countries by suggesting through its architecture any trace of imperial ambitions. A plan for a mural in the new Japanese embassy, which had depicted a landscape composed of Mount Fuji, the emperor's sacred bridge at Nikko, and a castle at Torii, was abandoned because sensitive American officials felt that the scenes of Fuji, Torii, and the bridge were widely separated geographically and that "their melange" in a single composite scene might offend the often inscrutable sensibilities of the Japanese. Instead, the State Department opted for an innocuous American scene depicting Mount Shasta and Mount Hood.

The plantation embassy, by contrast, never displayed such sensitivity. The use of southern colonial architecture in other parts of the world suggests that, rather than being approached as individual countries, the New World was considered virgin territory of insignificant cultural and political divisions upon which enterprising Americans could still make their mark without fear of arousing the wrath of any meaningful political entity.

Yet, by the 1930s, the embassy as plantation house appeared to be losing favor. Once again, the changing mood and growing disillusionment with the plantation manor as symbol of the nation was registered quite vividly in the literature of the times. Margaret Mitchell's epic saga of the South, *Gone with the Wind* (1936), ended dramatically with Scarlett O'Hara gazing at the charred ruins of Tara. The novels of William Faulkner, *The Sound and the Fury* (1929) and *Sanctuary* (1931), were littered with descriptions of rotting, almost fetid southern mansions.[41] Along these same lines, the reading public of the late 1920s and early 1930s was exposed to a new genre of picture book depicting melancholy, dilapidated southern mansions, beautiful in their own way, but nevertheless a thing of the past.

The plantation as symbol of a cheerless nostalgia in literature coincided with a disenchantment with southern values in political circles as well. In the first painful years of the new economic climate of the 1930s, the old plantation house evoked an uncomfortable memory of a retrogressive milieu in an era of anticipation. If the South represented anything, according to Franklin D. Roosevelt, it was the epitome of the infirmities of the nation. The South was the most economically backward and socially reactionary section of the country. There was, according to the newly elected president, a "southern problem" plaguing the United States.[42]

The plantation house as embassy lost favor for more practical reasons, too. Dissenting voices claimed that these and other attempts at self-aggrandizement were counterproductive. America's international relations were being jeopardized by the country's "attitude of the superior helping the inferior," warned James McDonald, the executive director of the Foreign Policy Association. "As long as Americans continue to boast that they are different from and better than other nations," he added, "they are sowing the seed of much ill feeling among other nations."[43] Misgivings about ostentatious images translated into a decision to halt the construction of a plantation embassy in Managua. The FSBC apparently adhered to the warnings of local diplomats to avoid a dominating site and a condescending structure for the future embassy. Finally, the use of the plantation house as symbol of America abroad lost a powerful ally with the death of Congressman Stephen Porter in 1930.

With the changing of the presidential guard in the early 1930s, and in the context of a new socioeconomic era, the State Department began to experiment with new forms of symbolism. The testing ground was Japan, a country that traditionally had aroused ambivalent reactions in the United States. Japan was an Asian nation, and by implication inferior. Yet, at the same time, Japan was indisputably an industrial giant and a world power to be reckoned with. Confused assessments of Japanese stature and, consequently, the politically correct form of diplomatic architecture for the country, were registered in the wavering prose of the American ambassador. In a letter to Secretary of State Kellogg, Ambassador Edgar Bancroft admitted that he had no firm ideas about the appropriate style. "The main thing is to have it beautiful," he summarized gratuitously after a rambling, tortuous discussion of architecture and image.[44]

Given these nebulous assessments, architectural strategies in Japan wavered between arrogance and appeasement, condescension and a grudging recognition of Japan's special status. During the years 1930–1932 the United States completed two projects, a consulate in Yokohama and a large multibuilding embassy compound in Tokyo. Both ventures departed significantly from palace and plantation, presenting instead new possibilities for diplomatic construction in the years to come.

Jay Morgan, an American resident of Japan, was the architect of the White House replica in Yokohama (Fig. 16). Situated on a hill in a neighborhood of nondescript western-style buildings, the edifice functioned as as lighthouse; its shining, incongruous classical design and elevated setting provided a strong American presence in this gateway to Asia. "Being of early American design," noted an admiring observer, "it is truly a welcome sight to American travelers approaching Yokohama, Japan, by ship, and looks just like a little bit of homeland in an oriental setting."[45] Impressive and peculiarly American in style, the White House in Yokohama had the obvious advantage of lacking the condescending symbolism of the plantation house. Indeed, the Yokohama consulate eventually became, as the following chapter will demonstrate, an important prototype for diplomatic symbolism in the 1940s. One can only suspect that resurrected interest in the executive mansion as a symbol of America was related, at least in part, to a new style of presidency brought on by the Roosevelt years.

A more complex but equally enduring model guided plans for the Tokyo embassy compound, the designer of which was Harold Van Buren Magonigle of New York, an architect with an extensive record of institutional and government buildings in the United States. Here the FSBC experimented with the fusion of a variety of symbolic elements: Japanese, American, and a generic type of pseudo-oriental design (Fig. 17). The buildings were constructed with reinforced concrete disguised with pure white stucco, which gave the massive concrete structure a light and airy

16. American Consulate, Yokohama, Japan, 1932 (Jay Morgan, architect)

17. American Embassy, Tokyo, Japan, 1932 (Harold Van Buren Magonigle, architect)

look. All openings were capped with pseudo-oriental mosaic patterns—whether these were "Persian," Hispanic, or Japanese was a matter of opinion. The copper roofs were reminiscent of local shinto shrines and, given their height, were the dominant element of the embassy compound. Curiously, this selective emulation of Japanese architectural elements set the building apart from its surroundings. In the aftermath of the 1923 earthquake, Tokyo had been rebuilt along modern western lines, with none of the trappings associated with Japanese building traditions.

The symbolic use of Japanese architectural elements, in a structure situated on the crest of a hill overlooking the soon-to-be-erected new Japanese parliament building, was an attention-grabbing device designed to display guarded respect for the traditions of the host country. Its eclectic architecture—Greek columns, Spanish colonial stucco, pseudo-oriental tiles, and a Japanese roof—reflected, perhaps, the uncertain image of Japan, a country that did not fit the comfortable division of the world into European superpowers and the stagnant cultures of the Old World.[46]

The Japanese projects were the last of the grand diplomatic structures designed in the 1920s. The Depression years halted projects in midstream and canceled others even before they had left the drawing board. Nevertheless, the foundations for using architecture as a tool of foreign policy had been laid. In the years following the Second World War, the federal government would initiate an unprecedented expansion of its political architecture abroad, the fundamental rationale of which was derived from the experiences of the 1920s. Building on the precedent of plantation embassies, but employing a different style, embassy buildings in the 1950s and 1960s would be used as a tool for both defining and controlling a unique Pax Americana. The elements of this process had been elaborated during the 1920s. The necessary infrastructure of a political advisory board and a supervising bureaucracy were already firmly in place and formed the basis for the expansion of the role of the State Department some thirty years later. The unassuming Republican administrations of the 1920s had quietly developed an important diplomatic mechanism to be used for years to come.

PART TWO

4

Interlude

MARKING TIME, 1933–1945

ON 19 JUNE 1942, more than six months after the United States had once again entered the arena of global warfare, an American army officer paid an official visit to enemy territory. Colonel T. Bently Mott, the former military attaché of the American embassy in France, arrived in Vichy by way of Lisbon on "a special mission in connection with American war cemeteries and battlefield monuments in France."[1]

In one of the most bizarre incidents of the conflict, Colonel Mott apparently persuaded his counterparts to absolve the dead from the horrors of war. Enemy forces in France and Belgium agreed to respect the sanctity of American shrines and graves under their occupation. The specter of destruction and annihilation that accompanied the Nazi occupation throughout Europe contrasted sharply with the inviolated resting places and untouched monuments of America's Great War dead. By October 1944, shortly after the liberation of France and Belgium, the American Battle Monuments Commission (ABMC) reported, with a certain degree of self-satisfaction, that the negligible damage to its property in Europe had resulted from neglect rather than wanton destruction.[2] In a macabre marking of time, the ABMC had been waiting patiently for the duration of the conflict in order to swing into action once again.

The ABMC had not been hovering in the wings alone. War and the Depression had also affected attempts to consolidate America's stature through diplomatic architecture. Yet even though events had slowed down the building of government-sponsored monuments abroad, a lively and continuous debate on the appropriate form of national symbolism in modern times and its manifestation abroad accompanied the ten-year lull. An energetic Commission of Fine Arts (CFA) and a president personally interested in the political value of architecture abroad defined the contours of the country's postwar projects. Most important of all, the bureaucratic infrastructures that had managed and devised these projects before remained intact; both the ABMC and the State Department were poised to reactivate their projects even before the cessation of hostilities.

The CFA initiated the redefining of America's symbolic image abroad as early as 1933. The commission's indefatigable secretary, H. P. Caemmerer, distributed surveys to all of the United States' diplomatic and consular missions requesting an inventory of monuments erected by private American citizens or the U.S. government. The results of the survey revealed a random collection of shrines, almost all of which were private affairs, many in a state of disrepair.[3] The most common type of monument to American achievements was the ubiquitous scientific institution donated by American philanthropists, the architecture of which rarely bespoke anything that was uniquely American. In a typical dispatch the American consulate in Jerusalem reported the existence of three major buildings that were the gifts of American citizens—the Strauss Health Center, the Jerusalem YMCA, and the Rockefeller Museum of Antiquities—all of which were built in the local British colonial genre because stringent building codes of the mandatory government prohibited deviation from a standard British Middle Eastern architecture. In other parts of the world, busts and statues of great and near-great Americans figured prominently as representations of the nation's spirit; statues of Lincoln and Washington were the most popular items. The commission also discovered a few military memorials, which had hitherto received no support from the ABMC, nor, for that matter, from any other federal agency. No clear sense of a uniquely American culture emerged from these mostly private, uncoordinated monuments. With the exception of the Great War battle monuments in Europe, America's symbolic image abroad was still a haphazard, undirected affair.

Revisions in random representations of America abroad began with the reduced yet still functioning embassy construction program. The program's all-powerful mentor, Franklin D. Roosevelt, had very strong opinions on the role of art and architecture in the service of the nation at home and abroad. Roosevelt encouraged the press to view him as a modern-day Jefferson: a gentleman farmer who, among other things, dabbled quite seriously in architecture as a medium for conveying the essence of American democracy.[4] At home the president became the champion of the Dutch Colonial revival movement along the Hudson River, where he personally supervised the architectural plans of more than a dozen public buildings. The president seized the opportunity of the dedication of a Roosevelt-inspired Dutch Colonial post office in order to expound upon his architectural theory: "We are seeking to follow the type of architecture which is good in the sense that it does not of necessity follow the whims of the moment, but seeks an artistry which will be good for all time to come. And we are trying to adopt the design of the historical background of the locality and to use, in so far as possible, the materials which are indigenous to the locality."[5]

Two crucial points emerge from these articles of faith. The virtues of the past that had made the country great, the president suggested, could serve well in defining America's symbolic image. Solid historical architecture in a modern context provided reassurance, stability, continuity. Yet a message from the past remained ineffective if it was unrelated to its surroundings. Hence, the president called for an environmentally sensible architecture, which implied disapproval of such practices as the 1920s construction of southern plantation house embassies in a variety of incongruous geographical regions.

Roosevelt had, indeed, specific thoughts on the appropriate historical styles for various embassies, the construction of which he intervened in routinely. His directions for the planned Moscow embassy reveal the essence of the symbolic diplomatic statement that he had hoped to convey in other parts of the world. After establishing diplomatic ties with the Soviet Union, Roosevelt dictated both style and architect for the important mission of expressing American culture to this somewhat tenuous ally. Roosevelt urged the Foreign Service Buildings Commission (FSBC) to allocate the then-extravagant sum of $1.25 million for an expressive embassy compound, which he felt was "essential for our government." His political motives were quite clear: "We can build an embassy on that hill in the city park overlooking the river which will be as simple and as beautiful as Monticello, and I myself should like to see a modern version of Monticello built there with subsidiary buildings patterned after those which fringe the lawn of the University of Virginia. I like the idea of planting Thomas Jefferson in Moscow. For this particular job, I know no one so well fitted as Harrie T. Lindeberg."[6]

Lindeberg, the fashionable architect of large country estates, did indeed receive the challenging assignment of presenting an updated, "modern" version of the Jeffersonian creed for display in the capital city of an alien political culture. For the record, it should be noted that, because of the war and subsequent tensions between the two superpowers, the project never advanced beyond the initial planning stage. Nevertheless, Roosevelt's utterances provide a rare glimpse of the ideological underpinnings of the construction of American monuments abroad.

The Jefferson paradigm for Moscow was part of a general revival of eighteenth-century Enlightenment thought and the rising popularity of Jefferson as a national symbol in the 1930s and 1940s. Commenting on the avalanche of popular and scholarly biographies of Jefferson, the impending publication of his complete writings, and the great public flurry surrounding the construction of the Jefferson Memorial in the capital, historian Ralph Gabriel pointed out the ostensible contradiction of a complex urban-industrial society celebrating the virtues of a man of agriculture and a critic of cities. There was a curious irony in the fact that Roosevelt, the creator of big and centralized national government, felt a kinship with a historical figure who had always insisted on marginal, decentralized government as a crucial attribute of a healthy democracy.[7]

This somewhat incongruous homage to Jefferson, Gabriel noted in a series of articles published in the late 1940s, reflected a selective revival of

Enlightenment political philosophy.[8] The swift demise of the principle of individual rights in many parts of the world, as well as the frightening rise of tribalism and anti-intellectualism associated with modern totalitarian regimes, had increased the attractiveness of the eighteenth-century proclamation that all men are created equal and that men everywhere have certain inalienable natural rights. The Jeffersonian revival expressed the country's commitment to the sanctity of fundamental civil liberties of all men everywhere. Roosevelt's neo-Jeffersonian endorsement of universal civil rights, according to political historian Albert Fried, legitimized intervention on behalf of the powerless and oppressed both at home and abroad.[9]

Guided by the urge to spread the gospel of American Enlightenment as counterweight to the various forms of totalitarianism throughout the world, the State Department devised a fresh scheme for America's diplomatic architecture. During the years 1936–1941, the department constructed ten large projects based on the Roosevelt-inspired guidelines. The embassy program of the 1930s and early 1940s utilized unspent funds from previous allocations and a five-year, $5-million grant to construct buildings in "foreign cities as typically American as they can possibly be."[10]

The theme of the revised project was the construction of early national edifices as symbols of the American political creed. The urge to produce potent, Enlightenment-inspired statements was strongest in those parts of the world where a firm commitment to any political ideology had yet to be established. In tropical regions, such as equatorial Africa, the State Department envisioned replicas of early national southern architecture "carrying out Jeffersonian ideas and employing Porte Cochères and classical strong white columns. In some hot countries the new American buildings will greatly resemble the old houses of New Orleans."[11] In practice, the form of monumental southern architecture as diplomatic structure was distinctly urban, the model being Baltimore rather than New Orleans. This reliance on the architecture of the urban South resolved the problems associated with plantation embassies as representations of the democratic aspirations of the United States. In cities, market forces had supposedly replaced deferential tradition and demeaning racial customs. Southern architecture, the most suitable style for tropical environments, was further purged of its pernicious connotations by the construction of edifices that would embody principles of the American Enlightenment.

Thus, in its first African project at Monrovia, Liberia, the State Department constructed a replica of the Baltimore home of Charles Carroll, Jr., the son of one of the signers of the Declaration of Independence and a supporter of the black colonization movement (Figs. 18 and 19). The architecture of the Monrovian building accomplished all of Roosevelt's

18. Artist's impression of American Legation, Monrovia, Liberia, 1938 (supervising architect of the Treasury Department)

19. Remodeled, present-day version of original Monrovian building

architectural objectives. First and foremost, it embodied much of the administration's internationalist worldview; the building was well suited to the climate, embodied the essence of the country's global vision, and was sensitive to local political conditions. Although the edifice was an accurate duplication of early national architecture from another continent, it was neither a political nor a technological anachronism. Paradoxically, the building could be seen as a relevant symbol of America's contemporary merits because it implemented ultramodern building techniques. Irrespective of its historical trappings, the local press in Liberia hailed the Monrovian legation as one of the most innovative buildings in the entire country. Its reinforced concrete frame—the epitome of modern building technique—solved the problem of fire hazards and blight that plagued timber structures in equatorial Africa. Concrete beams also allowed for the construction of extraordinarily deep porches and loggias for protection from the heat and heavy tropical rains.[12]

The endorsement of historically relevant diplomatic structures revived interest in the little White Houses as embassies. Indeed, during the course of the 1930s and 1940s the State Department experimented quite widely with reproductions of the White House. Whether motivated by convictions that uniform products were more marketable than a potpourri of forms, or merely at a loss to articulate the right version of Enlightenment symbolism for a diverse world, the FSBC constructed White House embassies and legations in disparate corners of the globe, from Baghdad (1938) to the Nationalist China capital of Chungking (1944).

This apparent quest to broadcast American commitment to universal human values through the medium of a uniform early national style was symptomatic of nagging difficulties in the United States' acceptance of cultural diversity; the White House embassies represented a somewhat naive belief in the universality of the American political experience. Behind the White House on the Tigris lay what Daniel Boorstin has interpreted as an expectation that "people of lesser nations," such as the inhabitants of the Middle East, would learn from this symbol and "seize the opportunity to deal with each other in the manner" of the "self-governing, self-determining" colonies that had forged the American political experience.[13] The diplomatic edifice of early national architecture suggested an unshakable faith in the universal appeal of the U.S. political system, as well as what George Kennan has observed to be an American "tendency to judge others by the extent to which they contrive to be like ourselves"[14] (Fig. 20). That the American historical way could indeed be exported was affirmed by the fact that the White Houses in the wilderness could adjust to contemporary circumstances. They were cooled by "that same American contribution to modern comfort which the White House in Washington enjoys."[15]

20. American Legation, Baghdad, Iraq, 1938 (architect unknown)

21. Charred remains of American Embassy, Chungking, China, after a fire, 1943 (architect unknown)

In Chungking, the construction of a permanent White House embassy in the temporary war capital expressed similar sentiments (Fig. 21). Upon arriving in China as an intelligence officer in 1942, sinologist John King Fairbank recalled a formless, chaotic collection of muddy streets and houses, a reflection of the unformed—and, by implication, impressionable—state in which China still appeared to be languishing. Like clay in the hands of the artist, Fairbank claimed that the country could be fashioned in the image of its benefactors. Fairbank and others advocated intervening in the factional bickerings of the Nationalist China political elite by persuading intellectuals to conform to the American way.[16]

The obsession with making over the Chinese, manifested by the construction of a White House on the rocky peninsula between the Yangtze and Chialing rivers, highlighted an important aspect of American foreign policy: the tendency to identify friends and allies through sometimes narrow American blinders. Jefferson, Roosevelt noted in a speech he had prepared for Jefferson Day, 13 April 1945, had actively pursued the exporting of America's concept of democracy to other countries. "As minister to France, then as our first Secretary of State and as our third President, Jefferson was instrumental in the establishment of the United States as a vital factor in international affairs." Nothing, he vowed, not even the scourge of war, would discourage the United States from bringing the gospel of Jefferson to others, and battling "for the rights of man all over the world."[17] Roosevelt never delivered the speech. He died the day before the event. His successor, Harry Truman, continued the spread of Jeffersonianism by advocating turning all American embassies into little White Houses.[18]

In practice, the architectural strategy of the State Department was much more diverse and attuned to varying political climates and a spectrum of foreign policy objectives. Beyond the shores of China, and closer to home, in Latin America, the State Department devised a separate policy, equally important for its departure from previous architectural decisions in this sensitive area of the United States' indisputable sphere of influence. In recognition of the region's special status, neither early national styles nor any other trappings of American politics and culture appeared appropriate for Latin America. A new generation of embassies constructed in indigenous architectural styles replaced the plantation house projects of the 1920s. As an integral part of the Good Neighbor policy, the new diplomatic edifices affirmed that the United States no longer approached Latin America as if it were "a waste of jungle and Andes where picturesque warriors relieved the primitive monotony of living by periodic Gilbert and Sullivan revolutions."[19] In Guatemala City (1939), Ciudad Trujillo (1939), Managua (1940), and Lima (1944), the State Department constructed an array of Spanish colonial–style legations and embassies.[20] The last of this batch of artful constructions, the embassy in Lima, was also the most impressive. The pet project of Leland W. King, the architect who would eventually become director of the office of Foreign Buildings Operations (FBO), this building epitomized the new approach to Latin America (Fig. 22).

Like the other Latin American embassies, the Peru structure adopted the Spanish colonial style of the eighteenth century. The model was the government palace, the Torre Tagle, a typical Spanish transplant of basically Moorish design.[21] Indeed, the central motif of carved and secluded balconies shielded by horizontally shuttered windows was of Moslem origin. The choice of a Spanish colonial style for the Latin American embassies was in tune with the Good Neighbor policy and did not affront local national sentiment. Moorish trappings in Latin America represented the unifying effect of a Spanish empire and the formation of the region's unique identity. Indigenous traditions and a shared Spanish heritage created an authentic Latino architecture with important nationalist undertones. The colonial period in Latin American architecture, architectural historian Roberto Segre has noted, had produced a homogeneous architecture reflecting a sense of regional self-determination. Spanish architectural elements, tempered by local environmental and cultural modifications, had nurtured and solidified a sense of self-worth, which had

22. American Embassy, Lima, Peru, 1944 (Leland King and Franz Jaquet, architects)

propelled the myriad of former colonies toward political and cultural independence.

The post-Spanish national period, by contrast, produced slavish architectural emulation of alien motifs. "Liberation from colonial dependence and the formation of the Latin American nations resulted in the loss of the homogeneous code elaborated internally by the local culture," Segre has observed. The high architecture of industrialized nations—in particular, England and France—replaced the former Spanish models. "The eclectic architecture of Latin America expressed cultural dependence on models developed by the European bourgeoisie and imposed by foreign designers without an assimilation of local traditions."[22]

In copying the style of seventeenth-century Spanish colonialism, then, the United States was not asserting itself as the New Spain. Instead, the architecture of the new embassies recognized the integrity of Latin American nation-states. These edifices acknowledged a cohesiveness of the region beyond the stereotyped image of South America as backyard of the United States. In this spirit, and in contrast to the garden theme of previous plantation house embassies, where foreign elements introduced order into a chaotic, uncivilized jungle, the gardens of the new Latin American embassies and legations showed respect for the environment and culture of the host countries. No trivialization of local flora appeared here.

INTERLUDE: MARKING TIME, 1933-1945   101

Hence, the architects of the Ciudad Trujillo embassy compiled a painstaking inventory of "hundreds of decorative Dominican trees, shrubs, and flowers" in order to surround the legation property with a "beautiful exposition of indigenous Dominican flora."[23]

Among western countries, the State Department adopted yet another strategy of environmentally sensible embassies of no single style. In western nations, where a strong statement of an American political creed appeared less critical, the FSBC paid particular attention to climatic considerations. These countries received variations of Dutch Colonial and American-style Georgian architecture.[24] For example, the FSBC built a brick American-Georgian edifice in Helsinki, Finland. The building was well suited to the region's harsh climate, yet was sufficiently different from local architecture in its vague resemblance to the White House. A Georgian structure, of larger dimensions but similar style, was built in London's Grosvenor Square for the new American embassy (1937); the State Department constructed other "environmentally correct" embassies in Ottawa (1933) and Canberra (1945). The long-overdue embassy in Paris, a polite building that harmonized with its surroundings on the Place de la Concorde, was also completed in 1934.[25]

The environmental approach, the Latin American strategy, and the policy of early national edifices were all linked by a tenacious belief in the power of symbols. Moreover, the building of embassies does not support the characterization of Roosevelt's foreign policy as a series of ad hoc improvisations. This interpretation of "foreign policy by makeshift," which has been passed down by historian James MacGregor Burns, asserted that an overworked Roosevelt, confronted with conflicting opinions among his foreign policy advisors, never really espoused any broad visionary approach to the art of diplomacy. The various forms of embassy construction suggest, by contrast, sophistication and a pattern of multiple strategies for diverse foreign policy conditions.

The significance of embassy construction in the 1930s and 1940s should, of course, be seen in the context of expanding cultural affairs for diplomatic purposes. Given the urgent tasks confronting the nation at the time—recovery from a debilitating and protracted economic depression, as well as management of the overwhelming demands on funds and attention associated with the war—it is tempting to dismiss the persistent presence of the embassy construction program as an eccentric sideshow, a pet project of the president, or perhaps the outmoded machinations of a bureaucracy continuing to perform outdated and unnecessary tasks. An alternative and more convincing explanation for this unremitting infatuation with diplomatic representation requires seeing this project in the context of a broad, visionary preparation for leadership in the postwar world. By 1945, the State Department's Office of Information and Culture (OIC) had established seventy American information libraries throughout the world, as well as seventy-one "cultural centers" in Latin American countries, for the purpose of providing "facts and documented explanations of the United States." Much like large American conglomerates that, in the throes of the war and with their eyes cast toward the future, advertised their wares for future product recognition rather than immediate sales, the State Department was actively concerned with "explaining the American scene" to prepare the ground for future diplomatic initiatives.

A concerted effort to spread information about the American way appeared quite urgent, because by entering the world conflict the United States had "deliberately chosen a policy of active participation in world affairs" from which there would be no retreat. Given this commitment to active involvement in the affairs of others, the State Department set its sights on enhancing an "understanding abroad of our motives, our desires, our ideals." Such a task was indeed imperative, noted a high-ranking State Department official, because the American democratic system,

> with its disagreements and its individual liberty, is bewildering to a world emerging from the throes of authoritarianism. It is easy for foreigners, without knowing the real situation, to get the impression that this is a land of strife and discord, with race set against race, class against class, religion set against religion, the rich oppressing the poor, the poor revolting against the rich, gangsters roaming the streets of our cities, cowboys shooting up wild west saloons, and Congress weltering in a whirl of filibusters and cocktail parties.[26]

By expanding an American presence through the establishment of information libraries, the Voice of America, academic exchange programs, and cultural centers, the United States hoped to influence the elites of the postwar years.[27] Elaborate legation buildings complemented this effort. They provided a condensed glimpse of American foreign policy objectives, particularly for the proverbial man in the street who had no access to the elite-oriented information programs of the State Department, and who was liable to construct a pistol-packing, gangster-ridden, Hollywood-inspired version of life in the United States.

And yet, in the final analysis, this new quest for "uniquely American embassies" as an effort to counterbalance distorted images of popular culture was quite tame and unexceptional. The policy was, in many ways, visionary, but its implementation was based on a regurgitated yet unproven formula. Bound by President Roosevelt's guidelines, the State Department maintained its adherence to historical styles. Harrie T. Lindeberg, perhaps the most important apologist for the FSBC, and the architect of the Monticello-style plans for Moscow and the post–planta-

23. Artist's impression of American Legation, Managua, Nicaragua, 1940 (Harrie T. Lindeberg, architect)

tion house embassy in Managua (Fig. 23), expressed quite clearly the rationale behind this tenacious clinging to historicism. The renowned architect of country mansions argued that historical styles were meaningless only if they were anecdotal or eclectic. By avoiding the "visual affliction" of multiple, "borrowed and half-assimilated" styles, and concentrating instead on the quiet, understated architecture of reason inherent in early American design, one could produce pertinent symbols of "order and authority."[28]

In this sense, both State Department officials and their architects deliberately ignored the winds of change sweeping through the architectural profession in the United States at that time. The International Style exhibition held at the Museum of Modern Art in New York in 1932 was the catalyst for this atmosphere of innovation that had bypassed government circles.[29] The show, the subsequent publication of a seminal book by the exhibition's organizers, and, of course, the immigration to the United States of many of Europe's founding fathers of architectural modernism challenged the parochial, inward-looking, historically oriented mainstream of American architecture. In searching for what one of its advocates called "an architectural expression which should not be in conflict with any form of modern activity," a new generation of architects produced a contemporary architectural lexicon heralding their professed liberation from the stranglehold of staid historical styles.[30] Such iconoclasm had no place in the arsenal of a State Department engaged in combating an image of the United States as a puerile "land of shiny automobiles, reinforced-concrete skyscrapers, and boorish millionaires who found their natural expression in Yankee imperialism."[31] According to architectural historians Christiane and George Collins, the International Style exhibition implied "that one style had come into being for all categories of architecture," from banks to churches.[32] This attempt to produce an architectural Esperanto clashed with the image of uniqueness that the United States had hoped to convey through its political architecture abroad. In the final analysis, however, the reliance on historical metaphors proved to be equally powerless and meaningless.

A similar tenacious endorsement of historical symbolism lingered among ABMC policymakers as well during this transitional period. However, in contrast to the State Department, the activities of the ABMC were of a much more theoretical nature during the Roosevelt years. The bodies of American casualties were laid to rest in temporary, makeshift sites for the duration of the conflict. Prior to the cessation of hostilities, neither Congress nor the president offered plans for permanent overseas burials. In fact, the ABMC lacked a congressional mandate to supervise new burial projects.

Given its state of limbo, the commission and its advocates devoted their energies to maintaining public support for the induction of military casualties into perpetual national service. A crucial feature of their agenda, one that became all the more significant as the war approached a triumphant conclusion, was the intense lobbying for a federal prerogative in deciding on the appropriate form for commemorating the war dead. Advocates of burial abroad accomplished this mission by attacking the alternatives, in particular, the efforts of individual communities to commemorate locally their sons and daughters.

Local commemoration of war dead after the previous global conflict, Librarian of Congress Archibald MacLeish lashed out in the pages of *Architectural Forum*, was "distinguished by singular inappropriateness." In a brief pictorial survey accompanying his article, MacLeish criticized what he thought was a banal form of monumentality in small-town monuments. The repetitive doughboy and the maudlin figurative statues of *Remembrance* and *Victory* had been taken from catalogues; they were not labors of love, but cranked-out models of the funeral industry. Even those statues and memorials produced by local artists did not accomplish their lofty goals, claimed MacLeish.

> A great monument is, next to a great poem, the most enduring means to make the minds of men remember. But great monuments demand great artists and great artists are not too numerous to begin with, nor, when they do exist, are they always the artists the town councils and the local chamber of commerce select. . . . A second-rate monument is, of all substantial objects, the least visi-

ble and least effective. A monstrosity may be visible in its ugliness, but a mediocre piece is merely not there—as the soldier statues in so many towns are merely not there.[33]

MacLeish and his supporters urged the establishment of a national policy in order to avoid repetition of town-square "bronzes of dumpy G.I.s of the last war in every conceivable posture from rigid attention to the limp droop of the final gasp."[34] The delegitimization of local community commemoration of war dead encountered stiff resistance, however. Local communities did not react with Great War compliance to government attempts to monopolize the commemoration of the war effort. The national organizations of architectural and landscaping professionals were inundated with projects from chambers of commerce and city and town governments that showed no sign of relinquishing their right to celebrate the local contributions to the national war effort.[35]

Grudgingly, supporters of the national position devised a compromise. The commemoration of war dead at the local level would be restricted to the construction of "living memorials." By this they meant community buildings, parks, and recreation centers dedicated to those who had made the ultimate sacrifice. The celebration of sacrifice through useful structures had developed slowly, and with much resistance from federal circles, during the 1920s. Now it was officially endorsed as the only possible way of meeting growing demands for local commemoration while keeping intact the government's prerogative to supply a unifying political interpretation of the war. Thus, according to the editors of *Architectural Forum*, local government would have to be persuaded to restrict themselves to the "useful memorial," leaving it up to the federal government to formulate the appropriate abstract symbols of the war.[36]

The ABMC, of course, could not avoid debate over the most suitable symbolism to be used in war memorials both at home and abroad. In line with prevailing sentiment within the State Department, America's most influential architects and public figures instinctively preferred historical styles for the proposed memorials and war cemeteries. Modernist trends in architecture, the architect Charles D. Maginnis warned, were guided by the principle that "people and things were better forgotten." During the course of a public debate that appeared on the pages of *Architectural Forum*, he asserted that modern architecture in memorials would have a pernicious effect: "It [modern architecture] has no provision for enduring things, no solicitude for posterity. The past already is dismissed as a distraction and a tyranny and only the passing hour is of consequence. In their turn the generations will henceforth make their fleeting imprint upon the sands and the little men and the big will be submerged in the heightened tempo of evolution."[37]

Architectural critic and renaissance man Lewis Mumford echoed these thoughts. "The very notion of a modern monument is a contradiction in terms," he stated unequivocally. "If it is a monument, it cannot be modern, and if it is modern, it cannot be a monument."[38] The consensus among the movers and shakers was quite clear. Modernity in national funerary architecture was out of the question, because it tended to "forget."

The creation of historical symbols without repetition of the clichés of Great War cemeteries promised to be problematic owing to the conspicuous lack of models and archetypes. The point of reference for defining national symbolism was still the nation's capital. But Washington was a city drowning in specious classicism. New opportunities to rethink the basic form of celebrating the national cause had produced bleak results. The same tired old men regurgitated the same tired old forms of symbolism. The completion in 1943 of John Russell Pope's Jefferson Memorial was ample testimony to the unlikelihood that any new form of pertinent symbolism would be enunciated in Washington. Pope's pantheon on the tidal basin was not only orthodox and unimaginative; it was also unoriginal. It was a virtual duplication of Pope's own design for the Henry E. Huntington Mausoleum at San Marino, California.

The problem, the *New York Times* lamented, was that "no architectural Huey Long, no sculptural Father Coughlin, no artistic Dr. Townsend" had passed through Washington to "startle conservatives with the 'new and untried.'"[39] Iconoclast Frank Lloyd Wright likened Washington's unwillingness to develop pertinent symbolism to the flight of the "floo-floo bird": "I am referring to the peculiar and especial bird who always flew backward. To keep the wind out of its eyes? No. Just because it didn't give a darn where it was going, but just had to see where it had been. Now in the floo-floo bird you have the true symbol of our government architecture, too, and in consequence how discredited American culture stands in the present time!"[40]

Joseph Hudnut enumerated the damaging implications of the capital's classicism in a scathing criticism of the formal architecture of Washington, D.C. Neoclassicism, he suggested, was a self-defeating form of American symbolism. "The philosophical basis of this architectural creed," he observed, was "the belief in an abstract and universal expression in art . . . untouched by changes in taste, unrelated to locality or time." In other words, such forms failed to convey contemporary American sentiments. Moreover, classicism had been appropriated by so many different types of political regimes that it could no longer be considered a "safe" and unequivocal sign of democratic aspirations. "The art of the Classic Revival . . . can be as readily despised as the art of Napoleon, as admired as the art of Jefferson . . . since to Napoleon the classic was a symbol of political absolutism and to Jefferson a symbol of the resolute republicanism of early Rome."[41]

These objections to classical styles for government symbolism were of particular concern for those involved in commemorating the war effort. With disapproval of the sterile classical architecture of Washington, D.C., still ringing loud and clear, academics and government officials cautioned against the reproduction of the ponderous and historically remote symbolism of the previous generation of war memorials and cemeteries. New war memorials, noted *Architectural Forum*, needed to be "in conformity with national temperament and taste." The symbols "befitting the conquests of a Roman emperor" that bedecked many of the artifacts of the Great War were "anachronisms."[42] Consequently, the ABMC approached its future projects with its sights set on implementing a more realistic scheme.

The eventual form of appropriate graphic symbolism for cemeteries as national monuments abroad was shaped in large part by the lively professional debate over government-sponsored art. The federal government's involvement in public art during the New Deal had produced working guidelines that eventually affected the content of postwar symbolism. Those federal agencies involved in public art projects had discovered through trial and error that contemporary realistic representations were the most effective form of iconography. The public reacted positively to projects that depicted ordinary citizens involved in the task of building a nation. According to one of the mural artists for a small Kentucky post office, the goal of persuading ordinary citizens to accept the implicit ideology embedded in these art projects was more likely to be accomplished "with a design having to do with their own activities than a mythological figure which the average man does not even understand and which may give him the feeling of the majesty and might of his government rather than the feeling of his own personal relation to it and the concern of the government towards him."[43]

New Deal art officials asserted that abstract symbolism or avant-garde art forms had alienating effects. Indeed, public reactions to New Deal–sponsored modernism confirmed that, frequently, incoherent abstract motifs were seen as, at best, imagistically illegible, or, at worst, an elitist attack on popular attitudes and broad democratic priorities. Abstract form, the meaning of which was not immediately apparent, was liable to elicit hostility rather than identification.[44]

Armed with these thoughts in mind, both the State Department and the ABMC approached their forthcoming missions with a clear sense of artistic priorities that had not existed previously. Strengthened by experience and having weathered an interlude in which both the theoretical and practical aspects of political architecture were thoroughly aired, these two agencies geared up once again for the mission of producing symbolic architecture as a tool of political persuasion.

The main issue facing both the ABMC and the State Department, therefore, would be how and under what circumstances one could escape the bear hug of restorational symbolism, without passing through the treacherous territory of modernism. The reliance on early American styles for the construction of embassies and legations lacked relevance. It was out of tune with the new acquired taste for modernism, which promised to be the trademark of postwar America. The classicism of national cemeteries abroad appeared to be equally inappropriate; it lacked anything that was unequivocally American. Moreover, there appeared to be little appreciation for or understanding of classical motifs in the postwar world. Washington, D.C., could not fulfill the role of guiding light. "When you come to think of it," an article in *Vanity Fair* stated in summation of the criticism leveled at the symbolism of Washington, "it is rather silly that a young and energetic nation which invented the skyscraper to solve the problem of Manhattan, which measures its powers in machines, dynamos, high-tension wires and internal combustion, should construct its capital in terms of Tiberius and Diocletian."[45]

Slowly, and sometimes painfully, the keepers of the flame launched the quest for relevant alternatives. The cessation of hostilities in 1945 would furnish the opportunity for the articulation of different, more appropriate symbolism of the nation on foreign soil. Once again, the military led the way in its construction of resting places and memorials for the nation's war dead.

5

"Our Own Land on Foreign Soil"

THE OVERSEAS MILITARY CEMETERIES
OF WORLD WAR II

IN 1966, at the high tide of America's ever-growing involvement in a new war of uncertain dimensions, an outraged chairman of the House Armed Services Committee issued a demand for the repatriation of all American war dead from France. His announcement was triggered by the breakdown of talks between France and the United States over the future of American bases on French soil. The impending withdrawal of American troops, Representative L. Mendel Rivers claimed, should include the bodies of the over 60,000 who had sacrificed their "lives to save that nation [France] from disgraceful defeat."[1]

Rivers, a South Carolina Democrat, apparently felt that the mere suggestion of this drastic gesture of displeasure would shock the French into rethinking their position. Moreover, his somewhat macabre demand implied a profound frustration with the function of America's military cemeteries in foreign lands. The concept of the American military cemetery abroad was based primarily on the assumption that these monumental structures would underscore American strength, grandeur, and authority in foreign nations. The demand to remove the American military presence from their soil intimated that the French were unimpressed with the inherent political overtones of American monuments and cemeteries.

The enhancement of America's global position through monumentality had been the primary motive for constructing all American military cemeteries abroad. However, certain differences set the two generations of cemeteries apart. To begin with, the styles employed in the cemeteries and monuments of the Second World War were the offspring of great internal dissension within the architectural profession in the United States. Unlike the monuments of the Great War, which reflected the tastes and education of an undisputed architectural elite, the second generation of cemeteries was built during a period of transition and passing of the guard from traditionalists to the apostles of the modern. The projects of the American Battle Monuments Commission (ABMC) at midcentury represented a rearguard effort to slow down the pace of change and forge some form of compromise between clashing concepts of government architecture.

As artifacts of political architecture designed primarily for foreign exhibition, the new cemeteries and monuments were markedly different, too. Great War cemeteries had displayed a certain tactfulness by blending into the general landscape of military cemeteries of both Allies and former enemies. The monuments of the Second World War, by contrast, cast aside such communal gestures of western fraternity. While the cemeteries of the Great War had wavered somewhat in defining a uniquely American form of imperial funerary architecture, those artifacts of the Second World War explicitly celebrated American power; they strove to elicit admiration for and acquiescence to an imperial America. The monuments and graves of the First World War were embellished with symbols of commemoration. By contrast, the new generation of cemeteries was future-oriented; the overseas monuments and memorials of the Second World War offered clues to how and by what means the United States had established and would maintain its Pax Americana. These cemeteries, according to their exponents, were meant to be explicit representations of the American spirit, "pieces of our own land on foreign soil," an American "foothold in Europe" and other continents.[2] Even though the military cemeteries had not fulfilled Congressman Rivers' expectations of eliciting unwavering homage from America's allies, the transition that occurred in the symbolism of death between the two World Wars illustrated some of the more salient changes in America's image abroad.

The establishment of American military cemeteries and monuments after the Second World War had all the qualities of a well-worn genre play. The unfolding plot was predictable, and while names had changed, the main characters were almost identical to those who had governed the overseas military cemeteries program after the Great War. As had been the case during the 1920s, the drama commenced with the dilemma over the very act of repatriating fatalities. The urge to commemorate the private individual, or, conversely, the focus on the abstract qualities of death in the national cause, appeared to have been lifted out of the pages of a Great War script. Even before the end of the war, the Quartermaster General of the Army reported that "the thought of leaving our boys in foreign soil as was done after World War I is not meeting with favor; in fact . . . ninety-nine percent of the letters received from parents ma[de] the request that the bodies of their boys be returned home."[3] This public sentiment clashed once again with a determined government campaign to retain the bodies overseas. The ABMC led the counteroffensive against repatriation. Board members contemplated lobbying for the amendment of "existing legislation so as to discourage next-of-kin from requesting the return of the dead," but decided instead to accomplish this mission by persuasion, complicated bureaucratic measures, and moral pressure.[4]

In addition to the conventional manner of persuasion through speeches and articles, the campaign to retain American military graves abroad received crucial support from the office of the Quartermaster General of the Army. Following the Second World War, and to anticipate the much-feared demand for repatriation of all casualties of this second bout of global conflict, the Quartermaster General developed a complicated process for repatriation requests. Each next-of-kin received a thick pamphlet of forms and information concerning burial options. The material quite blatantly suggested that "Option 1," burial in a permanent military cemetery overseas, represented the most appropriate form for final rites. Burial in the United States was implicitly discouraged. Each request for repatriation had to be notarized. In addition, the Quartermaster General made prominent note of the fact that the bodies were already buried and that their reinterment would require "many months, probably years to complete."[5]

The ABMC and its allies applied moral pressure on bereaved families through wide publication of the fact that the overseas cemeteries contained the bodies of some of America's most famous soldiers. General George C. Patton, perhaps the most charismatic leader of America's fighting forces, was buried in conspicuously ordinary fashion in the Luxembourg Cemetery. Two members of the Roosevelt clan—Brigadier General Theodore, Jr.,and his brother Quentin—were buried in the Normandy Military Cemetery. A third brother, Kermit, was a victim of the war, too; he was killed in a military accident in Alaska in 1943. Alice Roosevelt, the bereaved spouse of Theodore, Jr., lent moral support to those who sought burials abroad by becoming an active member of the ABMC and an outspoken opponent of repatriation. This concerted effort to minimize requests for repatriation through persuasion and bureaucracy succeeded in part. About 33 percent—approximately 94,000 of the war's casualties—were eventually buried in fourteen overseas complexes.[6]

Much like the discussion concerning the appropriate manner of burial, the membership of the ABMC was similar to that of the Great War committee. As was the case in the aftermath of World War I, a prominent and popular military hero served as the commission's chairman. General George C. Marshall, the former chief of staff, inherited AEF commander John J. Pershing's role as embodiment of the commission's mission. Marshall appointed General Thomas North, a member of his personal staff, as secretary of the commission. This appointment ensured a modicum of continuity, because as a young lieutenant North had been General John J. Pershing's liaison officer to the ABMC. In this capacity he had taken an active interest in the design of the cemeteries of the Great War.[7]

Marshall's concept of the role of the military cemetery abroad was quite clear. The soldiers buried within the confines of these cemeteries were still conscripts; their primary task was to serve national goals and objectives. In an article published in *National Geographic* magazine, the general summed up his feelings with an anecdote about the plight of an American mother at the Épinal Cemetery in northeastern France. The superintendent of the local military cemetery there had stumbled across an elderly American, sick, penniless, and alone.

> She did not speak French, and for some time she had been existing only on apples and cookies.... She was a widow with few friends and without close relatives. Her only son had been killed in the war. At his death the woman had vowed that someday she would visit his grave and for years she had scrimped and saved to make the journey. Then at Épinal, the vow kept, her funds ran out. Fortunately, the mother held a return ticket for passage home, but from their own pockets the American couple [the superintendent and his spouse] gave her money for food and railroad fare to a French port.[8]

This brave woman, the story stated, had sought her son, sacrificing her life for him as he had for her.

At a more profound level, however, the moral of the story had nothing to do with the noble plight of a bereaved parent separated from the grave of her son by countless miles and an insurmountable financial obstacle. Marshall's tale did not criticize the American government for its unwillingness to provide financial aid for those parents attempting to visit the graves of loved ones. Instead, he saw her ordeal as a symbolic sacrifice that all Americans should make. Whatever the sacrifice, all loyal citizens, "not only the war-bereaved," should aspire to this "Gethsemane of the spirit," for "in a higher sense" the war fatalities were "the sons of every free man."[9]

Having seen fresh flowers on the graves of America's war dead in France—a tribute paid by local villagers—Marshall elaborated further by invoking the well-worn example of Athens and the Battle of Marathon. Quoting Pericles' tribute to the Athenian dead, Marshall clarified the concept of national commemoration. "In foreign lands there dwells also an unwritten memorial of them, graven not on stone but in the hearts of men," he quoted. In other words, America's sacrifice knew no bounds, as it had occurred within the context of a just war, a moral crusade rather than a narrow political campaign. For this, an article in the *New York Times* stated bluntly, the nations of the world "owe[d]" the deceased representatives of the American nation "a little something."[10] Such tributes would be facilitated by the constant reminder of American graves on foreign soil.

Marshall's approach to the cemeteries abroad was translated into tangible form and directed single-handedly by supervising architect John Harbeson. Harbeson had been a close associate of the Great War's supervising architect, Paul Cret, at the University of Pennsylvania's architecture school. Harbeson subsequently became a partner in Cret's firm, and had assisted in the planning and supervision of the Great War overseas cemetery project.[11] He had been handpicked for the job by the Commission of Fine Arts (CFA). Prominent members of the commission had correctly assumed that Harbeson would unquestionably accept their guiding principles—in particular, their cautious approach to national symbolism. In order to avoid original and novel artistic ventures that might challenge the dictums of the art establishment, no competitions were held among the country's select artists and architects. All personnel were nominated "with the advice and recommendation of its consulting architect and of the national Commission of Fine Arts."[12]

Under the high-handed guidance of John Harbeson and General Marshall's representative, General Thomas North, the remains of American soldiers were removed from 250 temporary cemeteries and reinterred in fourteen large sites. The largest cemetery was in Manila, where over 17,000 soldiers were buried and 36,000 missing were commemorated. The smallest locale was in Tunisia, with its 2,840 graves and 3,724 names of the missing on a ceremonial wall. The remains of soldiers who had fallen in Germany were removed to the Margraten Cemetery in the Netherlands and the Luxembourg Cemetery.

These threads linking the commissions of the two World Wars did not entail a mere duplication of Great War cemeteries. Belatedly, and reluctantly, the keepers of American symbolism acknowledged the need to move away from the previous pedestrian duplications of classical architecture as representation of the American spirit. It was no longer possible to ignore the rumblings of discontent from within the architectural profession about the lack of creativity and the contested political overtones of neoclassical government architecture. Thus, the architectural scheme of the cemeteries was affected by public and professional yearnings for new forms of monumentality in the western world in general and the United States in particular.

As early as 1948, and under the auspices of the *Architectural Review*, the giants of the architectural profession analyzed the role, form, and shape of monuments in postwar society in a debate that architectural historian Talbot Hamlin described at the time as "the most significant contribution to recent architectural criticism." Participants in the symposium and subsequent debate were Gregor Paulsson, a leading architectural theorist from the University of Uppsala; Henry-Russell Hitchcock, coauthor of the now-famous exposition of modernism *The International Style*; William Holford, joint author of the new master plan for the City of London; Sigfried Giedion, author of two seminal architectural studies, *Space, Time, and Architecture* and *Mechanization Takes Command*; Walter Gropius, founder of the Bauhaus and professor of architecture at

Harvard University; Lucio Costa, leader of the modern architectural movement in Brazil; Alfred Roth, one of the leading American exponents of modern trends in architecture; and architectural critic and social commentator Lewis Mumford.[13]

Given their shared sympathy for dynamic architecture, the conference participants underscored their aversion to classical motifs as the idiom for monuments. It was the language of despots, they said. The totalitarian powers of the recent global struggle had used classical motifs quite frequently; consequently, neoclassicism as representation of democratic countries was liable to project the wrong message to a postwar world. Moreover, "reminiscent" styles spelled a lack of dynamism and reactionary thought. "Monumentality in the past," Gropius observed, was the symbol of a "static conception of this world," which, he implied, clashed with the egalitarian winds now emanating from the western world in general and the United States in particular. Most conference participants agreed that new and relevant forms of monumentality would crystallize as a result of experimentation with machines and engineering techniques rather than a repetitive reliance on the "frozen music" of "static symbols."[14]

As far as the United States was concerned, this quest for new, modern, and dynamic forms of symbolism was an academic affirmation of a well-established vernacular trend of the late 1930s and 1940s. Architectural historians have given this comprehensive flirtation with ahistorical styles a variety of names: Depression Modern, American Moderne, and Machine-Age Design, among others. They do, however, agree that the movement began among industrial designers and commercial artists and that it was a surprisingly self-contained American genre.[15] Industrial design in the 1930s and 1940s had effected a swing away from imported, ponderous styles toward streamlined, machinelike forms. The most eloquent spokesman of this contemporary American genre was furniture designer Walter Darwin Teague. He described its underpinnings as the utter rejection of decoration and a synonymous discovery of the sublime qualities of American materialism. "We have achieved a high degree of simplicity because we are a primitive people," Teague stated.

> We have no developed history behind us to use in our artistic creations. . . . This is why so much of our modern work today has a certain stark and simple quality that relates it very closely to the primitive work of . . . most people who were discovering their techniques and tools. . . . We should be very careful to deny ourselves the luxury of decoration in the things that we do because we have no decoration today that is significant to us, that has a meaning. The Greeks in their great day, in the design of the Parthenon, had at their command a vocabulary of ornament that they had inherited through years of work, that

had become significant to them and was very useful in the creation of their internal rhythm. But we have no ornament.[16]

The stark and simple design of the products of Teague and others, the total lack of decoration, was deliberate. In the brave new world that emerged from the Depression and global conflict, American industrial designers embraced a style that rejected "useless" decorative elements and outmoded, elitist values, preferring instead to celebrate their society's love affair with the machine. Curves, flowing lines, and a distinct lack of adornment were the main characteristics of this uniquely American brand of modernism.

The effect of the Contemporary American style in architecture was quite significant. Aversion to decoration and disapproval of size for its own sake translated into a movement from vertical to horizontal lines, a shift away from luxurious design toward elemental architecture to fit immediate needs, and, within this context, a deep suspicion of adornment. This stark architecture expressed an authentic social mood, a new materialism that found beauty in unadulterated form and the elimination of "wasted," ceremonial space.

The architecture of the Depression Modern differed from modern European counterparts, such as the Bauhaus, in its use of materials, its final form, and its source of inspiration. Instead of glass and metal, the Contemporary American relied on granite, limestone, and brick. The flowing lines of this American style departed from the "geometric, packing-box type" style of modern European design. Moreover, as opposed to European trends, the Contemporary American did not originate in the "Groves of Academe." It began with the demands of the most technically advanced sectors of the American economy to produce pure and functionally efficient architecture. Hence, James Marston Fitch has noted, "appearance and purpose, function and form" became so intertwined that it was "difficult to separate the two." In a departure from the European models of modern architecture, with their explicit attempts to translate altruistic ideas into building design, the aesthetic principles of the Depression Modern followed, rather than preceded, "the actual invention and development of the idiom."[17] This new style of building, noted two public works administrators in 1939, was an "evolution rather than a revolution."[18] By this they meant that the new imperatives constituted a gradual response to the desires of clients; there had been no sudden coup d'état within the architectural profession. The rejection of superfluous decoration in favor of simple lines was a cost-related, pragmatic decision; neither government nor academia imposed a standard style.

The problem, of course, was how to induct these modern trends into the service of monumentality. A monument implied a hierarchy of values.

Modern architecture recognized no such thing. Its prophets asserted that all architectural creations—whether government building or low-income housing project—were equally artistically significant. Here lay the crux of the obstacle facing government designers: A monument, by definition, was not always a functional structure, while new trends in architecture focused exclusively on function. A monument was a durable testimonial, a conscious symbol provided for future generations, while modern architecture rejected poetic overtones and anything beyond immediate structural needs.

The issue of monumentality could not be brushed aside, for, as Sigfried Giedion noted during the course of the *Architectural Review* symposium, "the people want buildings representing their social, ceremonial, and community life," an order that modern architecture was not yet able to deliver. Solutions aired at the symposium ranged from the somewhat daring suggestion to return to the classical formula to that of attempting to derive a new monumental language from the inspiring engineering achievements of the twentieth century. By all accounts, the question was far from settled.

Nowhere was the issue of monumentality more acute than in the development of American memorial plans for the war dead. Activities of the British provided little or no inspiration. A debilitated postwar Britain had chosen the most expedient course of reproducing the architectural and horticultural designs of Great War cemeteries.[19] Such a solution would never have succeeded in the United States, whose economic and political situations had improved dramatically. There was no place for nostalgic re-creations of images that had been challenged from the beginning as overly sterile. Moreover, illustrious war refugees had empowered the faction of innovation within the architectural profession. Pure duplication of classicism would not wash.

The solution adopted by the ABMC was in the spirit of compromise. Hoping to appease warring factions within the architectural profession, and seeking to relieve some of the political pressures associated with the unwarranted scrutiny of its designs, the ABMC developed a policy aimed at the partial accommodation of everyone. The ABMC formula was derived from the architectural achievements of its late architectural mentor Paul Cret. Since completing his Great War cemetery project, and in partial recognition of the criticism leveled against his apparently unwavering classical stance, Cret had become an advocate of a new approach, the so-called Scrapped Classicism. Beginning in the late 1920s and until his death in 1945, Cret gradually devised a new form of monumental architecture that retained the imperious overtones of classicism but avoided facsimiles of the icons of Athens and Rome.

In a series of federally commissioned buildings designed and constructed during the 1930s and early 1940s, Cret produced a forceful case for compromise. On the one hand, he remained loyal to classical tenets of symmetry and proportion, as well as the use of columns to define monumentality. Consequently, he took issue with what he saw as the modernist insistence on originality and newness for its own sake. On the other hand, Cret conceded to the modernist dislike of decorated surfaces, and accepted the principle of "empty surfaces as an integral element of a building's composition." In his Folger Shakespeare Library (1932), Federal Reserve Building (1940), and Bethesda Naval Medical Center (1940), Cret implemented this architecture of compromise.[20]

Cret's point of departure was the Vitruvian dictum that a building without columns was purely functional, while the columned structure was monumental. His ceremonial buildings of the 1930s and 1940s were all columned, but the columns were unornamented, with none of the frills accompanying the columns of the Beaux Arts school. By maintaining stripped-down classical symbols Cret hoped to retain the sense of power and durability of sound political architecture. At the same time, this terse, unadorned version of classicism removed anachronistic tensions from government architecture without relinquishing the aura of authority. Ahistorical columns implied a forward-looking concept of national power.

With its sights set firmly on Cret's modified governmental architectural archetype, the ABMC built a series of overseas chapels in the style of the Scrapped Classical. An excellent example of this type of monumental structure was Gardner Dailey's two hemicycles surrounding the chapel and memorial courtyard at the Manila Cemetery (Fig. 24). Here, as in most other architectural creations in the overseas projects, "Doric, Ionic, and Corinthian columns give way to capital-less rectangular posts; instead of pediments and sloping roofs, there are flat or shed roofs" with little or no historical allusions.[21] Other overseas monuments implemented the same concept of austerity and massiveness as a point of departure, but went so far as to discard columns altogether, seeking instead different symbols of durability and authority. The general design pattern of the Ardennes Memorial, the work of the architectural firm of Reinhard, Hofmeister, and Walquist of New York, belongs to this category (Fig. 25). The monolithic limestone memorial, perched on a gray granite podium, resembled an altar from which the sacrifice of the thousands would be commemorated. Its sheer bulk and austerity implied endurance and importance. Like a carved rock—the most fundamental form of monumentality—the square-shaped structure towered above the entire compound. The sculpture work attached to the bare facade announced the

24. Memorial chapel and hemicycle at Manila Cemetery (Gardner A. Dailey, architect)

contemporary political significance of the cemetery complex. The austere lines of the block channeled attention toward the seventeen-foot American eagle, the three personifications of Liberty, Justice, and Truth, and the thirteen-star representation of the origins of the American nation.

The sculptural work, by C. Paul Jennewein of New York, was a collection of clichés: a reiteration of the sublime qualities of American political culture in the three figures, the power of American nationhood represented by the New Deal–style eagle, and, of course, the convention of continuity—the validation of America's political origins through the representation of the thirteen original colonies in a modern setting. This somewhat unimaginative message did, however, constitute a significant departure from previous Great War motifs of nationhood in its focus on American ideals and the conspicuous absence of polite homage to the shared western values traditionally associated with neoclassicism.

This and other architectural attempts to evoke monumentality without resorting to obsolete classical conventions were not implemented merely

25. Memorial chapel at Ardennes Military Cemetery (Reinhard, Hofmeister, and Walquist, architects)

to satisfy the conflicting demands of competing factions within the architectural profession in the United States. They addressed, as well, clashes among the board members of the ABMC. As Americans who had been born for the most part in the previous century, many committee members displayed marked animosity toward modern architecture and sculpture and maintained a staunch loyalty to traditional representational solutions. During the course of a fact-finding mission to Europe, the commission's ruling faction—which included Vice Chairman Admiral Thomas Kinkaid and Alice Roosevelt—voiced strong support for the traditional formalism of the previous generation of American cemeteries abroad. They were somewhat less taken with the new generation of cemeteries, some of which, they thought, lacked "reasonably conventional design." Most of their wrath centered on plans for the Luxembourg Cemetery.

This ultramodern complex, designed by Ralph Walker, differed significantly from all other cemetery projects. Its main building, the centrally placed chapel, lacked the trappings of conventional monumentality (Fig. 26). The sacrosanct columns were there, of course. But, having adopted the modernists' aversion to decorated exteriors, Walker came up with the novel solution of doing away with external surfaces completely. Instead of massive granite, marble, or limestone walls—traditional symbols of permanence, solidity, and dignity—Walker used empty space and the natural view that met the visitor upon entering his modern-day Propylea. As a concession to those who pointed out the frequently inclement weather, Walker did agree to enclose the area with glass plates. However, he remained adamant in his refusal to use conventional walls.

Committee members rejected Walker's design as more reminiscent of a garage than a chapel.[22] Their objections stemmed primarily from a desire to produce cemeteries that would be meaningful for "ordinary people" who were unaware of the significance of symbols and styles.[23] They objected to both indecipherable modernism and esoteric classicism, saying that they were both elitist by nature. In its many apologetic explanations for adopting a policy of compromise, the ABMC claimed that it was indeed concerned mostly with producing easy symbolism for the masses. The ultimate rationalization offered for its safe solutions was the political folly of experimenting with taxpayers' money. In a typical statement, supervising architect Harbeson stated that "America's army was a citizen's army; its members came from every hamlet in the States, the great majority from areas far removed from the great centers of population, or of modern art movements. The Commission asks that all designs be such as would be understood by, and would have a meaning for, the relatives of the dead from these little communities . . . the Commission does not feel its purpose is to foster the evolution of art forms."[24]

26. Artist's impression of proposed chapel at Luxembourg Cemetery (Ralph Walker, architect)

At least as important as this professed sympathy for the untutored masses was the desire to avoid being targeted by the political crusade against modernist art in the United States of the 1950s. A vocal and influential group of supporters in Congress, led by the chairman of the House Committee on Public Works, Michigan Republican George Dondero, launched a highly successful campaign equating modern art with un-American values. Dondero and his supporters perceived iconoclasm in art, the rejection of conventional representations of form and space, as a repudiation of traditional worldviews, part of an international Communist-inspired conspiracy to undermine the American way. Congressional critics received crucial support from the embattled professional organizations of representational artists, in particular, the National Sculpture Society, which was fighting a rearguard battle to maintain their virtual monopoly over the government "gravy train" of the postwar years.[25]

And it was indeed lucrative. The chosen few for the ABMC projects received payments ranging from $12,000 to $45,000 per statue or frieze.[26] Bolstered by the combined pressure of powerful congressional supporters, the bastions of conservative art waged a vigorous campaign for the prized monopoly of government sculpture in general, and the overseas cemeteries in particular. By arguing that modern art works were foreign imports, the works of "newly-arrived" Americans who could not produce works reflective of the "true" American spirit, and by portraying the spirit of modernism as a "serious cancer in the culture of the nation," the National Sculpture Society and the CFA forced the hand of the ABMC to invest exclusively in representational works.[27]

While ostensibly free to pursue the calling of their own artistic leanings, the sculptors commissioned by the ABMC accepted the models dictated by the National Sculpture Society. In its 1946 booklet entitled *Enduring Memory*, the society presented the fundamental archetypes for its version of sound, national American funerary monuments. Ironically, the editors could not come up with any American model. They advocated modified versions of great works of memorial art—such as a Greek Metope from Periclean Athens, Ivan Mestrovic's modernized version of Michelangelo's *Pietà*, and French sculptor Emile Antoine Bourdelle's *La Vierge d'Alsace*, to name but a few. The book urged the remaking of the artwork in contemporary terms, or an alternative juxtaposition of more or less truthful renditions of the original pieces with modern scenes of the war effort so that "the common man" could digest their subliminal messages. Consequently, a Metope served as a model for Lee Lawrie's *Youth Triumphing over Evil* at the Brittany Memorial. A modern-day *Pietà*, Malvina Hoffman's *Resurrection*, adorned the facade of the Épinal Monument. A modified *Vierge d'Alsace*, *The Angel of Peace Nurturing a New Generation*, by Edmund Amateis, was the central piece of artwork in the Rhône Cemetery (Fig. 27). For their services in producing these guidelines for government-sponsored funerary architecture, four of the book's coeditors received commissions from the ABMC. They were Lee Lawrie, Donald DeLue, Malvina Hoffman, and Ralph Walker, who apparently underwent his unforeseen conversion to modernism only after receiving his commission.[28]

While conflicting artistic and political pressures had obvious impact on the final shape and style of the cemetery project, the intended political message of the architecture and art—in particular, the ultimate objective of winning over foreigners to the American cause—appeared to enjoy unanimous support. The secretary of the ABMC hammered home this theme in an internal memorandum that stated that the ulterior motive of the cemetery project was to produce "a psychological effect upon alien people of the sacrifices made by Americans."[29] In this sense the new batch of cemeteries broadened significantly the path blazed by the Great War shrines.

Indeed, even though both the First and Second World War cemeteries pursued the same fundamental objective of announcing an American

27. ABMC prototypes for memorial architecture. *Top left:* Lee Lawrie, *Youth Triumphing Over Evil*. *Top right:* Edmund Amateis, *Angel of Peace Nurturing New Generation*. *Bottom:* Malvina Hoffman, *Resurrection*

presence on foreign soil, some crucial differences in content set them apart. The symbolism of the World War II cemeteries revealed new cultural and political priorities in American society at midcentury. The differences in horticulture, layout, and iconography indicated significant shifts in the American mentality during the thirty-odd years separating the design and construction of Great War cemeteries from those of the Second World War; these changes, while mostly due to internal developments within American society, reflected a public climate that was receptive to a new unapologetic role of the United States as world leader. By 1945 many of the unresolved issues raised in Great War cemeteries had been decided. In contrast to the symbolism of the World War I sites, the new monuments and memorials did not express uncertainty as to whether victory meant the resurrection of time-honored tradition or, conversely, the inauguration of a brave new world. The question was no longer whether modernization had eclipsed traditional standards. The new issue in these shrines was the perceived implications of the new order of things—in particular, the role of the state in everyday life and the extent of government intervention abroad.

At their most fundamental level, the shrines of the Second World War were characterized by a series of structural patterns that set them apart from the Great War cemeteries and made it quite impossible to internalize the significance of the sites through a simple reference to past traditions. Even the actual plots hinted at the need for benevolent official guidance. Like the cemeteries of the Great War, the graves were laid out in symmetrical rows. However, owing to the elaborate geometrical shapes of the sites, any unguided attempt to find a particular grave was extremely difficult. If the Great War cemeteries were laid out mostly in simple rectangles or squares, the new generation of overseas burial grounds employed more intricate configurations, ranging from the trapezoid of the Netherlands cemetery in the village of Margraten to the petal-shaped Lorraine Cemetery in France (Figs. 28 and 29). Within each of these complex perimeters, the graves were divided into subplots, each arranged at a slight angle and sometimes of irregular shapes, so as to make the personal tracking of individual plots almost impossible. One needed instruction from an official source to make sense out of the blending patterns and shapes.[30]

The purpose of the intricate designs, according to supervising architect John Harbeson, was to divert attention away from "depressing" thoughts of death and sacrifice and evoke instead admiration for the great collaborative design that had produced these complex artifacts.[31] The underlying idea here was the diversion of attention from individual deaths to celebrate the sophisticated spirit of enterprise that had produced the American fighting machine. Just as the First World War cemeteries had conveyed a simplified sense of order in the terse rectangular layout of the

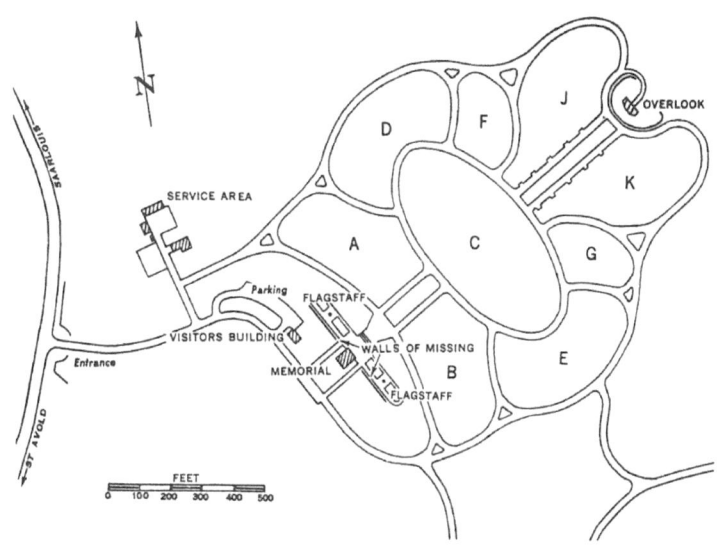

28. Lorraine Military Cemetery (Allyn R. Jennings, landscape architect)

29. Margraten Cemetery (M. Rapuano, landscape architect)

graves, the complexity of those of the Second World War underscored the role of collaborative enterprise rather than individuality in the war effort. The elaborate interplay of complex landscaping, with government-style architecture and strategically placed works of art, signified and gave "coherent form to that interdependence of the individual and the social group which is of the very nature of [American] democracy."[32]

In sharp contrast to the grave sites of the Great War, the landscaping of the Second World War cemeteries replaced commemorative conventions with horticultural symbols of rejuvenation. The lament and mourning that had embellished Great War shrines was replaced by the theme of resurrection. By means of an extensive use of multiseasonal flowers "an impression ... of life" replaced the Great War reliance on evergreens, which had given, according to John Harbeson, an "impression of austerity, an accent on the finality of death."[33]

A change in the standardized form of epitaphs also underscored the virtues of collaboration and the transcendent nature of death in an ideological struggle. The headstones of the unknown in Great War cemeteries had borne the inscription, "Here rests in honored glory an American soldier known but to God." In World War II cemeteries the term *comrade-in-arms* replaced the previous *American soldier*, thereby positioning the deceased within the context of a collaborative union in which the deeds of the individual were related to the actions of others. The overarching message of death in the national cause, which far outweighed any sense of personal tragedy, relied once again on the paradigm of the Battle of Marathon. Pericles' immortal words, inscribed at the Florence Cemetery, summarized the essence of American sacrifices: "They received each for his own memory praise that will never die and with it the grandest of all sepulchers, a home in the minds of men. . . . Therefore do not mourn with the parents of the dead who are with us. Rather comfort them. Let their burden be lightened by the glory of the dead."[34]

The frequent invocation of Marathon implied once again that the United States was the new harbinger of classic democracy. As such, the graves of its warriors were not odes to tragic deaths of young American men. The meaning of their sacrifices transcended the boundaries of kin; with their blood they had engraved their deeds in the pages of history. Pericles' exhortation to avoid mourning highlighted a previously covert message embedded in the Great War cemeteries that the ultimate manifestation of unwavering loyalty to a collective—death within the ranks of an army—was not a tragedy. The relinquishing of individuality and an allegiance to the state and its affairs deserved praise.

Paths and walkways of the cemeteries also echoed this theme of the precedence of the state. In a departure from the policies of Great War cemeteries, where visitors first encountered the sea of individual graves, the typical entrance to Second World War cemeteries was through the chapel area, where the official version of the war and its significance were expounded. The previous pretense of a mute official guidance in the war effort, the idea that government was only coordinating the collective will of the people, vanished from the cemeteries of the Second World War. In nine of the twelve Second World War cemeteries in Europe the visitor initially confronted an articulate and forceful official interpretation of the events before ever seeing the graves. In the new cultural climate of the postwar period, the American political establishment, through its agent, the ABMC, no longer bothered to disguise the role of a centralized authority in interpreting the complex events that had so affected the lives of its citizens. As Richard Polenberg points out, the Second World War led Americans to rely unabashedly on their government for guidance and solutions to their dilemmas. During the war, he notes, "the federal government employed more people, spent more money, and exerted wider control over people's lives than ever before." The dependence of Americans on their government for help in making sense out of the complex world in which they lived was now an irrefutable, acknowledged fact; naturally, it received bold representation within the cemeteries.[35]

As for the centerpieces of the cemeteries—the chapels and memorials—they, too, departed from the themes of the Great War. To begin with, the actual war memorial—an official governmental interpretation of events that had been suppressed at the cemetery sites of the Great War so as not to distract attention from the image of individual sacrifice—became an integral part of the Second World War cemetery complex. Thus, a communal celebration of the event literally and metaphorically overshadowed the individual grave sites. By avoiding a pedantic copying of the historical European styles of the preceding generation of shrines, the new architectural form expressed "spiritual values without resorting to the banalities of the past."[36] With the exception of the Norman-style chapel at the Brittany Cemetery, the new approach to ceremonial architecture within the cemeteries adopted Paul Cret's reductionist Scrapped Classicism modification of exclusive homage to tradition.[37] Although the buildings were not, by any means, boldly iconoclastic, their ahistorical architecture was certainly more politically coherent than the retrospective symbolism of Great War shrines. The cold, terse lines of most of the modernist shrines in the cemeteries of the Second World War suggested that future-orientation had become the new formal central motif in the American cemeteries. The new American global agenda demanded a departure from exclusively historical themes. New forms of political symbolism implied that, having once again tipped the scales of a global conflict, Americans now stood prepared to shake off the burden of an inhibiting past.

The significance of this new architecture and landscaping was underscored by the "modified-modern" sculptural works—the endowment of familiar symbols of classical origin with new meaning through the use of sleek, modern lines—a style that contemporary critics described as "consciously non-historical."[38] Moreover, the themes of the statuary in the new generation of cemeteries were almost exclusively resurrection and future-orientation. Typically, *The Spirit of American Youth* at the Normandy Cemetery, a modified version of an Athenian Kouros representing a comrade-in-arms rising from the waves upon which he had fallen, emphasized that these sites were devoted to the fate of the deceased beyond the grave (Fig. 30).

In contrast to the iconography of Great War cemeteries, which had dwelt upon the virtues of a broad Anglo-Saxon culture, the art of Second World War burial grounds celebrated things uniquely American. Gone were the knights in shining armor, the symbolic juxtaposition of European and American values, and the interpretation of the war as a latter-day crusade to save western civilization. Instead of the Great War monument of Marianne and Lady Liberty clasping arms in a gesture of sisterhood, the Second World War cemeteries focused on intra-American cooperation. The Nettuno Cemetery's representation of an American soldier and sailor, arm in arm, shoulder to shoulder, suggested that victory was an internal American triumph that was brought about through the synchronization of complex and functionally diverse enterprises of a sophisticated American society (Fig. 31).

This sense of the war triumph as the result of the smooth workings of a complex infrastructure was underscored through the prominent display of machinery in the iconography of the cemeteries. Unlike the instances of machines in the art of the Great War, where silent weapons were divorced from their operators, the machines of the Second World War were linked intimately to human beings, and were portrayed in realistic combat scenes. The side panels surrounding the war maps of the Ardennes Cemetery in Belgium emphasized men controlling and employing the elaborate tools of war. America's industrial capability had led to the success of the United States, and thus encouraged the perception of a positive relationship between industrialization, machines, and the American way of life (Fig. 32).[39]

The theme of the beneficial implications of industrial power appeared quite explicitly in the descriptions of battles within the cemeteries. Like those of the First World War, the new burial grounds had engraved battle maps. But, instead of the small medallion-like maps in the previous generation of shrines, the typical cemetery of the Second World War used an entire room to describe the feats of American troops at each particular site. These wall maps were accompanied by exhaustive texts deciphering the technical data engraved on them. The rhetoric of battle in the cemeteries of the Second World War interpreted military success as the result of complex and intricate coordination between various aspects of the

30. Donald DeLue, *The Spirit of American Youth*: Normandy Military Cemetery

31. Paul Manship, *Brothers in Arms*: Nettuno Military Cemetery

fighting machine. Each element of the large war apparatus employed a specific tool that complemented the efforts of other sectors. The inscriptions at the Luxembourg Cemetery, for example, noted that the amphibious landing of ground troops at Normandy had succeeded because of a preceding naval barrage and air attack, while the description of the liberation of France at the Épinal Cemetery documented in painstaking detail the complex joining of several army groups, each arriving from a different direction, in the attempt to isolate German units in the south of France.[40]

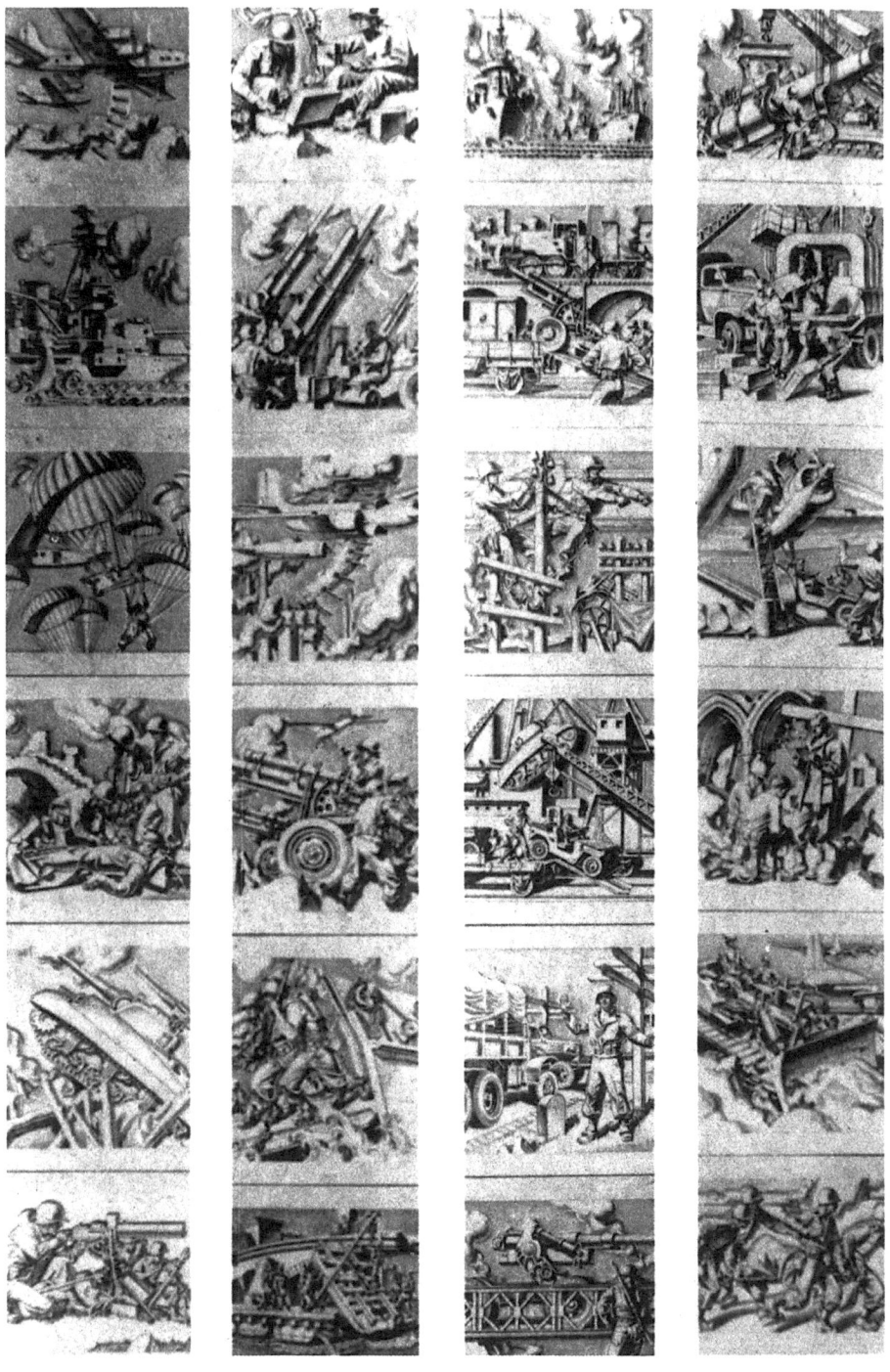

32. Side panels, Ardennes Military Cemetery (Dean Cornwell, designer)

The various campaigns invariably described American successes not as mere triumphs of will and valor but as the result of massive concentration of firepower and interaction between specialized units of a fighting machine. Descriptions of Great War battles had suggested that daring and personal valor were still the crucial elements of modern warfare; the texts accompanying Second World War battle maps gave victory to the side with a mechanically adept fighting force that attacked the enemy in overwhelming numbers and with superior weaponry.

It would appear that the cemeteries of World War II pointed quite explicitly toward the transitions that a second bout of world conflict had imposed upon American society. The new generation of military burial sites in Europe presented an America that seemed quite at ease with modernization. The iconography of machines announced openly that the tipping of the scales of global power had been brought about by the technological advantages of the United States, with little or no allusion to the anachronistic virtues celebrated at Great War cemeteries.

Having gone through a previous experience of total war, Americans no longer had to rely on anachronistic symbolism to articulate their sentiments. Within their complex and intricate society the new claims of government received explicit recognition. The new cemeteries celebrated coordinated leadership and rational organization. The Great War pretense of an ideal social order, based on minimal formal power invested in the state, was conspicuously absent. The formal interpretation of the war effort moved from the back of the cemetery grounds to the front, thereby transforming the role of government from coordinator to guiding light.

As far as the United States' global role was concerned, the symbolism of the cemeteries demonstrated great strides, too. In the cemeteries of the First World War, when the concept of a strong American leadership in Europe had not yet been unequivocally embraced, the cemeteries sought simply to announce a significant American presence. The cemeteries of the Second World War, by contrast, preached predominance and an imperial vision that went far beyond any previous self-representation of American aspirations and limitations in the global sphere of events. The iconography of the Second World War celebrated American values and institutions within a global arena. Rather than cloaking the significance of the war in vague metaphors of western culture, the art and architecture of the new cemeteries fashioned an American interpretation of events. A new role as leader, rather than partner or disciple, appeared here. These claims to leadership were derived not from time-honored western values but from the future-orientation of American society. The United States' technological edge, the iconography of the Second World War suggested, had brought about this revolution.

Indeed, in the figurative displays of overwhelming strength and massive firepower, one may see not only a documentation of the war effort but also the crystallization of an important political philosophy. The positive role assigned to massive force and technological superiority within the context of global confrontations was to become the hallmark of American foreign policy for years to come. Americans approached the foreign crises of the second half of the twentieth century with the same logic that had guided their role in the Second World War. International crises, large and small, could be solved with the introduction of massive firepower, the infusion of overwhelming numbers of troops, and the introduction of sophisticated new weapons.

And yet, the angry cries for the belated repatriation of the dead suggests that these cemeteries as artifacts of political architecture did not accomplish their mission. A cursory glance at newspapers from V-day during the 1950s and 1960s reveals that these cemeteries rarely figured prominently in the commemoration of the Allied war effort. Even before the last of the overseas cemeteries was dedicated in 1960, these sites appeared to have slipped from the public memory.

There are two reasons for the ineffectiveness of these cemeteries as tools of political propaganda. As far as the art and architecture was concerned, the critic John Canaday observed, "it was at best innocuous.... These memorials do not say 'remember'; they do not say 'forget'. They simply give no sign of awareness that anything at all has happened."[41] Contemporary observers charged that the dilution of symbolism brought about by the tepid compromise between tradition and modernity, as well as the overall philosophy of creating a simplified iconography that refrained from brooding over the personal, human dimensions of the war, had evoked nothing more than indifference. The problem with the artwork was that it was neither modern nor classical; the statues within the overseas cemeteries were "over-familiar dilutions of the Neo-Greek... a flabby modern rendering of this overworked mode."[42] In its efforts to produce works of art that would offend no one, the ABMC had avoided both avant-garde and strict classical styles. Instead it had encouraged works of pale compromise. The pallid pseudo-modernistic shrines, according to Canaday, were unimaginative "antiseptic wastes of marble suggesting the forms so dear to Hitler and Mussolini, but without the sheer brutal weightiness that made these monuments perversely impressive."[43] The lone attempt at originality—the proposed site for the Luxembourg Cemetery, made by Ralph Walker—had been rejected for not toeing the line of conventionality.

The primary problem with the architecture of the cemeteries was that it was conventional and overfamiliar to the point that it failed the fundamental test of monumental architecture: whether it rivets attention and evokes emotional response. In addition, the movers and shakers of the World War shrines had ignored another cardinal principle of monumental architecture; they had located the projects in the vicinity of crucial battles rather than within the context of significant tourist attractions. Based on notions derived from the cemeteries of the Great War, they approached their shrines as sites for "pilgrimage." The cemeteries were expected to fulfill the role of modern-day holy sites, which would draw devout pilgrims to their mostly remote locations. With few exceptions, the cemeteries were not situated in major urban centers nor in especially attractive areas. They were often built in areas that were unlikely to attract even the accidental tourist. If anything, the ABMC had sought pristine, bucolic surroundings, much like the locations of the rural cemeteries that were still in vogue in the United States. The Margraten Cemetery in the Netherlands was not the site of a major battle but the central repository for those who had died in Germany. Given this fact, the cemetery could conceivably have been built in a more appropriate area than this unimposing rural village near the industrial center of Maastricht.

Preconceptions about the positive linkage of placid rural surroundings and death kept the new generation of cemeteries hidden from high-density exposure. The assumption that the memory of the bloody tragedy would act as a magnet for veterans, tourists, and grateful locals bent on paying homage at the sites of crucial battles was proved wrong. Two rounds of global warfare had jaded the world; mass death was no longer a novelty and could not in itself attract public attention.

Aesthetically, the cemeteries of World War II were conservative and unimaginative. Owing to the tug-of-war between modernity and tradition in government-sponsored projects, the ABMC had produced nonconfrontational works that aroused little wrath but, by the same token, attracted little attention. In this sense, the architecture and art of the second generation of military cemeteries reflected the problems involved in enlisting architecture in the service of democratic nations. Democracy functions on compromise, on attempting to appease and please as many different groups as possible. Under these circumstances, the officially ordained projects of democracies produced undramatic artifacts of patriotism. Owing to its very nature, government reacted slowly and cautiously to changing cultural trends, lest it be accused of following pretentious vogues or abandoning the common man in favor of the elite.

The only viable way to produce forceful exemplars of political architecture was to remove government-sponsored architectural projects from public scrutiny, thereby allowing decisions to be made and messages to be enunciated without having to make peace between the conflicting crosscurrents that characterize the democratic political process. It was with these crucial lessons in mind that the United States approached its other major project of political architecture abroad. The contemporaneous efforts to construct embassies as artifacts of political architecture were of a much more didactic nature, because they were carried out by experts armed with explicit instructions to ignore public pressures and concerns about national symbolism abroad. Here the architecture was significantly more arresting, ideologically blatant, and centrally placed. For better or for worse, the new generation of American embassies promised, by discarding the uncertain symbolism of World War cemeteries, to induce anything but indifference.

6

Foreign Bodies

AMERICAN IMPERIAL ARCHITECTURE, 1945–1965

TIME MAGAZINE called the phenomenon a new international sport. In a condescending and, at times, mystified tone, the periodical documented the "corpus of ground rules" that governed this new activity wherever it occurred. The function of an early-warning system, according to *Time*, was provided by the appearance of sign painters,

> serious little men with paintpots and newly issued brushes, their lips moving soundlessly with the memorized slogans: 'Yankee Go Home' or 'Down with the Neocolonialists'. . . . Next come the marchers, swinging along with mob gaiety and waving their xenophobic standards at the white faces in the embassy window. . . . The next arrival is apt to be a riot truck, probably provided—though for different purposes—by U.S. Aid funds. . . . Out come the carefully collected stores of cobblestones, brick halves and rocks. And then the fun begins.[1]

Damage was usually inflicted on the glass exteriors of embassies and U.S. information libraries. In other instances, especially in Third World countries where elaborate decorative screens protected the windows, it was the flag as symbol of a foreign presence or books as representations of the power of foreign knowledge that were destroyed. Regardless of the ostensible reason behind the various outbursts of anti-Americanism, the attacks did indeed follow an almost identical pattern.

In Ghana, where demonstrations were orchestrated by Kwame Nkrumah's ruling Convention People's party, demonstrators lobbed a few stones toward the protective mahogany window screens, but channeled most of their wrath at the American flag. Given the tone of the threats to "massacre" Americans, just as Americans had "massacred the people in Korea and Germany, in Cuba and Panama," the actions of Emerson Player, a black embassy attaché, suggest that both sides, American diplomats and Ghanian protestors, understood the rules of the game. Upon observing that the American flag was about to be burned, he rushed out into the crowd of demonstrators, grabbed the flag, and ran it back up the flagpole. Player came out of the incident unscathed. The most serious incident in the Ghanian demonstrations involved an economic attaché whose camera was snatched by a demonstrator.[2]

In Indonesia, where the ruling party instigated the demonstrations, the American government had not built a monumental embassy. Here, demonstrators attacked American information libraries and burned books, the symbols of the power of superior knowledge that the United States wielded so casually in its dealings with developing nations. As in Ghana, neither American personnel nor local employees suffered injuries.[3]

Radical opposition groups observed the etiquette of anti-American demonstrations, too. Students and Moslem fundamentalists in Khartoum shattered embassy windows and burned library books, while studiously avoiding contact with any of the seven hundred American personnel in the city.[4] "Communist-inspired" student groups in Santa Cruz, Bolivia, burned the American flag in front of the offices of the United States Information Service, but ignored the handful of defenseless Americans in the city.[5]

This channeling of anti-American sentiment into attacks on buildings rather than Americans themselves led growing numbers of observers to the conclusion that the physical representations of American power abroad—in particular, a new generation of architecturally innovative embassy structures—were uncomfortable symbols of intrusion. Mass assaults on American diplomatic buildings, rather than personnel, focused attention on the edifices themselves, their architecture and ubiquity. Third World countries, in particular, according to critics of the State Department's postwar strategy of embassy construction, interpreted the architecture of American power as representations of colonial designs. "In the popular mind," Ada Louise Huxtable observed, "the new embassies have two strikes against them; they are big and they are different. In some countries these massive structures symbolize what we have in power and plenty as opposed to what they have not."[6] The cultural chauvinism embodied in the new diplomatic structures, so this argument went, made them obvious targets of anti-American sentiment. Indeed, during a five-month period, from October 1964 to March 1965, American embassies, consulates, and cultural centers bore the brunt of twenty-five frontal attacks; the overwhelming majority of these diplomatic outposts had been constructed in the late 1950s and early 1960s.[7]

It is, of course, difficult to corroborate the theory that these attacks were symbolic enactments of dissatisfaction with America's new global presence. However, there is little doubt that the monumental embassies erected by the United States in the aftermath of the Second World War represented an architecture of imperialism. Rather than merely announcing the coming of age of a new power, the new American symbols abroad were intrusive, and mostly antinationalist. They presupposed the fundamental inferiority of other nations. By trivializing the customs and traditions of others and, at the same time, celebrating an exclusive American control over the technological secrets of the future, the embassy buildings demanded adherence to the policies and priorities of the United States.

There is substantial physical evidence for examining this case. The State Department spent $215 million in embassy construction during the first fifteen years after the war and another $200 million in the 1960s. This lavish spending contrasted sharply with the less than $20 million spent for embassy construction between 1900 and 1945.[8] The interpretation of official American edifices abroad as an architecture of imperialism is substantiated by revealing comments in State Department files in the National Archives, the *Congressional Record*, and the architectural press. However, the literary evidence in support of this interpretation is far from overwhelming; there is no smoking gun. A close reading of official documents has not produced any blatant statement to the effect that the architecture of embassies was seen as a tool to be used for the tightening of American control and domination in foreign lands.

This lack of incriminating literary evidence does not destroy the case for an architecture of imperialism. It is not necessary to prove that such a policy developed consciously. The velocity and profound nature of change in the postwar years produced its own dynamic. The sphere of international relations—in particular, the power vacuum created by the demise of traditional empires—thrust the United States into a position that led inevitably to a haphazard and sometimes erratic effort to assert global priority. Under these circumstances, the official language of power was sometimes evasive, and often unclear. The written material is replete with hints and suggestions, rather than blatant statements. In contrast, the language of architecture is significantly less ambiguous.

This expansion of American diplomatic construction abroad was, of course, a by-product of the United States' changing international situation in the postwar period, expressed in particular by its massive physical presence on foreign soil. A mere ten years after the war, 580,000 American civilians—one in every three hundred American citizens—resided abroad. Together with close to one million military personnel and dependents, and periodic waves of mass tourism, these citizens gave the United States "millions of ambassadors over the earth."[9]

By 1957 the number of official nonmilitary emissaries had reached an all-time high of close to 99,000. Most were associated with the Foreign Service and the administration of a wide variety of programs that were initiated, strengthened, and revamped to meet the challenges of the postwar era. The U.S. government launched foreign aid programs, both military and civilian, on a grand scale in order to bolster the regimes of Allies and to court the new political entities of the postwar period. An ambitious propaganda network aimed at cultivating a favorable impression of the United States among elites and intellectuals led to the expansion of American cultural institutions abroad, mostly through the establishment of libraries, cultural centers, and academic exchange programs.

The initial reasons behind the construction of federally owned edifices abroad were primarily practical. Many American government functions abroad were centered in European cities that had been devastated by the war. As for the Third World in general, and Africa in particular, the United States sought to establish a presence in countries where the necessary infrastructure of office space and western-style housing was scarce. Here, the government had little alternative other than building from scratch.

But, above all, the massive construction effort overseas reflected the realization that the theater of war in which the United States was now engaged had shifted from armed conflict to economic and political maneuvering, from actual warfare to the battle for hearts and minds. The United States expanded its global radio network and created a new independent network of cultural disseminators—the United States Information Service (USIS)—whose task it was to encourage knowledge and acceptance of American culture and values through libraries, traveling cultural exhibitions, and academic exchange programs.[10]

The decision to erect impressive diplomatic edifices in just about every nation-state of the postwar period was an integral part of this information strategy. According to the editors of *Life* magazine, the United States did not need to resort to "traditional imperial" practices in order to hold its own. What was required was manifest and uniquely American "outposts of order" in which "the lives Americans lead or would like to lead" would be symbolically represented.[11] Embassy buildings—a visible manifestation of what John Foster Dulles had called "the good fruits of our freedom"—figured prominently in this scheme of things.[12] Much like the variety of cultural programs initiated by the USIS, the embassy structures were indicative of a nagging American sense of underculture, the desire to demonstrate that military and economic power were not unaccompanied by achievements in the arts. A massive foreign presence now allowed this quest to demonstrate American cultural prowess to spill over into architecture.

Ambitious designs to further the American cause through architectural symbolism enjoyed the luxury of a generous budget as well as diminishing public and congressional scrutiny. Funds were acquired outside of the usual budgetary process, owing to the accumulation of credits abroad. Large American war credits in countries unable to repay these debts led the State Department to establish a barter program through which host countries supplied building materials and labor in return for debt forgiveness.

Thus the United States was able to build an impressive array of foreign legations at bargain rates. Ninety-seven percent of the 1946 appropriation of $110 million for overseas construction was met by host countries seeking to reduce their obligations to the United States from "lend-lease," surplus property, and other aid programs.[13] In 1954 the overseas building program received a ten-year, $200-million allocation. These funds came from two sources: local currency and the disposal of surplus American properties abroad.[14] Congressional opponents, both the cautious spenders and the isolationists, were reduced to sniping at the program. Given the fact that these allocations did not seem to consume a portion of the budget that could have been used for other, "safer," purposes, critics could not muster support, anger, or much dissatisfaction among their colleagues.

The quest for unambiguous political architecture abroad led to the dismantling of the interdepartmental Foreign Service Buildings Commission (FSBC) after World War II and the subsequent rehauling of the building procedures. By separating the architectural process from the inevitable crosscurrents of an interdepartmental agency, the State Department could now pursue its own agenda with no outside interference. A new internal division in the State Department, the Office of Foreign Buildings Operations (FBO), enjoyed almost complete autonomy in deciding upon relevant styles, as opposed to the mostly technical duties of State Department building officials during the reign of the FSBC.

In presenting their program to Congress, FBO officials used a two-pronged argument. First, they claimed, the massive construction effort abroad provided "a maximum recovery of foreign credits owed to the United States." The State Department contended that the construction funds came from otherwise uncollectible debts abroad, the conversion of "substantial local currency credits into tangible and valuable assets." In addition, the State Department carefully avoided presenting the massive plans to construct embassies as a personal crusade of the executive branch. Foreign countries, especially among the developing nations of the Third World, the State Department informed Congress, expected—indeed, demanded—such exercises in public diplomacy. They "attach great significance to the scope and nature of American operations, including physical facilities.... They regard dignified, adequate facilities not only as a show of friendship ... but a reflection of the U.S. role as a major world power."[15] Opponents occasionally managed to invoke mild rebuke of the free-spending mentality of FBO officials. But for the most part they looked on helplessly as the State Department presented its plans to the appropriate congressional committees as a fait accompli.[16]

Abundant funds, with few strings attached and with only nominal congressional supervision, reduced the need to compromise with and accommodate various pressure groups, political or artistic. In stark contrast to the bickering and subsequent appeasement policies that had characterized America's monuments-abroad project throughout the previous fifty years, the FBO now had the funds, discretion, and necessary confidentiality to develop schemes that served only one purpose: the creation of a forceful American image for foreign exhibition. For the first time since the United States began devising intricate plans for political architecture, government officials were freed from the shackles of public debate and compromise.

The State Department's formula for successful symbolic architecture abroad may be pieced together by reading through the comments of the bureaucrats in charge of the program. These officials were concerned almost exclusively with appearances rather than function. A now-familiar argument of FBO proponents reiterated that the encounter with the facade of American institutions was bound to be practically the only time that most people would ever confront any representation of the United States. "To a great many people our official buildings are the only physical embodiment of our culture they are likely to see other than automobiles or refrigerators," a regional supervisor of the FBO declared.[17] Frederick Larkin, the ranking building official in the State Department from 1935 through 1950, stated in a presidential report that embassies should be approached as "oases of American soil in foreign" lands.[18] Larkin's choice of words underscored the cardinal principles of the embassy-as-symbol program. As an oasis, the embassy edifice needed to introduce refreshing concepts into otherwise parched and desolate landscapes. The replenishing oasis spelled hope; by implication, its surroundings were wilderness, emptiness. Above all, and as a point of departure for the whole program, the oasis needed to stand out from its surroundings. Thus the architecture of embassies was designed to superimpose aspects of a uniquely American worldview on a distinctly foreign territory. It was with these thoughts in mind that the State Department launched its massive construction effort abroad. From 1946 through 1953 the FBO executed two hundred projects in seventy-two countries. In subsequent years, hundreds of additional projects followed, most with the explicit purpose of expressing "a physical symbol of our Government and our people" abroad.[19] During the fiscal year 1963–1964 alone, the FBO proposed 130 separate projects.[20]

Given the political context of the postwar years—in particular, the growing urge to think in global rather than local terms—as well as the United States' self-image as harbinger of progress, the historical style of embassy architecture lost favor; it was introspective to the point of being esoteric. Classicism was equally inappropriate because of its retrospective nature and authoritarian connotations. The poor reception of the Scrapped Classicism of the cemetery projects ruled this style out as well. New forms of government symbolism seemed inevitable.

Significant flux within the architectural profession hastened the reassessment of style in the immediate postwar era. In contrast to the situation in the earlier years of this century, America's architectural establishment had irrevocably shed its conservatism and introspectiveness. This was due in large degree to the empowerment of illustrious architectural iconoclasts who had immigrated to the United States from war-torn Europe. A veritable revolution occurred within the architectural profession by means of swift takeovers of the country's major architecture schools. The modernist "coups d'état" at the country's major architecture schools were frequently supported by sympathetic university administrators seeking a more progressive image with which to promote their schools in the postwar years. Moreover, the rapid expansion of higher education in the 1950s produced hundreds of contracts from academic institutions seeking a visionary architectural blend of progress and traditional values in the spirit of postwar higher education. The prolific architectural creations on the campuses of the 1950s and 1960s announced quite explicitly that the age of safe, rehashed solutions to the challenges of symbolic architecture was over.[21]

This new flamboyant spirit of the architectural profession dovetailed neatly with the rehauling of the FBO's administrative and professional frameworks. Immediately after the war, Frederick Larkin, who for twenty years had directed the State Department's program of colonial embassy building, retired. His recommendation for a successor was his chief architect, Leland King, the creator of the 1946 Spanish colonial embassy in Lima. Together with the departing Larkin, King had devised the plan for expansion by using local currency credits abroad. In order to handle the deluge of projects, King decentralized his office. He divided the FBO into nine regional offices. Regional supervisors had the dual responsibility of overseeing projects and recommending the appropriate style for diplomatic structures in their region. Paradoxically, decentralization did not lead to any great architectural diversity. Since building the Lima embassy, King had undergone a conversion to modernism, and his handpicked regional supervisors were mostly apostles of the International Style.

Indeed, this first experimentation with political architecture abroad in the postwar years relied entirely on the International Style, characterized by a standard boxlike design, a lack of any ornamentation, and an unabashed display of basic building materials. This first batch of postwar embassies was the product of the so-called functional school of modernist design. The architects were disciples of Ludwig Mies Van Der Rohe, a German fugitive from nazism who had brought with him to the United States the concept of *Neue Sachlichkeit*, an architectural philosophy of problem-solving and objectivity. According to the "New Objectivity," function and efficiency had to be the dominant features of buildings. This meant that structures should be reduced to skeleton and unadorned outer surfaces—a "skin-and-bones" architecture of pure form. Advocates of the New Objectivity emphasized technical perfection and proportion as aesthetic qualities and eschewed the decorativeness of the previous generation of monumental construction.[22] Impressive variations of these "skin-and-bones" embassies of the early postwar years were the embassy buildings in Rio de Janeiro and Havana, both products of Harrison and Abramovitz, the creators of the United Nations complex in New York. In both of these structures the architects used granite rather than the more orthodox steel facade, perhaps playing upon the metaphor of durability associated with stone; in other respects both embassies were very much in line with the reigning minimalism of the time (Fig. 33). The FBO built an array of other minimalist embassies throughout the world, from Copenhagen to Madrid.[23]

These International Style embassies had the distinct advantage of exposing the differences between the two superpowers of the postwar era. Soviet political architecture espoused elaborate historical styles. As of the early 1930s, Soviet architectural ideologues had condemned modern architecture as dangerously "subjective" and incapable of producing unambiguous political statements. Historical imperial styles—ranging from the indigenous imperial Russian to neoclassicism—were sanctioned as the proper media for transmitting "ideologically saturated" messages on the "grandeur," "permanence," and "might" of the collective state.[24] Thus in a discussion of the modern embassy in Havana, a leading architectural magazine noted that the FBO had "presented to the rest of the world a colorful picture of a young and progressive-minded" America, which contrasted quite sharply with the Spanish colonial–style Soviet embassy building. "Note the pretentious classicism of official Soviet architecture abroad, then compare it with the clean and friendly embassies" of the United States, the magazine commented.[25]

Ideological contrast was not the only reason for embracing the International Style during the early 1950s. The choice of boxlike embassies of clean glass and naked steel was influenced, too, by contemporary architectural theories derived from the Gestalt school of psychology. According to this school of thought, human beings were more likely to appreciate and remember simple symmetrical shapes—squares and rectangles—than asymmetrical, complex forms. The observation that most people possessed a tendency to appreciate fundamental shapes and stim-

33. American Embassy, Rio de Janeiro, Brazil, 1953 (Harrison and Abramovitz, architects)

uli lent support to champions of modernist architecture, who argued that rectilinear architectural expressions projected an attention-grabbing and positive American image abroad.[26] Basic forms were seen as "positive visual fields" from which information was most likely to be seen and absorbed. Designers argued that any attempt to incorporate irregular or complex structural devices was liable to have a disorienting effect and generate confusion.[27] Conversely, functional and terse embassy structures, based on modern technologies and frank display of state-of-the-art building materials, promised to produce "beauty through clarity, . . . dignity without pomposity," as well as "a sense of importance but not of overbearing officialdom."[28]

Terse, modern embassies were not the immaculate conceptions of a consortium of architects and foreign policy strategists. The minimalist architecture of embassies reflected prevailing social tides at home. The style's popularity drew inspiration from the prevalent buoyant sentiments in the United States during the immediate postwar years. The undecorated surfaces of these ahistorical structures, their simple shapes and deliberately conspicuous display of modern building materials, were the communal representations of a future-oriented society completely at ease with new technologies, a society that would not repeat the mistakes of history. In this sense the buildings served the ultimate purpose of portraying a nation unshackled by the past, and commanding the technological knowhow of the future.

"Like an Edsel or a Toastmaster," Allan Temko has noted in his ambivalent critique of this school of architecture, the buildings could "function almost anywhere in the United States, and in much of the rest of the world as well, in any size or model."[29] In their frank display of their components, the embassy buildings implied that there was no closely guarded secret to American success. America's triumph was duplicable. Conspicuously simple designs and the absence of ornamentation refuted traditional concepts of hierarchy in architecture. The modular form of architecture drew no distinctions between classes, did not differentiate between geographical center and periphery; it presented a more democratic, less authoritarian aura, the antithesis of secretive diplomacy.

The International Style embassy served the dual purpose of portraying the United States as an innovator and providing a billboard for American business. Indeed, the embassies were identical in style to the headquarters of monolithic American conglomerates that were simultaneously arising throughout the world. Unconsciously or otherwise, the striking similarities between the embassy designs and the architecture of corporations conveyed to beholders that the United States envisioned a global economic arena of unrestricted commerce, and harbored a deep conviction in the intrinsic ties between free trade and free government. The fundamental idea behind this prototype of embassy buildings, according to its advocates, was to duplicate the architectural logic of the "headquarters of a small corporation."[30] Asked what these buildings were meant to impart to the rest of the world, the FBO listed two main points in business jargon: "a) better organization of the job and b) better integration of the building process."[31] According to FBO chief Leland King, the essence of the American way as displayed through International Style architecture was discipline, flexibility, and a simple and economical approach to all types of problems, big and small.[32]

The reign of the International Style was, however, short-lived, owing to both theoretical and political questioning of its validity. On a purely practical level, the similarities between prevailing corporate architecture and diplomatic edifices proved quite problematic. The ultimate objective had been to produce forceful and uniform artifacts of political architecture; but the resemblance between corporate headquarters and diplomatic edifices resulted in the identification of government and big business rather than any tangible proof of a distinct American national image.[33] No clear distinction existed between a national style and a private style; no purpose for the American presence abroad could be found in the architecture. The International Style of government architecture, warned architectural critic Peter Blake, conveyed the message that "the most acceptable civic or governmental character is no character at all." A corporate style was unable to produce "a government building symbolic of more than bureaucracy," nor could it translate the essence of modern western-style democracies into pertinent symbolism.[34] When the State Department's political hierarchy expressed these misgivings, they managed to infuriate FBO head Leland King by suggesting, as an alternative to the disappointing results of minimalist embassies, a return to historical styles. Historicism, they argued, at least had connotations of prestige. In his final and ultimately unsuccessful rearguard battle, King urged his superiors to "conform to this world-wide contemporary trend" of the International Style if they wanted the country's diplomatic buildings to be "truly representative of the progressive and characteristic way of American life."[35]

The catalyst for change at the theoretical level came from a more general questioning of the concept of "style"—the idea that the final shape of a structure should adhere to philosophical guidelines that predetermined form. A new generation of architects, the products of the academic revolution of the postwar era that encouraged experimentation and skepticism, now abandoned the favored architectural form of the founding fathers. They leveled their attack against the concept of functionalism in modern architecture; it was denounced as too mechanistic, restrictive of individual expression, and artistically repressive. Behind this denouncement lay the ambitious goal of rejecting the concept of a reigning style altogether. Style was regarded as a superficial solution to profound architectural problems. A primary theoretical goal of the International Style architecture had been the replacement of individual expression with a repetitive modular pattern. The new rebels advocated a diametrically opposite direction. They urged creative freedom, which took into account local environmental conditions and the architect's own personal vision and drew upon customs and traditions past and present.

Richard Bennett, an articulate spokesman of the new generation and a soon-to-be advisor for a revamped FBO strategy, called the new school of thought "the architecture of relativity." Just as Einstein had "caused the absolute world of the scientist to disappear," so too the Young Turks of the profession had abandoned the concept of building according to preordained rules.

> They know that the solution to the architect's problem is not the simple choice of following Wright or Mies; deciding to expose construction; to suppress the mechanical plant; to eliminate crafts—to revere craftsmanship; to seek to develop a regional style—to lose themselves in international clichés; to base their work on some dynamic module; to copy the Swedes; or to go back to Vitruvius. Perhaps the solution is not to be found in architecture at all, but in observation of the world around us—the social, economic, and scientific forces and ideas of our time which our architecture must reflect even as all other architectures have been reflections of theirs. . . . If we see contradictions in our architecture, it is because our time in history is beset with a variety of contradictions.[36]

In other words, variety was not a sign of weakness but an indication that architecture had adopted the most fundamental of contemporary scientific theories that "mass, energy, space and time are interchangeable, straight lines bend, and . . . systems can be made up."[37]

This dramatic about-face in the architectural profession in the United States has often been called a revolution. But this was not the case. The founding fathers of the International Style never tried to indoctrinate their students; they never suggested that their particular solutions to architectural problems should be canonized. In fact, the abandonment of the principles of "skin-and-bones" architecture represented a validation rather than a rejection of the new ways in architecture. According to Walter Gropius, founder of the Bauhaus movement, from which the International Style had received its inspiration, the modernist approach was to teach a way of thinking, a methodical approach to problems according to existing conditions rather than rigid adherence to style.[38] Indeed, as we will see, Gropius himself produced a highly expressive embassy, one that was far removed from the terse style of his own Bauhaus.

Dissatisfaction with the unhappy liaison of geopolitics and the International Style, as well as the rejection of the concept of a fixed, universal style, led to an alternative and even more ambitious strategy. The final months of 1953 represented a turning point for the architectural presence of the United States abroad. The new secretary of state, John Foster Dulles, urged that the United States present itself in more nationalistic terms as part of its strategy of fighting the cold war. The drive to counteract the presence of a large and formidable adversary necessitated constant reminders of the differences between the rival superpowers.[39] The architecture of embassies was one of the most conspicuous means by which Dulles hoped to impress upon the world both the might and the uniqueness of the United States. Both Dulles and his right-hand man, Under-Secretary of State Christian Herter, met and corresponded with the country's premier architects and, in a series of telegrams to U.S. missions abroad, Dulles informed them of impending plans to produce a new generation of politically meaningful and architecturally aesthetic structures in foreign lands.[40]

In accordance with the new order, Leland King, director of the FBO and champion of the International Style of architecture as symbol of America's foreign presence, was dismissed.[41] The FBO's regional supervisors, who during the King administration had enjoyed wide discretionary powers, were relegated to mere supervisory roles. In their place the State Department instituted a new policy body, the Architectural Advisory Panel (AAP). Between 1953 and 1959, the AAP approved a crash program of hundreds of diplomatic edifices, not as mere abodes for diplomatic activities but as expressive "physical symbol[s] of our government and our people."[42]

In forming the panel and in granting it wide discretionary powers, the State Department sidestepped the federal Commission of Fine Arts (CFA), which had previously dealt with the standards of American architecture at home and abroad. The stinging criticism that had accompanied the commission's high-handed treatment of the overseas American military cemeteries—the government's most ambitious construction project in foreign lands—discouraged any further reliance on their services. Charges of favoritism, lack of creativity, and abuse of government funds encouraged the State Department to seek advice from experts whose loyalties and livelihood were not necessarily related to government projects. Given the availability of discretionary funds, and lacking the need to accommodate lobbyists, the State Department went about forming the AAP, composed of members who, according to testimony of the director of the FBO before a House subcommittee, had "no axe to grind," meaning that they did not espouse "any specific architectural cause."[43]

The policy governing the composition of the committee as well as the choice of members neutralized political and artistic pressures, thereby allowing the State Department to pursue the singular goal of translating political symbols into effective architectural form. A committee based on the revolving-door principle (members served for a two-year term) ensured that the only long-term vested interest governing the style of embassies abroad would be that of the State Department. A brief glance at the list of committee members suggests that the State Department consistently chose people who rejected the concept of building according to a set style. Thus they were able to rely on experts who considered the objectives of clients—in particular, environmental and political considerations—to be the only legitimate concerns. An even more striking fact is that only two architects received more than one commission from the State Department. Fifty-five different architects were awarded contracts during the halcyon years of 1954–1959.[44]

In order to avoid accusations of relinquishing its authority to architectural cliques, the chairmanship of the AAP remained constantly in the hands of an influential State Department individual. The first chairman was Colonel Harry McBride. As an assistant secretary of state and former chief administrator of the National Gallery of Art, McBride was the perfect choice as leader of a team whose task it was to enlist the fine arts in the service of politics. His diverse background as both senior official in the State Department and one of the chief figures in devising an official version of a representative national art in the United States set the tone for the elaborate policies that emanated from the AAP. Harry McBride's successor was Joseph C. Satterthwaite, assistant secretary of state for African affairs; he was followed by Waldermar J. Gallman, director-general of the Foreign Service. Over the years the head of the FBO received the rank of deputy assistant secretary for foreign buildings, and it was this official who ultimately relayed to the AAP the technical, financial, and ideological requirements that the State Department sought in its embassies-as-symbols.[45]

The first panel's most prominent ideologue was Pietro Belluschi, dean of the School of Architecture and Planning at the Massachusetts Institute of Technology and a private practitioner of great skill. Two other members from private firms with a history of government contracts were Henry R. Shepley of Boston and Ralph T. Walker of New York, the latter being the first institutional architect to challenge the concept of a set style for government in his proposed model for the Luxembourg Cemetery. Throughout the years the State Department used the same basic criteria for AAP membership: two members of private firms with some but not exclusive foreign or governmental experience, a member with an academic background, and a chairman who represented the views of the Department's hierarchy.

Contrary to its rather tame appellation, the functions of the panel were far from advisory. Its members wielded full power over the choice of architects; they vetoed unsatisfactory designs; and, guided by the lay hierarchy of the State Department, the AAP insisted upon an unyielding deference to the objectives of their political clients. The terse policy statement of the panel declared that American architecture abroad needed to reflect the high standards of architecture and construction that existed in the United States as well as "increase goodwill by intelligent appreciation, recognition, and use of the architecture appropriate to the site and country."[46] In an addendum to this instruction sheet, Pietro Belluschi elaborated on the implications of the Department's guidelines. The architect's task, he stated, was twofold. First and foremost, the various buildings should demonstrate a sound understanding of both the historical conditions and the building customs of the host country. Once mastered, local techniques and customs were to be reinterpreted by infusion with a "distinguishable American flavor."[47]

The ulterior cultural motive of these projects as communicated through the language of the guidelines and addendum was quite explicit. Local construction practices were faintly praised as "customs." As such, they were unchanging, stagnant, and, by implication, inferior. American architectural practices, on the other hand, were "achievements" to be accomplished with a "free mind without being dictated by obsolete or sterile formulae or clichés, be they old or new."[48] In other words, the buildings were intended to demonstrate American control and knowledge of stagnant foreign forms, while simultaneously demonstrating the power of the United States through the innovative fusion of old and new, local and imported. For all practical purposes this meant relegating native elements to the level of decorations for buildings based on uniquely American "new techniques or new materials." Indeed, the FBO instructions warned architects that they were not dealing with abstract problems but with issues that affected the course of nations and events that were far beyond the sphere of architectural problem-solving.

Further understanding of the philosophy of the AAP may be gained by reading the theoretical utterances of Belluschi and other influential committee members. In 1950, and prior to his State Department nomination, Belluschi had described the mission of the American architect as twofold: First and foremost, the architect had to be a "lively interpreter of the new social order and . . . a prophet of his age"; methodical design, he implied, could change societies and shape public opinion. In addition, Belluschi challenged the validity of an architecture that had stripped away explicit symbolism and ornamentation, replacing them "with stark utilitarian [forms] . . . which give little nourishment to the senses." According to Belluschi and other influential committee members, "cold functionalism" was self-defeating, because architecture—both public and private—needed to evoke emotion, "which pervades our actions, our political motives, our very happiness."[49] In an elaborate discussion of the role of "symbols of American life" in architecture, AAP charter member Ralph Walker added: "We are apt to forget in our proud moments of being pure rationalists, of being hard-boiled realists, that we are ruled sentimentally by the symbol. The European world unfortunately learned that the Fasces, the Swastika, the Sickle and the Hammer, were as potent as the cross and the crescent ever were, and in their rule architecture was just as much affected as it was in Rheims or in Constantinople."[50]

Walker added that it was "vitally important in any cultures which the United States may touch that its buildings achieve a new look—one totally unrelated to the concepts of the factory engineer—one indicating both the power and richness of American life."[51] American symbolic architecture had to abandon the "strange symbols" of the starkly "mechanist and material," which served no other purpose than the introduction of "further chaos" into the process of distilling the American way of life into architectural form.[52] But, by the same token, Belluschi told an audience of students at Reed College, the rejection of the International Style did not entail a rapprochement with reactionary forces. "Conservative architects have looked in vain to the past for ready-made solutions . . . unfortunately the social order which produced such appealing forms no longer exists."[53] The solution lay in adapting, modifying, and reshaping traditional symbolism for modern purposes.

Additional clarification of how revamped symbolism could enhance the architecture of the State Department came from Walter Gropius, at that time dean of the School of Architecture at Harvard University, and perhaps the most influential architect in the United States. Gropius, who was to execute the impressive glass and steel modern-day Parthenon embassy in Athens, quoted Goethe in explaining the place of tradition in modern architecture, and the ultimate strategy behind America's imperial architecture:

> There is no past which we should long to resurrect,
> There is eternal newness only, reconstituting itself
> Out of the extended elements of the past,
> And true yearning should always be toward productive ends,
> Making something new, some better thing.[54]

In other words, historical elements were appropriate inasmuch as they underscored progress and innovation. The introduction of indigenous customs and styles was justified only when its juxtaposition with or modification by nontraditional methods and symbols highlighted the inadequacies of stagnant forms. Architecture for the State Department, Gropius asserted, should abide by the "spiritus loci" but in modified "contemporary terms" that reflected the progressive "political attitude of the United States."[55]

The way to avoid clichés, according to Eero Saarinen, designer of the seminal London embassy and subsequently a member of the AAP, was to treat the embassy as an exercise in expressionism. "A church must have the expression of a church. An airport should be an expression related to flight," and an embassy needed to have "a federal character" that differed from country to country.[56] Another cardinal aspect of diplomatic architecture, according to Edward Stone, designer of the American Embassy in New Delhi and one of the most influential members of the AAP in the 1960s, was the concept of endurance and permanence, the idea that the United States had a long and solid stake in the host country, through the use of explicit symbolism and monumental architecture.[57] In sum, the ultimate objective of AAP and the State Department hierarchy was to avoid standard styles, seeking instead to impart "to the building a quality reflecting deep understanding of conditions and people." "Conditions" appears to have been a euphemism for the political objectives of the client, the State Department; "people" implied the need to adapt any solution to particular cultural settings.

In order to achieve this goal of demonstrating the advantages of a uniquely American vision by contrasting American techniques with indigenous customs, the AAP consistently handed out commissions to the "expressionist" school of modern architects. These architects were, for the most part, disciples of the Swiss architect and philosopher Le Corbusier, who used the plasticity of modern building material to turn structures into pieces of expressionist sculpture. Even though Le Corbusier had experimented with a variety of styles over the years—he had collaborated with Harrison and Abramovitz on the functionalist United Nations headquarters—he is most remembered for his expressionist use of reinforced and prestressed concrete, which allowed the architect to treat the facades of buildings sculpturally. Some of the basic principles from his expressionist period were almost tailored to suit the needs of architecture for symbolic political purposes. He represented a particularly attractive role model, with his brilliant fusion of tradition and progress, East and West, in his parliament building for Chandigarh, the newly formed state capital of India's Punjab.[58]

Le Corbusier had argued that institutional buildings, in particular, should be placed on stilts in order to allow free access beneath. Placing a building on a podium, as the subsequent analysis of the new embassies will show, produced a temple-like effect, endowing the structure with an almost mystical quality. Le Corbusier also urged the use of horizontal strips of glass windows, an effect that would be used by embassy architects in their attempts to devise a symbol of openness toward and, conversely, constant monitoring of the host environment.[59]

Le Corbusier's sculptural approach to architecture found a receptive audience in the United States because of prior experience with this concept. In the field of commercial architecture, in particular, designers had toyed quite extensively with the idea of structures that advertised their functions.[60] The most visible and memorable experimentation in this field occurred at the 1939 New York World's Fair, where architects were encouraged to build edifices that would "speak" of their intended purpose. Consequently, the fair sported numerous flamboyant artifacts of sculptural architecture, including a marine transportation building that looked like a gigantic oceanliner, a powderbox-shaped cosmetics building, and an RCA structure shaped like a giant radio tube.[61] The fair's sculptural architecture, as well as its legitimization in academic circles through the work of Le Corbusier, provided the AAP with a precedent of sorts for the use of expressive architecture for American embassies.

While it comes as no surprise that sculptural architecture was used as a tool for demonstrating power and control in the new nations of the Third World, this new philosophy appeared also in western Europe, which might almost have been considered home turf. Irrespective of country and geographical region, the basic philosophy of demonstrating power through architecture characterized all of the State Department's ambitious construction efforts. In fact, the very first of the new generation of structures was the new American Embassy in Great Britain, perhaps the only country in Europe where the United States was never challenged as the dominant superpower of the postwar period.

Designed by Eero Saarinen—better known for his Dulles International Airport on the outskirts of Washington, D.C., the St. Louis Arch, and the CBS building in New York—this edifice embodied all of the cardinal elements of architecture as a symbol of power (Fig. 34). Commissioned in 1956 and completed in 1960, the London embassy illustrated vividly the departure from previous American procedures of embassy construction. A principal tenet of modern postwar architecture, and a guiding light for previous American embassy projects, had been the use of simple form and austere surfaces, free of elaborate ornamentation. But Saarinen's building, a critic noted, was a complex, highly decorative enterprise, that drew attention to the almost billboard qualities of the facade.[62]

In attempting to keep with the historic flavor of the surrounding Grosvenor Square architecture while at the same time demonstrating American ingenuity, Saarinen turned the entire facade into an elaborate geometrical display of interlocking panels modeled after a typical Georgian-shaped window. The simple requirement of holding a windowpane in place was abstracted and turned into a decoration. This architectural exercise was not meant to pay respectful homage to a particular historical

34. American Embassy, London, Great Britain, 1956 (Eero Saarinen, architect)

style. Naked grids of exposed reinforced concrete on the ground level was, instead, an ingenious modern technique for holding together the seemingly independent conglomerations of pseudo-periodic frames. The gilded tips of the beams and the unusual color scheme that complemented the innovative geometrical patterns bespoke progress rather than tradition. In other words, a mundane element of a period style was elevated to the heights of didactic art through the use of innovative construction methods, modern building materials, and an iconoclastic color scheme.

The image of the building as a monument to American progress and the eclipse of British tradition was enhanced by placing the entire structure on stilts. Saarinen stated that he had created this "false podium" to endow the embassy with the aura of a "Greek temple."[63] In addition, the building did not take up the entire block; hence it could be admired from all sides and in its entirety. It was isolated further by a surrounding dry moat, which, malicious tongues speculated, was meant to be filled with poison ivy. The entire edifice, raised off the ground and physically separated from its environment, had all the trappings of a colonial monument; it advertised the skills of its builders at the expense of its beholders. "For all its sham politeness," noted the architecture critic of the London *Ob-*

server, "this building has also to be American, new, crisp, and glamorous. Hence the rather aggressive, staccato modeling of the facade, the perpetual gilding, the costume jewelry that overbedecks it all. Every detail contradicts the original and overpolite intentions."[64]

As for the "xenophobic," heroic-sized golden eagle that hovered over the entrance, it, too, appeared to be consistent with the basic tone of the architecture, which was meant to glorify American technology, wealth, and power rather than pay homage to an indigenous architectural tradition.

The London embassy possessed the fundamental characteristics of this new generation of American embassies: an elevated and isolated position, modern materials designed to "improve" upon historical form, thereby trivializing local tradition, and numerous windows. Indeed, almost the entire facade was made up of glass panels, ostensibly to convey a sense of openness. In actual fact, heavy curtains veiled the windows so as to allow the occupants to scrutinize their surroundings without revealing too much of themselves.

Much of this same philosophy of American monument building overseas guided the construction of the embassy in Dublin. In 1958, architect John M. Johansen was charged with the difficult task of constructing a monumental embassy on a pie-shaped lot bounded by intersecting streets. The receding width of the lot ruled out the use of a conventional rectangular or square shape for the embassy. In addition, Johansen felt the need to avoid the use of Georgian architecture, prevalent in Dublin, because of associations with its despised English origins. Johansen's solution, his "sinewy drum for Dublin," was in the true spirit of monumental architecture (Fig. 35).[65]

Technically, the circular shape of the embassy solved the problem of multisided visibility. It did not bulge asymmetrically in any one direction, and it could be seen equally well from a variety of angles. Didactically, the idea of "a continuous facade" fulfilled the crucial political mission; the building faced "all directions . . . and thus doesn't turn its back on anyone . . . in keeping with US democracy."[66] Like the London embassy, a surrounding moat underscored the edifice's monumentality. The historical roots of the architectural design were supposedly the round Celtic coastal towers of the ninth and tenth centuries. The interlacing beams that held the structure together were ostensibly reminiscent of Celtic carvings and jewelry. Yet this circular structure and its intricately shaped beams departed in one striking respect from traditional architecture: the entire structure was made of precast concrete.

Above all, the building demonstrated how progressive architecture could endow defunct traditions with a new and modern meaning. The

35. American Embassy, Dublin, Ireland, 1959 (John Johansen, architect)

style—the decorative motifs—was supposedly Irish; but it was all kept together and endowed with contemporary significance by modern American technique. Indeed, as local Irish newspapers noted, the embassy "was the nearest that automation has come to the building industry in Dublin."[67] "What I tried to do," observed the architect in explaining the meeting of minds on political and technical objectives, "was to incorporate Irish tradition and culture along with modern American building techniques and concepts as well."[68] Modern techniques had redeemed ancient motifs from obscurity.

American political architecture in the British Isles was all the more conspicuous because it contrasted sharply with contemporary British strategies. Great Britain, the predecessor of the United States as western superpower, produced a deliberately banal diplomatic architecture in the postwar years. Of the twenty-one chancery buildings constructed between 1950 and 1970, none was meant to serve a symbolic role. "Though functionally never less than adequate," noted the *Architectural Review*, "none is architecturally distinguished and none would qualify for inclusion in an anthology of the best British buildings of the last twenty years."[69]

In contrast to the American strategy, the British Foreign Office did not farm out its projects to outstanding private firms. Moreover, the office in charge of British government structures abroad, the Directorate of Estate Management Overseas (DEMO), was part of the Department of the Environment, formerly the Ministry of Public Works. Its architects were tenured civil servants, with little incentive for innovation, and no knowledge of foreign policy objectives. These designers and architects received no encouragement from the Foreign Office, where, given Great Britain's continuously contracting global objectives in the postwar years, "old fashioned attitudes to matters of design remain deeply ingrained, and ... the decision to build rests essentially on economic and practical grounds."[70]

A sharply different American policy of "prestige embassies" was not confined to the British Isles, of course. American embassies as monuments appeared all over Europe, from The Hague to Athens.[71] Indeed, in the Athens embassy (1961), Walter Gropius abandoned the terse architectural canons of his Bauhaus in order to demonstrate quite figuratively and explicitly the primacy of political goals over architectural style in the decision-making process of the AAP. There, the father of the antitraditionalist and machine-like Bauhaus school subordinated his concerns for avoiding symbolism and monumentality in order to enhance the State Department's political objective of demonstrating to the nations of the world how the American mentality could propel ancient customs into the twentieth century (Fig. 36).

His model, of course, was the Acropolis, the well-worn symbol of western democracies. In paying homage to the original Greek monument, Gropius implemented the fundamental elements of classic Greek temples—podium, quadrilateral plan, interior patio, and exterior columns. But the materials used were distinctly modern: glass, steel, and reinforced concrete. His most explicit statement of the transformation of tradition was through his use of columns. Rather than providing the basis for the structure, the reinforced concrete columns supported a series of vertical girders from which the upper stories hung like a suspension bridge. Thus, columns, which over the years had become redundant signs of monumentality, were now once more integral parts of the structure, thanks to American ingenuity.

Monumental embassies were constructed in locations other than Europe, of course. But regardless of the differing local strategies that defined American geopolitical goals in other corners of the globe, this same fundamental philosophy of producing imperial embassies that glorified American techniques by trivializing local motifs governed all construc-

36. American Embassy, Athens, Greece, 1962 (Walter Gropius, architect)

tion projects. In Africa and Asia the same Janus-faced architecture that at once looked backward to tradition and forward to a millennial transformation characterized America's foreign presence.

In one major respect, however, the embassies in the Third World differed from their European counterparts. Familiarity with western historical form had allowed the State Department to manipulate authentic indigenous styles in each of its European embassies. In nonwestern countries, by contrast, ignorance led to the invention of a stereotypical pseudo-traditional architecture that the FBO used uniformly in countries and regions that had little in common with each other. Most embassies in Asia, Africa, and Latin America used decorative screens to veil their glass facades. In the Middle East, the screens served as trappings of Moslem architecture, while in Latin America they were supposedly modeled on Hispanic traditions; in reality the screens were almost identical.[72] Curved portals and roofs were used interchangeably, too. Thus, the pseudo-Moslem roofs of the buildings in the Iraqi embassy compound bore striking resemblance to the pitched oriental roof of the consulate in Fukuoka, Japan (Figs. 37 and 38).

This pseudo-historical architecture reflected the imposition of new divisions of politics and culture. The world, according to this architecture,

37. American Consulate, Fukuoka, Japan, 1961 (Clark, Beuttler, and Rockrise, architects)

38. American ambassador's residence, Baghdad, Iraq, 1961 (José Luis Sert, architect)

comprised two distinct groups: complex, nuanced western European cultures and, by contrast, a backward, somewhat faceless Third World, in which differences between nations were of little importance. Indeed, as Melvin Gurtov has pointed out in his study of American political attitudes toward the developing nations, American policymakers consistently ignored the unique national identities of individual Third World countries; American policies implicitly questioned the legitimacy of nationalism in the new nations of the postwar years.[73]

The dimensions of this attitude toward Third World nations were explicitly articulated in a congressional hearing concerning the erection of embassies in Africa. State Department officials insisted on the necessity of providing physical evidence of American interests in all of the new African nations, but appeared to agree with the statement that many of the new countries were culturally indistinguishable and had been carved out of the British Empire arbitrarily in order to "satisfy the vanity" of local despots and sycophants.[74] This ambivalent attitude toward the national identity and integrity of individual African countries contributed to the development of a stereotypical architecture that trivialized African culture and tribal lore while dismissing the unique political aspirations of individual nations.

Among the various monumental structures constructed in Africa, the State Department regarded the embassy in Accra, Ghana (1959), as an archetype. Beyond its distinctively African context, the Accra embassy incorporated many of the fundamental elements that had guided embassy construction in other parts of the world. The building was raised above the ground, dominated by screened fenestration rather than solid walls, and isolated from surrounding structures so as to enhance appreciation of its theme. The embassy embodied the trivialization of non-European cultures by means of political architecture.

Initially, architect Harry Weese had found little to inspire him in the boomtown capital of the newly independent Ghana. The monotonous urban sprawl of Accra comprised mud houses, tin shacks, and, in the more affluent neighborhoods, trite "masonry clichés" that had been "imported" from Europe. An ordinary office building, along the lines of the graceless structures that characterized the downtown area, would not have fulfilled the purpose of displaying the United States' diplomatic goals in stone.[75] A chance visit to a rural village, together with a robust dose of stereotypical views of the African mentality, eventually provided the necessary inspiration. Weese designed a structure perched upon a set of spearlike posts resembling the white-spiked palace of an African chief he had come upon during one of his site visits. The strange buttresses of the African palace, according to the architect, recalled two distinctive elements of the mythic African landscape: the towering anthills of the African bush and the elongated spears of the African warrior (Fig. 39).

39. American Embassy, Accra, Ghana, 1959 (Harry Weese, architect)

Weese displayed American control of these native elements by inverting the anthill-palace cones. In a distinct departure from local indigenous forms, the structure did not climax in tapered form; instead, like inverted pyramids, the cones supported the main body of the structure, thereby raising the building off the ground and endowing it with the same temple-like qualities of the London and Dublin embassies. The building had some gratuitous wood paneling; but a close look at the building material revealed bare, prestressed concrete beams. The base of the structure looked like basketwork, but instead of straw, the exposed surface proved to be an intricate weave of concrete beams.

In its entirety, the structure demonstrated once again how modern American techniques could manipulate local customs. The various native elements used in the building, Weese noted, conveyed "some of the richness of imagery and decoration in the African psyche"; architectural ingenuity, a distinctively American contribution, demonstrated how these decorative effects could be made useful through innovative and imaginative building methods.[76] This neotraditionalist architecture, then, was meant to create a meaningful past for a new African nation that appeared to have lost its way in an age of rapid change. The architecture asserted American mastery of the mysteries of that past in particular and the new order of things in general.

Similar strategies of manipulating native techniques through American knowhow also characterized American embassies in the Islamic world. Legations and embassies constructed in Moslem countries during this period relied on stereotypical elements of pseudo-Moslem architecture:

"screen walls against the glare (and marauders) and vaulted roofs."[77] When possible, the embassies would incorporate decorative features that were reminiscent of local religious art, or the architecture of the country's Golden Age. Richard Neutra's Karachi embassy (1962) used a series of golden pseudo-Islamic vaulted roofs, which, according to the architect, resembled "the Mogul architecture of the Golden Mosque of Amritsar."[78] The fact that Amritsar is a Sikh shrine and not a mosque apparently did not bother the architect.

The basic formula in Moslem countries, as explained by Edward Larrabee Barnes, who had designed the American consulate in Tabriz, Iran (1962), was to show how "modern technology" could benefit "native tradition": "All we added to the local aesthetic [of brick vault construction in northern Iran] was, we hope, a sophistication and refinement not found in peasant architecture. Our buildings are disciplined, the engineering is true."[79]

In designing embassies and legations in Moslem countries, the FBO was guided by what Edward Said has called the "myth of arrested development."[80] Oriental traditions were seen as timeless, eternal, immobile. The gulf between the stagnant East and a progressive West could be bridged only by implementing superior American knowledge and power. Along these lines, seemingly meaningless sets of oriental curves at José Louis Sert's embassy compound in Baghdad (1961) were endowed with significance in their function of separating the two layers of a double, sun-protective roof; the waters of the Tigris, which flowed sluggishly by the embassy compound, were turned to modern purposes with the diversion of the current through a maze of canals that moved the water ingeniously uphill to provide irrigation as well as a protective moat in front of the main entrance (see Fig. 38). In this, perhaps the most critically acclaimed of all FBO projects, Sert fulfilled the desires of his clients to "draw up plans that would reflect an artistic combination of Eastern and Western motifs . . . modern yet conservative."[81]

All of the newly constructed legations in Moslem countries displayed the trappings of monumental diplomatic architecture. A temple-like building based on extensive yet veiled fenestration, isolated from contact with neighboring edifices, and surrounded by a protective moat vividly expressed American power through architecture. Effective control demanded a display of knowledge of indigenous customs, on the one hand, and an explicit demonstration of how a modern nation could apply local elements to progressive needs, on the other. The embassies highlighted the ostensible benefits inherent in the imposition of an efficient American way of life on societies that were "fettered by tradition."

But by 1961, after the construction of the Rabat embassy, which ranked among the most ostentatious American edifices in the Moslem

40. Model for American Embassy, Rabat, Morocco, 1961 (Ketchum, Gina, and Sharp, architects)

world, the limits of this particular diplomatic philosophy of architecture were quite evident. The sprawling structure of precast vaulted roofs and imitation oriental aluminum sunscreens proved to be uninhabitable (Fig. 40). A scathing report by the comptroller general of the United States included a long list of flaws—the result of the precedence of symbolism over functional design. The building had been completed in July 1961, but as late as 1963 it remained unoccupied because the ambassador objected both to its condescending "oriental" aesthetics and to its design.[82] The precedence of ideology over function had produced a building that, despite the pleasant climate and the breathtaking view from the hilltop site, had no provisions for windows in the main office annex. The demands of the State Department to produce a didactic piece of political architecture had led the architects to ignore the fundamental function of an embassy—to provide comfortable quarters for the conducting of routine business.[83]

Similar problems plagued the ambassador's residence in India, which Edward Stone had built to accompany his 1959 "modern Taj Mahal" embassy building (Fig. 41). This $700,000 "modified Mogul" design drew sharp criticism from Ambassador John Kenneth Galbraith, who objected to the building's monumentality at the expense of functionalism. Stone's use of grills rather than solid dividers within the residence pre-

41. American Embassy, New Delhi, India, 1959 (Edward Stone, architect)

cluded privacy. Both the ambassador's living room and the main guest suite had grills instead of walls, thereby giving birth to the quip that "people who live in Stone houses should get dressed in the dark." A multijetted fountain in the main reception room did not live up to its intended role of a trapping of imperial architecture. As far as the ambassador was concerned, it merely served to emit the annoying sound of "a toilet permanently out of order."[84]

Consistent complaints about the uncomfortable and often offensive features of palatial embassies prompted revisions in the guidelines of the AAP. The new objectives of the program, articulated as early as 1961, stated that:

>   1. the department did not wish to serve as a vehicle for experimental or ostentatious design;
>   2. the practical kind of building would be stressed as opposed to the monumental;
>   3. buildings should be economical to build and maintain, and should be planned for expansion.[85]

Complaints from within were not the only reason for these revisions in the FBO's architectural strategy. The architectural presence of the American political entity at a time when its policies and programs were unpopular, and the rise of accusations against the United States as harbinger of western neocolonialism, drew attention to the insidious nature of the resonant symbolism. Wittingly or otherwise, the embassies of the 1950s and 1960s had given rise to a genre of imperial architecture that clashed with the prevailing atmosphere of self-determination. *U.S. News and World Report* echoed a widely held opinion in stating that the best "cure for anti-American violence" would be to minimize the diplomatic profile of the United States, which was "a cause for anxiety and suspicion in small foreign capitals."[86]

The United States' diplomatic edifices in the 1950s and 1960s were representations of power in a foreign land, visible signs of an unequal relationship between the United States and host countries. This philosophy of imperial architecture produced a species of what Octavio Paz has called "pseudo-modernity" in which a uniquely American modern culture condescendingly highlighted the deficiencies of the past. The incorporation of stagnant elements of local culture into futuristic, uniquely American designs underscored "the worst of two worlds": strident cultural imperialism coexisting with trappings of archaic and often repressive sociopolitical infrastructures of the host country.[87]

The imperial architectural policy suffered a fatal blow in the early 1960s, when its major source of revenue, the reservoir of local currency debts, showed signs of drying up. The State Department sought supplemental sources of local currency for its embassies-abroad project through disposal of surplus agricultural products in target countries. But by 1962, State Department officials admitted that there appeared to be no other recourse than to turn to Congress for direct dollar allocations. Once again, then, a public scrutiny of embassy construction policies was restored.

To the great misfortune of the FBO, the House Committee on Foreign Relations was in the hands of Representative Wayne Hays of Ohio, who objected not only to the ostentation of the new diplomatic structures, but to the very concept of "sending innumerable people out there."[88] After years of living with the fact that his objections carried little weight, Hays now eagerly attacked and curtailed the spending and design policy of the FBO. Hays's stance was that the FBO tended to construct heavy-handed, ostentatious, and unnecessary buildings, and he censured their projects routinely. His committee scuttled numerous projects, such as the $300,000 residence in Cyprus and a $1.4-million apartment building for Japan.[89]

Changing circumstances in the funding of overseas construction forced State Department officials to disavow publicly their previous independent procedures. "Buildings are not sculptures; neither are they monuments,"

Deputy Under-Secretary of State Roger W. Jones recanted in front of an inquisition-like hearing on amendments to the Foreign Service Buildings Act. The State Department, he promised, would now "insist that our buildings be functional" and would see to it that the appropriate committees were kept "informed during the course of our program development, and not just when we come up here for an authorization bill."[90]

Given the poor reception of the embassy edifices abroad, congressional suspicion of State Department autonomy, and growing budgetary constraints, the FBO set about revising its architectural strategy—indeed, its whole concept of symbolic diplomacy. As would be the case with the unfavorable response to its sister project of military cemeteries abroad, the demise of conspicuously expressive embassies signaled an uncertain future for all efforts to enlist architecture in the service of foreign policy.

7

Epilogue

RETREAT

ON 26 NOVEMBER 1950, Chinese troops launched a massive attack against American forces in Korea. By March 1951, the Eighth Army—America's main fighting force in Korea—had been driven back from positions deep in the northern half of the country to the thirty-eighth parallel. The debacle in Korea ranked among the United States' most significant military setbacks in modern times. The rout was all the more painful because of some unexpected side effects. Not only had the American armed forces experienced a serious military defeat; to make matters worse, the retreat to new positions entailed the loss of two major American military cemeteries. The burial grounds at Pyonyong and Suchon were now under enemy control. Two evocative symbols of American power in foreign lands had been snatched from the very hands of their keepers.

Anticipating a public outcry, the U.S. government swiftly reversed its previous policies on burials abroad. In the midst of battle, Americans buried at all United Nations temporary cemeteries in Korea were disinterred, sent to Japan for final identification, and shipped home. In a somewhat empty gesture, the remains of a number of unknown American dead were left at the Allied cemetery at Tongyok; all other caskets were withdrawn hastily. "Never in the history of the United States or any other nation," noted the graves registration officer in charge of this operation, "has there been a mass evacuation of the remains of men killed in action while hostilities were still in progress."[1] Never again would the United States leave its fallen soldiers in foreign fields. The monuments and burial grounds of new conflicts were now placed on sovereign American territory only.

The Korean incident was not the first time that an American military cemetery had fallen into enemy hands. And yet, the Nazi occupation of American cemeteries in Europe did not entail a similar about-face; the preceding pages have documented the almost benign reactions to the loss of Great War cemeteries during World War II. What factors, then, induced this reassessment of the political significance of battle monuments?

In part, the changing sentiment toward military cemeteries abroad was affected by the diminishing importance of symbols in international relations. During the latter half of the twentieth century the United States no longer invoked abstract moral issues as an exclusive prerequisite for intervention. The Korean conflict was in essence a civil war in which the United States had intervened in order to consolidate its private agenda of regional strategic objectives. Intervention had not been decided upon in answer to an appeal from an embattled people facing an outside aggressor. Korea was a country at war with itself; the divided country would remain politically unstable even after the battle had been decided.[2] In order to consolidate its goals, the United States could not rely on symbols and token monuments. These different circumstances demanded a large and permanent military garrison in Korea. Here, the military cemetery as symbolic reminder of the power and intentions of the United States and as proxy for the actual deployment of troops was a redundant feature.

In addition, the Korean burial issue represented the very beginning of what would eventually be a profound reassessment of the role of political architecture. Even while the final touches were being put on the battle monuments and cemeteries of World War II, and just as the massive campaign to produce expressive embassies began, the return of bodies from Korea represented the first sign of a new, limited approach to American symbolism abroad. To begin with, the American Battle Monuments Commission (ABMC) made no effort to orchestrate a campaign against repatriation of the war dead, as it had done previously. The conspicuous absence of such a debate in the nation's newspapers suggests that this silence was quite prudent and in line with public sentiment.

Perhaps the most significant step of the ABMC was the abandonment of its previous mandate to focus exclusively on American symbolism abroad. The commission completed its task of commemorating the casualties of World War II with three monuments erected within the United States. In New York City's Battery Park, it erected a monument for the 4,596 American soldiers who had perished off the coasts of the Americas but outside of the territorial waters of the United States. At the Presidio in San Francisco, a similar monument marked the death of 412 Americans who had lost their lives off the west coast. The final grand gesture of the ABMC was the Honolulu Memorial. Here the ABMC commemorated the 18,000 missing of World War II from the Pacific area, the 8,194 Korean missing, and the 2,489 missing from the Vietnam War.

Built within the perimeters of the Veterans Administration's National Memorial Cemetery of the Pacific, the Scrapped Classical monument in Hawaii demonstrated a radically different agenda now assigned to the concept of death in the service of the nation, one that departed significantly from previous ABMC policies. The memorial did not celebrate the sacrifice of one particular national military effort, as had been the case in the past.

Ostensibly, the symbolic significance of this gesture was quite straightforward. The intrusion of Vietnam and Korea into what had previously been an exclusive memorial to World War II proclaimed that the fight for freedom had not ended in 1945. New challenges had arisen, and, the monument implied, Americans were still willing to make the ultimate sacrifice to preserve freedom both at home and abroad.[3] However, the importance of the Honolulu Memorial, and its most significant innovation, was the decision to broadcast these sentiments internally, signaling the abandonment of the original function of the ABMC of enhancing America's international image.

Rather than using its leverage as a tool for consolidating support for the United States abroad, the ABMC now returned to the Civil War custom of using the nation's war dead to manufacture and consolidate a sense of nationhood for internal purposes. When viewed against the background of great social turmoil and revisions in American values during the late 1950s and 1960s, the return of national military monuments from abroad reflected growing concerns about the cultural and political integrity of the bonds of nationhood, an issue of far greater urgency than the implanting of symbols of America abroad.

The futility behind this invocation of a Civil War ethos in the latter half of the twentieth century was perhaps best demonstrated by the negligible attention paid to these ABMC monuments at home and, by contrast, widespread popular fascination with a new form of military memorial, best represented by the introspective, antinational, and artistically iconoclastic Vietnam Memorial in Washington, D.C. The work of a Yale undergraduate, Maya Ying Lin, this was the only national memorial to be erected in the United States after the completion of the ABMC projects.[4]

In stark contrast to the conventional approach to military memorials, Lin stripped her monument of all forms of traditional symbolism. The national relevance of the conflict was nowhere to be seen; the divisive war, her monument implied, produced no redeeming legacy. Having been removed entirely from the confines of a national cemetery, the memorial did not preach. It avoided the use of conventional imagery. The pallor of youthful death dominated the site, its resonance heightened by the roll call of countless victims. "Here there is no patriotic inscription," George Mosse notes, "just a long list of the names of the dead engraved in the low-lying black wall, names to touch and honor in private and public grief."[5]

Nearby, Frederick Hart's statue of three American soldiers does little to counteract the sense of tragedy and futility that envelops the monument (Fig. 42). The three soldiers in battle fatigues, Spiro Kostof has observed, "look a little lost, or just plain tired; too knowing in any case to

42. Frederick Hart, *Three American Soldiers*

strike brave poses."[6] The soldier figures represented the three large racial groups in American society, but they suggested divisions rather than common values. While ostensibly meant to commemorate the contribution of all Americans to the national cause, their dispirited postures highlighted the drama of an old man's war fought by the young, a white man's conflict waged by people of color.

Belatedly, but quite predictably, changes in the national agenda at home and abroad affected the sister project of monumental embassies as well. Beginning in 1965, dissatisfaction with the course of America's foreign policy, as well as a resurgence of isolationist sentiment in Congress—euphemistically referred to as budgetary prudence—led to the rejection of anything that smacked of monumentalism. The scuttling of the coy, self-effacing design of John Carl Warnecke for an embassy in Bangkok exemplified the changing fortunes of expressionist projects (Fig. 43). In distinct

43. Model for American Embassy, Bangkok, Thailand, 1959 (John Carl Warnecke, architect)

contrast to most other efforts of the monumental embassy era, in which hypermodern buildings were adorned with trivialized native ornaments, Warnecke planned an embassy based almost exclusively on local style. The designer sought to reflect traditional Thai architecture, rather than the blending of an American-style building with local decorative elements. The best way of symbolizing America, according to Warnecke, was by paying unadulterated homage to "the site and the climate and rich cultural heritage of Thailand." Warnecke's model for the embassy paid tribute to the pagoda architecture of Thailand; its final shape was the result of an exhaustive study of traditional architecture, both secular, governmental, and residential. Its distinctive American quality was articulated through the use of reinforced concrete slabs rather than indigenous building material.[7]

But Warnecke's polite pagoda was not to be. Growing doubts about America's long-term objectives in the region as well as a reassessment of the role of monumentalism in foreign policy confined his plans to the drawing board. Guided by Secretary of State Dean Rusk's personal admonition to limit new embassies to terse "functional requirements," and to avoid at all costs experimentation with the "ostentatious and the controversial," the Architectural Advisory Panel (AAP) canceled Warnecke's mandate.[8] Panel member William Wurster summed up the new policy of the AAP by describing the Bangkok model as too "theatrical." Bearing Rusk's comments in mind, Wurster reminded his colleagues that "our architecture should not be a circus."[9] These attacks on expressionist political architecture abroad hastened the arrival of a new architectural strategy in the Office of Foreign Buildings Operations (FBO). By the late 1960s, the magazine *Industrial Design* noted in its survey of new and very private embassy compounds in various parts of Latin America that the State Department had institutionalized a new architecture of simple structures and compounds, some of which were tucked behind high walls, all deliberately inconspicuous, a "standing decree and part of the 'low profile' of Americans" abroad.[10]

The timing of this change coincided with growing sober assessments of the price of empire. In addition to sparking off violent dissent at home, America's entanglement in Vietnam had, by the mid-1960s, inflicted irreversible damage on the country's stature abroad. The nagging presence of a Communist state just off the coast of the United States, as well as an escalating arms race, heightened further the debate over the emotional and economic price of empire.

The subsequent questioning of the symbols of empire and the mobilization of art and architecture for global display came after sixty years of frustrating experimentation with visual statements of the country's political power. The preceding pages have identified many of the obstacles that hampered these designs. In the case of the military cemeteries, we have seen how three fundamental problems—uncertainty over the correct form of symbolism, poor choice of location, and a faulty liaison between the concerns of architects and those of their clients—undermined the program. In lieu of forceful government guidelines as to the desired content of symbolism in foreign lands, the final form of Great War cemeteries was unimaginative and stilted. Given the strength of tradition and Eurocentricity, the buildings and cemeteries relied heavily on unsuitable classical forms.

In the aftermath of the Great War, when the dimensions of mass destruction and high numbers of casualties were still fresh in the minds of a shell-shocked Europe, the United States had avoided any forceful articulation of its contribution to Allied victory. Of course, the actual decision to erect large American cemeteries abroad demonstrated an urge to alert the world to a new and omnipresent global power. However, the symbolism employed was self-defeating. By emulating the classical designs of others, by failing to take the opportunity to produce a uniquely American symbolism, the United States failed to capitalize on its war effort.

EPILOGUE: RETREAT 173

The cemeteries and memorials of World War II adjusted accordingly. They did indeed display a new, modified form of symbolism. The results, however, were equally disappointing. This new form of symbolism did not produce the expected effect, partly because of the great autonomy given to a group of unexceptional architects and sculptors. Rather than reflecting the concerns of their clients, the professional staff used the project as leverage in an internal power struggle within the architectural profession. Attempts to produce forceful exemplars of political architecture were thwarted, also, by public scrutiny. The need to accommodate conflicting tastes, as well as the patronizing attitude that ordinary people could appreciate only simplistic art forms, led to an art and architecture of compromise.

Moreover, the outmoded notion of a cemetery as a site of pilgrimage diminished the effectiveness of the already-diluted symbolism of the projects. Based on notions derived from the Great War—in particular, the idea of the cemetery as a modern-day version of a holy shrine upon which grateful pilgrims would descend on festive occasions—the graves and monuments of the Second World War were located near battlefields, most of which were not in highly visible areas. Rather than situating the cemeteries in the vicinity of large-scale tourist attractions, or upon other well-worn paths, the ABMC stubbornly placed them within the context of soon-to-be-forgotten battles. The concept of pilgrimage was ineffective because a second round of world war had produced a society accustomed to the pathological aspects of global conflict in modern times. Widespread death and destruction were now the norm, not the exception. As such, Memorial Day celebrations and the commemoration of V-day did not draw large crowds to the cemetery sites.

A similar litany of ineffective symbolism plagued the construction of embassies as artifacts of political architecture. After toying with two different strategies in the 1920s—the palatial style, which avoided any display of unique American qualities, and the plantation house, the features of which were overtly pernicious—the State Department turned toward a sometimes esoteric early national style that had no political meaning outside of the United States. The advent of markedly different administrative conditions in the aftermath of World War II—in particular, the availability of large budgets unchecked by public scrutiny—led to the development of explicitly American and contemporary symbolism.

Initially the immediate postwar period of embassy construction produced a series of modernistic outposts that seemed unaware or free of political constraints; they were pure examples of modern aesthetics or technology. Closer scrutiny of the nature of the cold war encouraged a more elaborate architectural philosophy, one that sought to impress foreigners with symbols of American knowledge, power, and control. But the political climate of a world that had only recently experienced the heavy hand of despotism proved to be uninviting terrain for these trappings of neocolonial architecture. The move from a corporate architecture to the imperial structures of the early 1960s and, finally, the retreat behind the wall of inconspicuous designs in the late 1960s reflected a growing awareness among America's professional policymakers of the complexities and nuances involved in maintaining the role of global leader in troubled times.

A sincere belief in universally shared values had permeated all efforts of political architecture abroad. By removing linguistic barriers and translating principles into graphic symbols, the United States expected to touch the hearts and minds of a divided world. American efforts at political architecture revealed a mixture of liberal idealism and self-righteous faith in the physical and moral power of this nation. These instances of political architecture also brought into focus the convergence of cultural factors with foreign policy. To the extent that America's international objectives were anchored in the political culture of the nation, these artifacts of Americana abroad were also expressions of important internal developments—in particular, they showed the impact of modernization on American society. But frequent changes in the form of America's political architecture abroad demonstrated the difficulties, internal and external, involved in encoding an American creed into a concise and universally attractive iconographical formula.

These exercises in political symbolism hinged upon a tenacious faith that monumental architecture could indeed consolidate authority and induce cohesiveness. Such assumptions were neither novel nor an exclusive by-product of foreign relations. Historically, the most evocative instances of the use of architecture for political purposes in modern-day America were the City Beautiful movement of the turn of the century and the colonial architecture of the Philippines. Both ventures were based on the assumption that the behavior of ordinary people could be controlled by means of uplifting, symbolic architecture.

This trust in the power of architectural symbols was misguided. Given the many alternative sources of information to which twentieth-century global villagers were exposed, monumental architecture lost much of its resonance; it was no more an exclusive source of information about the design of rulers and empires than in previous historical periods. Single-minded design of monuments could not elicit the desired responses in a multimedia epoch. Nevertheless, whatever marginal effect might have been accomplished through the construction of military cemeteries and symbolic embassies was thwarted by an erratic and banal symbolism.

It would appear, then, that at least some of the difficulties experienced in articulating cohesive and enduring symbols of empire were due to the fluid and contentious nature of America's political culture. Given the

EPILOGUE: RETREAT

great incessant jostling of diverse interest groups hoping to influence, change, and modify the decisions of government, all attempts to produce enduring, universally shared artifacts of political architecture were doomed to failure. Symbols do not produce cohesive societies; cohesive societies produce forceful symbols that reflect political conformity and common causes.

To clarify this point, we should return to the 1948 symposium, "In Search of a New Monumentality," where the giants of the architectural profession groped for a reconciliation between the intrinsic need for symbolism in politics, on the one hand, and the democratic ways of the postwar period, on the other. A lone voice, that of Gregor Paulsson, professor of the history and theory of art at the University of Uppsala, urged his colleagues to scrutinize the pages of their history books before making any rash recommendations. He observed that, historically, monumental architecture succeeded only in the hands of despots. Leaning on a comfortable crutch provided by Renaissance historian Jacob Burckhardt, Paulsson observed how the condottieri of northern Italy had created the awe-inspiring "re-birth of antiquity" in order to legitimize "their (mostly illegal) power and to induce fear among their subjects." Within this same context, the magnificent architecture of Rome under Nicholas V (1447–1455) was not produced "for the sake of the wise ... but for the *turbae populorum* whose feeble faith" could be maintained only through fear induced by majestic symbols.

> If we look more closely into the question of when the monumental quality was particularly sought for we find it was in anti-democratic times. Democratic Greece did not aim at the magnificent in dimensions and outlay; on the contrary, its temple buildings are strikingly intimate. Monumentality arose with the Hellenistic princes. ... So strong a word can only mean, for our generation, buildings of vast dimensions, such as those created by Imperial Rome ..., or Versailles, or the Empire State Building or the Parteigelande in Nuremberg. The monumental, whether one likes it or not, must be identified with the Imperialistic. ... Genuine monumentality can only arise from dictatorship because it is an adequate expression of its emotional complexes. ... Monumentality is able to have this social function because it is an expression, in a special category, of domination, of arrogance, and other forms of the basic emotion, wrath, or its inversion, fear.[11]

In other words, America's inability to "reconquer the monumental expression" in its public architecture in foreign lands might conceivably be interpreted as a vindication of its political system, an indicator of a functioning democratic culture, rather than another example of human failings, political ineptitude, or lack of foresight. Under these circumstances, the quest for stable monumental forms of political architecture—to instruct, supervise, and restrain—was unsuccessful.

Fluctuating objectives in foreign fields were responsible for the intriguing lack of theoretical literature accompanying the ambitious intrusion of monuments in other lands. The American experience never produced visionary imperial architects. No Edwin Lutyens or Herbert Baker emerged to translate national ambitions into stone. The country's political architects were ideologically constrained by the confusing directives of their political clients, as well as a fundamental populist aversion to empire. Therefore, the monuments tended to be trite reproductions of classical statements of power, imitations of the imperial experiences of others, or unmodified transferrals of internal American symbols, all of which affected the target audiences in unforeseen ways. Ironically, perhaps predictably, the few American architects who produced original concepts were foreign-born—from Paul Cret to Walter Gropius.

No clear-cut and enduring guidelines emerged from government to cultivate a homegrown imperial school of architecture. The major political figures who guided the course of political architecture abroad were uncharacteristically tongue-tied when called upon to explain their preferences for any particular imperial style. Such eloquent figures as Congressmen Porter and Linthicum, as well as Secretary of State Stimson, could only mouth tired clichés. In July 1929, during the course of a closed committee meeting, they used the following language to describe the construction of a monumental embassy in Paris:

> CONGRESSMAN PORTER: There is a political angle to this that I can't lose sight of, and I might pause temporarily to say that with a good advertisement, and we agree that this would be a good advertisement, the easier it would be to get additional appropriations.
>
> CONGRESSMAN LINTHICUM: What is the word the State Department uses for advertisement?
>
> SECRETARY OF STATE STIMSON: Representation?
>
> CONGRESSMAN LINTHICUM: What was that word you used the other night?
>
> COMMISSION SECRETARY MERRILL: Prestige.
>
> CONGRESSMAN LINTHICUM: Prestige! That's it![12]

And so this typical patter of adjectives droned on. This nebulous approach to the nexus of power and architecture was reminiscent of the practices of nineteenth-century railroad magnates who foisted a jumble of foreign-looking prestige mansions upon Nob Hill. Beyond a vague desire to express prestige, power, and opulence, San Francisco's newly rich never clearly explained why they had built brick mansions imported from New York or reconstructed, pillaged castles from Europe.

Clearly bothered by the same nagging inability to express the implications of success, the country's foreign policy experts implanted symbolic, larger-than-life artifacts of America on foreign soil to demonstrate prowess, although they were quite unsure about the significance of it all. When the government stood before the elusive mirror of foreign policy, it donned the cloak of grand art to improve its image, only to discover that the reflection belonged, in actual fact, to someone else.

Politicians received little inspiration from architects, who, even behind the closed doors of committees, remained stubbornly silent on the significance of particular styles for the country's architectural monuments abroad. These architects preferred exhaustive discussions of technical and financial details to ideological discourses. Their publications and explanations were overwhelmingly technical, with almost no meaningful remarks about their fateful choice of styles. When, in September 1928, a reluctant Cass Gilbert was coerced by members of the Foreign Service Buildings Commission (FSBC) to explain why he had suggested a Palladian-style building for the new chancery in Ottawa, Canada, all he would say was that he had aimed for a "dignified" but not "boastful" statement on an American presence in Canada. A frustrated archivist has jotted down near this quotation that these "were the first real adjectives of any meeting."[13]

Such evasive concepts of architecture, power, and prestige inevitably led to the reproduction of safe classical formulas or modifications of the designs of other imperial powers, even when the symbols were glaringly inappropriate. Only after World War II, when the debilitated powers of the Old World signaled their withdrawal from empire and had abandoned architecture as a political tool, did Americans begin to invent their own style of imperial architecture. Ironically, American innovations in monumental architecture and their ephemeral results were basically imported merchandise, the products of a cadre of refugees who had infiltrated the country's major architecture schools.

Paradoxically, then, "failure" might be construed as a triumph of the American political system. Attempts to use monumental architecture failed because a democratic American society could not accommodate the inherent imperialism of single-minded political symbols in other countries. The frustrating attempts to implant a stable, symbolic presence abroad suggests, perhaps, an intrinsic conflict between American political culture and imperial practices. The United States could not sustain potent forms of political architecture because its contentious factional structure, with its constant reliance on appeasement of and compromise between conflicting political forces, seldom fostered unyielding, time-resistant guidelines for its foreign policy. The volatile cultural fabric of a nation wedded to change undermined the ability of its architectural artifacts to announce enduring ambitions of power and dominance in foreign fields.

Notes

Introduction

1. Richard B. Morris, "Is the Eagle Un-American?" *New York Times*, 14 February 1960, sec. 6, pp. 30, 32, 37–38.
2. Eero Saarinen, letter to the editor, *New York Times*, 6 March 1960, sec. 6, p. 19.
3. Donald DeLue, President, National Sculpture Society, to Gilmore D. Clarke, Chairman of the Commission of Fine Arts, 27 June 1946, box 6, Lee Lawrie Papers, Library of Congress; Edward Shenton, "They Will Never Be Forgotten," *Saturday Evening Post*, 14 August 1954, 59.
4. United States Commission of Fine Arts, *Art and Government: Report to the President by the Commission of Fine Arts on Activities of the Federal Government in the Field of Fine Arts* (Washington, D.C., 1953).
5. Jules David Prown, "Style as Evidence," *Winterthur Portfolio* 15 (Autumn 1980): 198.
6. Peirce F. Lewis, "Axioms for Reading the Landscape," in Donald Meinig, ed., *The Interpretation of Ordinary Landscapes* (New York, 1980), 15.
7. Spiro Kostof, *America by Design* (Oxford, 1977), vii.

Chapter One
Prologue: Hesitant Beginnings

1. The story appears, among other places, in American Embassy Association, *American Embassies, Legations, and Consulates Mean Better Foreign Business* (New York, n.d.), 15–17.
2. George B. Forgie, *Patricide in the House Divided* (New York, 1979), 1–16.
3. David Sopher, "The Structuring of Space in Place Names and Words for Place," in David Ley and Marwyn S. Samuels, eds., *Humanistic Geography: Prospects and Problems* (London, 1978), 251–68.
4. Stephen Kern, *The Culture of Time and Space, 1880–1918* (Cambridge, Mass., 1983).
5. Merle Curti, *American Philanthropy Abroad: A History* (New Brunswick, N.J., 1963), 620–21.
6. Henry Nash Smith, *Virgin Land: The American West as Symbol and Myth* (New York, 1956), 260.
7. Morrell Heald and Lawrence S. Kaplan, *Culture and Diplomacy: The American Experience* (Westport, Conn., 1977).
8. This discussion of the development of an American diplomatic presence in Persia is derived from Department of State, Historical Studies Division, "The American Consulate at Tabriz: Historical Highlights, 1851–1944. Research

Project No. 492" (May 1967). I am grateful to Michael Metrinko of the State Department for bringing this document to my attention.

9. Merle Curti and Kendall Birr, *Prelude to Point Four: American Technical Missions Overseas, 1838–1938* (Madison, Wis., 1954), 205.

10. Richard Werking, *The Master Architects: Building the United States Foreign Service, 1890–1913* (Lexington, Ky., 1977), 9–10.

11. Waldo H. Heinrichs, Jr., "Bureaucracy and Professionalism in the Development of American Career Diplomacy," in John Braeman, Robert Bremner, and David Brody, eds., *Twentieth Century American Foreign Policy* (Columbus, Ohio, 1971), 127–28.

12. The most eloquent expositions of this economic interpretation of American involvement in foreign affairs are William Appleman Williams, *The Tragedy of American Diplomacy* (New York, 1962), and Walter LaFeber, *The New Empire: An Interpretation of American Expansion, 1860–1898* (Ithaca, N.Y., 1963).

13. Jerry Israel, "A Diplomatic Machine: Scientific Management in the Department of State, 1906–1924," in Jerry Israel, ed., *Building the Organizational Society: Essays on Associational Activities in Modern America* (New York, 1972).

14. Heinrichs, "Bureaucracy and Professionalism," 128.

15. American Embassy Association, *American Embassies, Legations, and Consulates Mean Better Foreign Business*, 5–6.

16. James B. Townsend, "Report on the Conditions of Embassies and Legations in Europe," in ibid., 37.

17. E. Clarence Jones, "Better Embassies Mean Better Business," in ibid., 23–25.

18. William Barnes and John Heath Morgan, *The Foreign Service of the United States: Origins, Development, and Functions* (Washington, D.C., 1961), 173–77.

19. Robert Wiebe, *The Search for Order, 1877–1920* (New York, 1967), 224–55.

20. The changing nature of government architecture is the subject of Lois Craig, *The Federal Presence: Architecture, Politics, and National Design* (Cambridge, Mass., 1984).

21. Ibid., 203, 213.

22. John Bassett Moore, "American Diplomacy: Its Influence and Tendencies," *Harper's* 111 (October 1905): 695.

23. See, e.g., Captain F. M. Barber, "The Government Ownership of Diplomatic and Consular Buildings," *North American Review* 190 (September 1909): 359; Perry Belmont, "The First Line of Our National Defense," *North American Review* 201 (June 1915): 886.

24. Heinrichs, "Bureaucracy and Professionalism," 143–54, 159–60.

25. Barnes and Morgan, *The Foreign Service of the United States*, 177.

26. Stanley Karnow, *In Our Own Image: America's Empire in the Philippines* (New York, 1989), 196–226.

27. The definitive study of Burnham is Thomas Hines, *Burnham of Chicago:*

Architect and Planner (New York, 1974). For a brief review of Burnham's work in the Philippines see Hines's article "The Imperial Facade: Daniel H. Burnham and American Architectural Planning in the Philippines," *Pacific Historical Review* 41 (February 1972): 33–53.

28. Burnham quoted in Jon Reps, *The Making of Urban America: A History of City Planning in the United States* (Princeton, 1965), 497–98.

29. Robert R. Reed, *City of Pines: The Origins of Baguio as a Colonial Hill Station and Regional Capital* (Center for South and Southeast Asia Studies, University of California, Berkeley, 1976), xxi.

30. Paul Wheatley, foreword to Reed, *City of Pines*, ix. See also Virginia Benitez Licuanan, *Filipinos and Americans: A Love-Hate Relationship* (Manila, 1982), for a discussion of the development of Baguio.

31. Paul Boyer, *Urban Masses and Moral Order in America* (Cambridge, Mass., 1978).

32. Daniel H. Burnham, "Report on Proposed Improvements at Manila," in *Proceedings of the Thirty-ninth Annual Convention of the American Institute of Architects* (Washington, D.C., 1906), 144.

33. For an interpretation of the architecture of the British Raj during this period see Thomas Metcalf, *An Imperial Vision: Indian Architecture and Britain's Raj* (Berkeley, Calif., 1989); Jan Morris and Simon Winchester, *Stones of Empire: The Buildings of the Raj* (New York, 1983).

34. Glenn A. May, *Social Engineering in the Philippines: The Aims, Execution, and Impact of American Colonial Policy, 1900–1913* (New York, 1980) documents the incoherence of American colonial designs.

Chapter Two
Incident at Sivry–sur–Meuse: Great War Monuments and Cemeteries in Western Europe

1. *New York Times*, 14 December 1931, 21.

2. Charles Moore, Chairman of the Commission of Fine Arts, to the Quartermaster General, 12 May 1923, Files of the Commission of Fine Arts, Record Group 66, project files 1910–1952, National Archives, Washington, D.C. (hereafter RG 66); "Proceedings of the American Battle Monuments Commission," 2 October 1923, 4–5, Files of the American Battle Monuments Commission, Record Group 117, National Archives, Suitland, Maryland (hereafter RG 117).

3. James S. Curl, *A Celebration of Death: An Introduction to Some of the Buildings, Monuments and Settings of Funerary Architecture in the Western European Tradition* (New York, 1980), 317–18.

4. On the Gettysburg Cemetery see Henry S. Burrage, *Gettysburg and Lincoln: The Battle, the Cemetery, and the National Park* (New York, 1906), 81–142; John S. Patterson, "A Patriotic Landscape: Gettysburg, 1863–1913," *Prospects* 7 (1983): 315–32.

5. Edward Steere, *Shrines of the Honored Dead: A Study of the National Cemetery System* (Washington, D.C., 1954), 10–12.

6. Ibid., 23.

7. Patterson, "A Patriotic Landscape," 315.
8. Curl, *A Celebration of Death*, 25.
9. Sharon Scholl, *Death and the Humanities* (Lewisburg, N.Y., 1984), 68.
10. Lillian B. Miller, *Patrons and Patriotism: The Encouragement of the Fine Arts in the United States, 1790–1860* (Chicago, 1966); Barry Schwartz, "The Social Context of Commemoration: A Study in Collective Memory," *Social Forces* 61 (December 1982): 374–402.
11. William Leuchtenberg, *The Perils of Prosperity, 1914–1932* (Chicago, 1958), 108–12.
12. *New York Times*, 14 February 1926, 21.
13. Henry Reilly, "Pershing's Job Today," *The World's Work* 57 (November 1928): 34.
14. U.S. Congress, House Committee on Foreign Affairs, *Hearings on H.R. 9634 and H.R. 10801: American Battle Monuments Commission*, 67th Cong., 1922, 6.
15. James Mayo, *War Memorials as Political Landscape: The American Experience and Beyond* (New York, 1988), 143.
16. Steere, *Shrines of the Honored Dead*, 24–25.
17. Ibid., 22.
18. Ralph Hayes, "A Report to the Secretary of War on American Military Dead Overseas," 1920, 14, RG 66.
19. For examples of the rhetoric of supporters see *New York Times*, 16 January 1920, 8; 18 January 1920, 9, 11; 20 January 1920, 6; 26 February 1920, 10.
20. "Minutes of the Fine Arts Commission," 21 November 1919, RG 66.
21. Hayes, "A Report to the Secretary of War," 15, RG 66.
22. Ibid., 14–15.
23. On veterans' organizations see Donald J. Lisio, "Bread and Butter Politics," in Stephen R. Ward, ed., *The War Generation: Veterans of the First World War* (Port Washington, N.Y., 1975), 38–58; Wallace Davies, *Patriotism on Parade: The Story of Veterans' and Hereditary Organizations in America* (Cambridge, Mass., 1955). For an example of veterans' support for the overseas cemeteries project see *New York Times*, 26 January 1920, 11.
24. U.S. Congress, *Hearings on H.R. 9634 and H.R. 10801*, 51.
25. Ibid., 57; *New York Times*, 7 September 1926; 7 November 1926, sec. 9, p. 16.
26. U.S. Congress, *Hearings on H.R. 9634 and H.R. 10801*, 14, 57.
27. The material in the files of the ABMC suggests that the decisions were often voted on by correspondence, and that the voting ballots were usually accompanied by recommendations of the permanent staff.
28. The controversy surrounding the "rearrangement" of graves is aired in a letter from Senator Reed to Major X. H. Price, 22 September 1925, and "Draft for ABMC's 1925 Report," 9–16, RG 117. The controversy was omitted from the final printed edition of the ABMC report.
29. Ibid.
30. John Burchard and Albert Bush-Brown, *The Architecture of America: A Social and Cultural History* (Boston, 1961), 265.

31. James Marston Fitch, *American Building: The Historical Forces That Shaped It* (New York, 1973), 207–13.

32. On Paul Cret see Elizabeth Grossman, "Paul Philippe Cret; Rationalism and Imagery in American Architecture" (Ph.D. diss., Brown University, 1980). On the official Washington style of architecture as developed in turn-of-the-century Washington, D.C., see Thomas Walton, "The 1901 McMillan Commission: Beaux Arts Plan for the Nation's Capital" (Ph.D. diss., Catholic University of America, 1980). For an overview of the federal style, see Craig, *The Federal Presence.*

33. On the Commission of Fine Arts see Sue Kohler, *The Commission of Fine Arts: A Brief History, 1910–1976* (Washington, D.C., 1977). The superimposing of official federal styles on the World War cemeteries is discussed in Elizabeth Grossman, "Architecture for a Public Client: The Monuments and Chapels of the American Battle Monuments Commission," *Journal of the Society of Architectural Historians* 43 (May 1984): 119–43.

34. On innovations in the celebration of death and the design of cemeteries see James Farrell, *Inventing the American Way of Death* (Philadelphia, 1980); Kenneth T. Jackson and Camilo José Vergara, *Silent Cities: The Evolution of the American Cemetery* (Princeton, N.J., 1989).

35. "War Memorials," *Bulletin of the Municipal Art Society of New York City* 17 (1919): 10.

36. See the text and debate of this proposed bill in U.S. Congress, *Hearings on H.R. 9634 and H.R. 10801*, 1–11.

37. Egerton Swartwout, "Memorial Buildings," *Architectural Forum* 45 (December 1926): 325–28.

38. Paul Cret, "Memorials—Columns, Shafts, Cenotaphs, and Tablets," *Architectural Forum* 45 (December 1926): 333.

39. Swartwout, "Memorial Buildings," 329–30. See also Harvey Wiley Corbett, "The Value of Memorial Architecture," *Architectural Forum* 45 (December 1926): 323.

40. The highway bill is discussed in U.S. Congress, *Hearings on H.R. 9634 and H.R. 10801*, 1–12.

41. Ibid., 20, 57.

42. Gavin Stamp, *Silent Cities: An Exhibition of the Memorial and Cemetery Architecture of the Great War* (London, 1977), 6. A pictorial survey of British war cemeteries in Europe appears in a book with a similar title: Sidney Hurst, *The Silent Cities: An Illustrated Guide to the War Cemeteries and Memorials to the "Missing" in France and Flanders, 1914–1918* (London, 1929). See also Rose Coombs, *Before Endeavours Fade* (London, 1983).

43. "An Empire's Gratitude," *The Times: War Graves Number*, 10 November 1928, ii.

44. Stanley Baldwin, "A Revelation and a Comfort," *The Times: War Graves Number*, 10 November 1928, iii.

45. Field Marshal Lord Plumer, "The Holy Land: Influence of the Cemeteries," *The Times: War Graves Number*, 10 November 1928, xiv.

46. "Help from Parliament," *The Times: War Graves Number*, 10 November 1928, viii.

47. "The Holy Land," xiv.

48. "World-Wide Labours," *The Times: War Graves Number*, 10 November 1928, viii.

49. Prince Edward, "Gratitude of the Empire," *The Times: War Graves Number*, 10 November 1928, iii.

50. "The Imperial War Graves Commission: Story of Its Work," *The Times: War Graves Number*, 10 November 1928, vi.

51. This eradication of racial distinctions in British military cemeteries was applied systematically in Europe only. I have noticed that British military cemeteries in the Middle East, where racial distinctions were a cardinal aspect of the British colonial policy, were segregated.

52. "Memorandum to the Fine Arts Commission," n.d., RG 66.

53. Major X. H. Price to General John J. Pershing, 1 February 1924, RG 117. See also General Pershing to Major Price, 18 February 1924, RG 117. The graves of Jews were marked by carved Stars of David.

54. ABMC, "Record of Proceedings, Twenty-third Meeting," 8 February 1927, 74–78, RG 117.

55. A picture and brief description of the St. Mihiel Monument is contained in ABMC, *St. Mihiel American Monument and Memorial* (Washington, D.C., 1986).

56. ABMC, *Aisne-Marne American Cemetery and Memorial* (Washington, D.C., 1983), 15–16.

57. Henry May, *The End of American Innocence: A Study of the First Years of Our Time, 1912–1917* (Chicago, 1964).

58. David Kennedy, *Over There: The First World War and American Society* (New York, 1980), 229.

59. Paul Cret, "United States Monument Near Chateau Thierry," 30 September 1927, RG 117.

60. Cret, "Memorials—Columns, Shafts, Cenotaphs, and Tablets," 335.

61. James Early, *Romanticism and American Architecture* (New York, 1965), 17.

62. Reilly, "Pershing's Job Today," 30.

63. John Pershing, "Our National War Memorials in Europe," *National Geographic*, January 1934, 5.

64. Grossman, "Paul Philippe Cret," 175.

65. ABMC, *American Armies and Battlefields in Europe* (Washington, D.C., 1938), 248–49.

66. On the different genres of battle descriptions see John Keegan, *The Face of Battle: A Study of Agincourt, Waterloo, and the Somme* (London, 1976), 28–29, 35–45, 61–67.

67. Descriptions of the Pegasus statue and other statues of Great War cemeteries may be found in Pershing, "Our National War Memorials."

68. For pictures of British tombstones in Europe see Hurst, *The Silent Cities*.

69. Grossman, "Architecture for a Public Client," 135.

70. *New York Times*, 15 September 1926, 5.

71. Ida Treat, "Is This America?" *Nation*, 19 October 1927, 422.

72. Cited in Lawrence Levine, "Progress and Nostalgia: The Self-Image of the 1920s," in Lawrence Levine and Robert Middlekauff, eds., *The National Temper: Readings in American Culture and Society* (New York, 1972), 298.

Chapter Three
From Palace to Plantation House: The Political Architecture of American Embassies, 1926-1932

1. Leuchtenberg, *The Perils of Prosperity, 1914–1932*, 107. See also Selig Adler, *The Uncertain Giant, 1921–1941: American Foreign Policy Between the Wars* (New York, 1965).
2. Robert Freeman Smith, "American Expansion and World Order," in Thomas G. Paterson, ed., *Major Problems in American Foreign Policy* (Lexington, Mass., 1984), 2:121–35.
3. Reinhold Niehbur, "Awkward Imperialists," *Atlantic Monthly*, May 1930, 670–75.
4. Charles Beard, "The American Invasion of Europe," *Harper's*, March 1929, 470–79.
5. *New York Times*, 14 February 1926, 21.
6. Barnes and Morgan, *The Foreign Service of the United States*, 177.
7. U.S. Congress, House Committee on Foreign Affairs, *Hearings on H.R. 15774*, 71st Cong., 1931; Frederick Larkin to Miss O. L. Nelson, 4 April 1932, Files of the Department of State, Record Group 59, National Archives, Washington, D.C. (hereafter RG 59), 124.01/633.
8. U.S. Congress, House of Representatives, *Report No. 1332, Purchase of Embassy, Legation, and Consular Buildings*, 64th Cong., 1917, 8.
9. John Ziolkowski, *Classical Influence on the Public Architecture of Washington and Paris* (New York, 1988), 169.
10. On the obsession with the architectural opulence of both great and second-rate powers see U.S. Congress, *Report No. 1332*, 4–7.
11. See various reports in the *New York Times* on the acquisition of palaces for American diplomatic posts: 22 March 1922, 16; 8 March 1923, 9; 1 January 1926, 11; 28 May 1926, 21; 16 July 1926, 4.
12. "United States Government Building, Rio de Janeiro," *American Architect* 122 (30 August 1922): 183–84; "Building for the United States Embassy, Rio de Janeiro, Brazil," ibid., 124 (10 October 1923): 325–26.
13. "New Embassy Building at Mexico City," *American Foreign Service Journal* 2 (October 1925): 336–37; "United States Embassy at Mexico City," *Bulletin of the Pan American Union* 59 (December 1925): 1247–49.
14 *New York Times*, 11 June 1923, 6. See also ibid., 12 June 1923, 18; 14 June 1923, 18.
15. William A. Du Puy, "Uncle Sam's Homeless Diplomats," *New York Times Magazine*, 10 February 1924, 4.
16. *New York Times*, 16 March 1926, 15.
17. Ibid., 18 February 1926, 27; 8 May 1926, 6.
18. U.S. Congress, *Hearings on H.R. 15774*, 2.

19. American Embassy Association, *American Embassies, Legations, and Consulates*, 7.

20. See the introduction to Hellmut Lehmann-Haupt, *Art Under a Dictatorship: Using Architecture as a Triumphant Symbol of Conquest* (New York, 1973), for an interesting discussion of the use of political architecture in the twentieth century.

21. Horace G. Knowles, Minister to La Paz, Bolivia, to the Secretary of State, 15 September 1911, RG 59, 124.01/66.

22. *New York Times*, 17 May 1928, 42. See also ibid., 18 March 1928, sec. 5, p. 4.

23. John Taylor Boyd, Jr., cited in William B. Rhoads, "The Colonial Revival and American Nationalism," *Journal of the Society of Architectural Historians* 35 (December 1976): 250–51.

24. Warren Susman, *Culture As History: The Transformation of American Society in the Twentieth Century* (New York, 1984), 18.

25. Ibid., 14.

26. *New York Times*, 16 August 1926, 14.

27. Du Puy, "Uncle Sam's Homeless Diplomats," 15. The article attributes the idea of White House embassies to Senator Robert La Follette. This is a mistake, as all other material suggests that the idea was presented by Senator Porter. See, e.g., "White House for Tokio," *American Architect* 118 (13 October 1920): 484.

28. Du Puy, "Uncle Sam's Homeless Diplomats," 15.

29. "Our Buildings in Foreign Countries," *American Foreign Service Journal* 8 (February 1931): 51–53.

30. Congressman Henry W. Temple in U.S. Congress, *Hearings on H.R. 15774*, 20.

31. "The British Embassy, Washington," *Country Life*, 14 January 1939, 41–42. See also "New Embassy at Washington," ibid., 24 December 1927, 943–46; "The British Embassy–Washington," ibid., 21 January 1939, 64–68.

32. William R. Taylor, *Cavalier and Yankee: The Old South and American National Character* (New York, 1957), 201, 334, 341.

33. Davidson cited in F. Garvin Davenport, Jr., *The Myth of Southern History: Historical Consciousness in Twentieth-Century Southern Literature* (Nashville, 1967), 61.

34. Gunther Stone, "Modern Architecture and the Plantation Nostalgia of the 1930s: Stone's 'Mepkin' and Wright's 'Auldbrass Plantation,'" *Journal of the Society of Architectural Historians* 34 (December 1975): 318; Harrie T. Lindeberg, "The Design and Plan of the Country House," *American Architect* 99 (12 April 1911): 133–37; Lindeberg, "A Return of Reason in Architecture," *Architectural Record* 74 (October 1933): 252–55; "Country Houses by H. T. Lindeberg," *Architectural Record* 74 (October 1933): 289–312.

35. *New York Times*, 23 May 1927, 10.

36. FSBC, *Report of the Progress on the Purchase of Sites and Construction of Buildings for the Foreign Service of the United States*, 1929.

37. Foreign Service Officer Matthew Hanna to the Secretary of State (report), 8 December 1926, RG 59, 124.

38. Estill Curtis Pennington, "The Climate of Taste in the Old South," *Southern Quarterly* 24 (Fall–Winter 1985): 7–31.

39. "Memorandum from K. Merrill Concerning the Construction of a Legation in Aden," 18 September 1928, RG 59, 125.1171/23. See also FSBC, *Report of the Progress on the Purchase of Sites and Construction of Buildings.*

40. *New York Times*, 26 September 1922, 17; 15 February 1931, 77.

41. For an analysis of the symbolism of the plantation house in Faulkner's novels see Davenport, *The Myth of Southern History*, 85–91.

42. Roosevelt quoted in ibid., 92.

43. *New York Times*, 23 May 1929, 24.

44. Ambassador Edgar Bancroft to Secretary of State Kellogg, 6 March 1925, National Building Museum, Embassy Files (hereafter NBM), folder 35.

45. Richard Boyce, "Evolution of a Consular Office: Yokohama," *American Foreign Service Journal* 13 (May 1936): 256–57, 291; Lawrence E. Allison, "Architecture in Other Climes: Japan," *Federal Architect* 9 (October 1939): 18.

46. Allison, "Architecture in Other Climes"; *New York Times*, 28 February 1932, sec. 9, p. 5; "The American Embassy, Tokyo," *Architecture* 61 (February 1930): 73–74.

Chapter Four
Interlude: Marking Time, 1933–1945

1. *New York Times*, 20 June 1942, 6.
2. Ibid., 2 October 1944, 5.
3. The responses to the commission survey are in RG 66.
4. *New York Times*, 15 March 1942, sec. 4 p. 3.
5. Ibid., 8 December 1940, sec. 7, pp. 9, 23.
6. Franklin D. Roosevelt to Secretary of State Stimson, 11 February 1934, quoted in minutes of the FSBC, February 1934, NBM, folder 33.
7. Ralph Gabriel, "Thomas Jefferson and Twentieth-Century Rationalism," *Virginia Quarterly Review* 26 (Summer 1950): 321–35.
8. A selection of these articles appears in Ralph Gabriel, *American Values: Continuity and Change* (Westport, Conn., 1974).
9. Albert Fried, *The Jeffersonian and Hamiltonian Traditions in American Politics: A Documentary History* (New York, 1968), 406.
10. *New York Times*, 26 June 1938, sec. 4, p. 10. On plans and priorities for building embassies during this period see F. Larkin to the Bureau of the Budget, Department of the Treasury (memorandum), 3 September 1938, RG 59, 124.01, and "Memorandum on New Projects," 27 May 1939, RG 59.
11. *New York Times*, 22 August 1937, sec. 6, pp. 21, 31.
12. *New York Times*, 5 January 1937, 24; 22 August 1937, sec. 6, pp. 21, 31; 26 June 1938, sec. 4, p. 10; 3 April 1941, 12.
13. Daniel Boorstin, *America and the Image of Europe* (New York, 1960), 22.
14. George Kennan cited in George Black, *The Good Neighbor: How the United States Wrote the History of Central America and the Caribbean* (New York, 1988), xviii.

15. George Allen, "New Legation and Consulate General at Baghdad," *American Foreign Service Journal* 15 (May 1938): 315–16.

16. John King Fairbank, *Chinabound: A Fifty Year Memoir* (New York, 1982), 202–9.

17. Franklin D. Roosevelt, "Speech for Jefferson Day, April 13, 1945," in Fried, *The Jeffersonian and Hamiltonian Traditions in American Politics*, 485–86.

18. *New York Times*, 19 May 1948, 7. On Truman's taste in institutional architecture see Cabell Philips, "Truman Likes These," ibid., 17 June 1951, sec. 6, pp. 18–19.

19. Paul Hadley, "United States Cultural Institutes in Other American Republics," *Publishers Weekly*, 14 April 1945, 1552. On the inordinate amount of attention given to cultural and public diplomacy in Latin America see Frank Ninkovich, *The Diplomacy of Ideas: U.S. Foreign Policy and Cultural Relations, 1938–1950* (New York, 1981), 35–50.

20. Frederick Larkin, "The American Legation, Guatemala City," *American Foreign Service Journal* 16 (November 1939): 630; Larkin, "New Legation at Managua, Nicaragua," ibid., 17 (February 1940): 88; Larkin, "The American Legation at Ciudad Trujillo," ibid., 16 (May 1939): 291; "La Residencia de EE. UU. de N.A.," *Arquitecto Peruano* 9 (May 1945): 8–20.

21. On the architecture of the Torre Tagle see Harold E. Wethey, *Colonial Architecture and Sculpture in Peru* (Westport, Conn., 1971).

22. Roberto Segre, "Communication and Social Participation," in Roberto Segre, ed., *Latin America in Its Architecture* (New York, 1981), 175–76.

23. Larkin "The American Legation at Cuidad Trujillo."

24. *New York Times*, 22 August 1937, sec. 6, pp. 21, 31.

25. On the embassy in Ottawa see *American Foreign Service Journal* 10 (February 1933): 49. The embassy in Canberra is described in the *New York Times*, 31 January 1937, 7. For a brief description of the Paris embassy see "The New U.S. Government Building in Paris," *Architecture* 70 (September 1934).

26. Comments of Assistant Secretary of State William Benton cited in Department of State, Office of Public Affairs, *America, a Full and Fair Picture: The Government's Information and Cultural Relations Program Overseas*, 1947, 34–35.

27. The development of American cultural and public diplomacy is described in Ninkovich, *The Diplomacy of Ideas*.

28. Lindeberg, "A Return of Reason in Architecture"; "Country Houses by H. T. Lindeberg." On Lindeberg's designs for the Moscow embassy see "Our Buildings in Moscow," *American Foreign Service Journal* 11 (April 1934): 176–77. On Lindeberg and the Managua embassy see *New York Times*, 6 March 1937, 6.

29. Henry-Russell Hitchcock and Philip Johnson, *The International Style Since 1922* (New York, 1932).

30. Fitch, *American Building*, 247–50.

31. Hadley, "United States Cultural Institutes," 1552.

32. Christiane C. Collins and George R. Collins, "Monumentality: A Critical Matter in Modern Architecture," *Harvard Architecture Review* 4 (Spring 1984): 16.

33. Archibald MacLeish, "Memorials Are for Remembrance," *Architectural Forum* 81 (September 1944): 111–13, 170.

34. Francis Cormier, "Comment on 'Worthy Memorials of the Great War,'" *Landscape Architecture* 34 (July 1944): 124.

35. For an example of the type and scope of local designs to commemorate the war dead, see a sample of letters reproduced in *Landscape Architecture* 34 (July 1944): 126.

36. "War Memorials," *Architectural Forum* 81 (December 1944): 96–100. See also "War Memorials," *The American City* 58 (January 1944): 35–36.

37. Charles D. Maginnis, "The War Memorial," *Architectural Forum* (September 1944): 106.

38. Lewis Mumford, cited in Cecil D. Eliot, "Monuments and Monumentality," *AIA Journal* 41 (March 1964): 69–71.

39. "Symbolism in New Deal Washington," *New York Times*, 4 August 1935, sec. 7, p. 10.

40. Frank Lloyd Wright, address to the Association of Federal Architects, cited in Craig, *The Federal Presence*, 292.

41. Joseph Hudnut, "Twilight of the Gods," *Magazine of Art* 30 (August 1937): 480–81.

42. "War Memorials," *Architectural Forum*.

43. Carl L. Schmitz cited in Marlene Park and Gerald E. Markowitz, *Democratic Vistas: Post Offices and Public Art in the New Deal* (Philadelphia, 1984), 8; see also 10–28. See also Karal Ann Marling, *Wall-to-Wall America: A Cultural History of Post-Office Murals in the Great Depression* (Minneapolis, 1982), 28–80.

44. Marling, *Wall-to-Wall America*, 293–326.

45. Vladimir Potts, "The Romanization of Washington," *Vanity Fair*, October 1931, 80.

Chapter Five
"Our Own Land on Foreign Soil": The Overseas Military Cemeteries of World War II

1. *New York Times*, 16 September 1966, 18. See also ibid., 15 May 1966, sec. 4, p. 15; 29 May 1966, sec. 4, p. 13.

2. Shenton, "They Will Never Be Forgotten"; *New York Times*, 30 May 1945, 20.

3. H. P. Caemmerer to Professor Gilmore Clark, Cornell University (memorandum), 13 November 1943, RG 66.

4. "Proceedings of the American Battle Monuments Commission," 19 November 1946, 138, RG 117.

5. U.S. War Department, Office of the Quartermaster General, *Disposition of World War II Armed Forces Dead*, 1946, 2.

6. ABMC, *Netherlands American Cemetery and Memorial* (Washington, D.C., 1986), 20–21.

7. Shenton, "They Will Never Be Forgotten," 37, 59.

8. George C. Marshall, "Our War Memorials Abroad: A Faith Kept," *National Geographic*, June 1957, 733.

9. Ibid.
10. *New York Times*, 30 May 1945, 20.
11. Ibid.
12. Brigadier Thomas North to Miss Dorothy Grafly, 16 March 1950, RG 117.
13. "In Search of a New Monumentality," *Architectural Review* 104 (September 1948): 117–28; Lewis Mumford, "Monumentalism, Symbolism, and Style," ibid., 105 (April 1949): 173–80.
14. "In Search of a New Monumentality," 127.
15. See David Gebhard, "The Moderne in the U.S., 1920–1941," *Architectural Association Quarterly* 2 (July 1970): 4–20; Martin Greif, *Depression Modern: The Thirties Style in America* (New York, 1975); Jeffrey L. Meikle, *Twentieth Century Limited: Industrial Design in America, 1925–1939* (Philadelphia, 1979).
16. Cited in Greif, *Depression Modern*, 34–35.
17. Fitch, *American Building*, 260.
18. C. W. Short and R. Stanley-Brown, *Public Buildings: A Survey of Architecture of Projects Constructed by Federal and Other Governmental Bodies Between the Years 1933 and 1939* (Washington, D.C., 1939).
19. Philip Longworth, *The Unending Vigil: A History of the Commonwealth War Graves Commission* (London, 1967), 187–237.
20. Craig, *The Federal Presence*, 294–97.
21. Aline Louchheim, "Memorials to Our War Dead Abroad," *New York Times*, 15 January 1950, sec. 2, p. 10.
22. "Memorandum for the Chairman from Admiral Thomas C. Kinkaid (Ret.), Honorable John Phillips, Mrs. Theodore Roosevelt, Mrs. Wendell Willkie, Brigadier General Benjamin O. Davis (Ret.), 1 November 1953, RG 117. See also Ralph Walker, *Ralph Walker, Architect* (New York, 1957), 121–22, 128–48.
23. For an example of this call for contemporary symbolism rather than classical allusions, see "Memo from Commission Member Keates Concerning Figurative Statues of Lee Lawrie," 11 March 1952, RG 117.
24. John Harbeson, "Our Memorials Abroad," *National Sculpture Review: American Battle Monuments Issue*, Winter 1955, 5. See also Thomas North, "American Memorials and Military Cemeteries of World War II," ibid., 14 (Spring 1965): 5, 25.
25. Jane De Hart Mathews, "Art and Politics in Cold War America," *American Historical Review* 81 (October 1976): 762–87.
26. Charlotte Devree, "Is This Statuary Worth More Than a Million of Your Money?" *Art News* 54 (1955): 34–37, 65.
27. "Souls of Clay," *Art News* 54 (1955): 17; Mathews, "Art and Politics in Cold War America," 773–78, 782.
28. National Sculpture Society, *Enduring Memory in Stone, in Metal, in Beauty* (New York, 1946).
29. Brigadier General Thomas North to Quartermaster General Major-General Thomas Larkin, n.d., RG 117.
30. Howell Walker, "Here Rest in Honored Glory," *National Geographic*, June 1957, 740.

NOTES TO CHAPTER SIX 191

31. ABMC, "Report on Survey in Europe, August–September, 1946," RG 66.
32. John Harbeson, "A Collaborative Undertaking," *AIA Journal* 36 (August 1961): 34.
33. ABMC, "Report on Survey in Europe," 2.
34. ABMC, *Florence American Cemetery and Memorial* (Washington, D.C., 1960), 7–8.
35. Richard Polenberg, *War and Society: The United States, 1941–1945* (Westport, Conn., 1972).
36. "War Memorials," *Architectural Forum*, 100.
37. For a sense of the debate on monuments, monumentality, and modernism see the comments of the founding fathers of the International Style in "In Search of a New Monumentality." See also Mumford, "Monumentalism, Symbolism, and Style."
38. Mumford, "Monumentalism, Symbolism, and Style"; "Memorials to Our War Dead Abroad." See also Devree, "Is This Statuary Worth More Than a Million of Your Money?"
39. For other examples of positive representations of machines and the American war effort see the south side of the Épinal Memorial and the ceiling at the Cambridge Memorial.
40. ABMC, *Luxembourg American Cemetery and Memorial* (Washington, D.C., 1961), 9–12, and *Épinal American Cemetery and Memorial* (Washington, D.C., 1957), 8–11.
41. John Canaday, "Our National Pride: The World's Worst Sculpture," *New York Times*, 25 July 1965, sec. 2, p. 10.
42. Devree, "Is This Statuary Worth More Than a Million of Your Money?" 34–37, 65.
43. Canaday, "Our National Pride"; "War Memorials," *Architectural Forum* 91 (December 1949): 116.

Chapter Six
Foreign Bodies: American Imperial Architecture, 1945–1965

1. "Those Do-It-Yourself Spontaneous Riots," *Time*, 18 December 1964, 27.
2. *New York Times*, 5 February 1964, 1; 6 February 1964, 1; 8 February 1964, 4, 22; 9 February 1964, sec. 4, p. 4.
3. Ibid., 8 December 1964, 1, 15; 9 December 1964, 3; 10 December 1964, 6.
4. Ibid., 11 November 1964, 1; 15 November 1964, 15; 25 October 1964, 8; 27 October 1964, 7.
5. Ibid., 28 October 1964, 1, 16.
6. Ada Louise Huxtable, "Sharp Debate: What Should an Embassy Be?" *New York Times Magazine*, 18 September 1960, 44.
7. "The Record of Outrages and the Protocol of Protection," *Life*, 19 March 1965, 39.
8. Carleton Knight, "Significant Clients: Slayton at State," *AIA Journal* 72 (February 1983): 36–42; U.S. Congress, House Committee on Foreign Affairs,

Foreign Service Buildings Act Amendments, 1959: Hearings Before the Subcommittee on State Department Organization and Foreign Operations, 1959, 4–5.

9. "The Nation's Commitments All Around the Earth," *Life,* 23 December 1957, 20–21. This entire issue was devoted to the United States' role as global cultural and political leader.

10. The expansion of the United States' "public diplomacy"—cultural programs and propaganda—is documented in Ninkovich, *The Diplomacy of Ideas.*

11. "Our New and Vaster Frontier," *Life,* 23 December 1957, 18.

12. John Foster Dulles, "Our Cause Will Prevail," *Life,* 23 December 1957, 13.

13. U.S. Congress, House Committee on Foreign Affairs, Subcommittee on State Department Organization and Foreign Operations, *Foreign Service Buildings Act Amendments, 1962,* 87th Cong., 1962, 10–11; "Architecture for the State Department," *Arts and Architecture* 70 (November 1953): 14–18.

14. U.S. Congress, *Foreign Service Buildings Act Amendments, 1962,* 10–11; "Architecture for the State Department"; *New York Times,* 26 January 1958, sec. 8, p. 1; *New York Times,* 16 June 1962, 22.

15. U.S. Congress, *Foreign Service Buildings Act Amendments, 1959,* 6, 11, 209.

16. For an example of the peripheral "sniping" of congressional opponents, see Blake Clark, "This Congressional Trip Paid Off," *National Review,* 13 October 1956, 15–16. On the ineffectual criticism of the heart of the program, the design policy, see the abortive attempts to scuttle the design of the embassy in Dublin in U.S. Congress, *Foreign Service Buildings Act Amendments, 1959,* 234–37.

17. Regional FBO Supervisor Ides van der Gracht to Deputy Secretary Lourie, 3 August 1953, RG 59, 110.4-FBO/8-353

18. United States Commission of Fine Arts, *Art and Government,* n.p.

19. U.S. Congress, *Foreign Service Buildings Act Amendments, 1959,* 10.

20. U.S. Congress, *Foreign Service Buildings Act Amendments, 1962,* 13–17.

21. On the architecture of American universities and colleges see Paul Venable Turner, *Campus: An American Planning Tradition* (Cambridge, Mass., 1984), esp. pp. 249–307.

22. Allan Temko, "American Architecture: Down to Skin and Bones," *AIA Journal* 30 (November 1958): 19–23. On the architectural philosophy of Van Der Rohe see Arthur Drexler, *Ludwig Mies Van Der Rohe* (New York, 1960), and Ludwig Hilberseimer, *Mies Van Der Rohe* (Chicago, 1956).

23. For other examples of U.S. minimalist embassies in the immediate postwar period see "U.S. Embassy Buildings," *Architectural Review* 118 (October 1955): 240–47.

24. Paul Willen, "Soviet Architecture: Progress and Reaction," *Problems in Communism* 6 (1953): 24–32.

25. "U.S. Architecture Abroad," *Architectural Forum* 98 (March 1953): 115.

26. Kent Bloomer and Charles Moore, *Body, Memory, and Architecture* (New Haven, Conn., 1977), 31–33.

27. Rudolph Arnheim, *Visual Thinking* (London, 1969); Donis A. Dondis, *A Primer of Visual Literacy* (Cambridge, Mass., 1973), 21–35; Margaret A. Hagen, *The Perception of Pictures* (New York, 1980), 10–12.

28. *New York Times*, 7 October 1953, 27, contains an analysis of the Museum of Modern Art's exhibition "Architecture for the State Department."

29. Temko, "American Architecture," 20.

30. "Architecture for the State Department," 16–17, 31, 36.

31. "U.S. Architecture Abroad," 115.

32. These thoughts of Leland King were articulated after his dismissal and during the course of his private practice in "Disciplined, Bold, Flexible, Simple, Economical," *Architectural Record* 151 (January 1972): 105–10.

33. The symbiosis between American corporate architecture abroad and the design of embassies is discussed in "U.S. Architecture Abroad," 101–15.

34. Peter Blake, "What Is 'Government Character'?" *Architectural Forum* 89 (January 1959): 76–83.

35. Leland King, "Notes for Statement at Conference with Assistant Secretary of State, Mr Wailes, and Mr Wilber/budget," 9 July 1953, NBM folder 180.

36. Richard M. Bennett, "The Architecture of Relativity," *Architectural Record* 111 (July 1952): 144–48.

37. Ibid.

38. Fitch, *American Building*, 278.

39. On the revamping of American cultural and public diplomacy to suit the strategic aims of the cold war see Ninkovich, *Diplomacy of Ideas*, 113–84.

40. John Foster Dulles to various embassies and legations, 13 August and 2 October 1953, RG 59, 124.01/8-1353. On Herter's involvement in the program see his exchange of letters with AAP member Henry R. Shepley, June–August 1958, RG 59, 120.5/6-458.

41. On the circumstances surrounding the dismissal of Leland King see Regional FBO Supervisor Ides van der Gracht to Deputy Secretary of State Lourie, 3 August 1953; Edmund Purves, Executive Director of the American Institute of Architects, to Secretary of State John Foster Dulles, 15 December 1953, RG 59, 110.4-FBO/12-1553 and 110.4-FBO/8-353. King's own somewhat hazy account of his dismissal may be found on tape in NBM.

42. U.S. Congress, *Foreign Service Buildings Act Amendments, 1959*, 10.

43. Ibid., 14.

44. U.S. Congress, *Foreign Service Buildings Act Amendments, 1962*, 15–16.

45. The procedure of the AAP and its relationship to the departmental hierarchy is discussed in U.S. Congress, *Foreign Service Buildings Act Amendments, 1959*, 16–18. For a different interpretation that places greater emphasis on the input of architects, see Jane Loeffler, "The Architecture of Diplomacy: Heyday of the United States Embassy-Building Program, 1954–1960," *Journal of the Society of Architectural Historians* 49 (September 1990): 251–78.

46. U.S. Congress, *Foreign Service Buildings Act Amendments, 1959*, 10–11.

47. "Architecture to Represent America Abroad," *Architectural Record* 117 (May 1955): 188.

48. Ibid. See also Pietro Belluschi, "Notes on Trip to Near and Middle East, April 26 to May 15, 1955," NBM, folder 43, for a typical collection of condescending remarks on the building techniques of other nations.

49. Pietro Belluschi, "Architecture and Society," *AIA Journal* 15 (February 1951): 85–91; Edward Relph, *The Modern Urban Landscape* (Baltimore, 1987), 107.

50. Walker, *Ralph Walker, Architect*, 145.

51. Ralph Walker to Harry A. McBride, Henry R. Shepley, and Pietro Belluschi (memorandum), 11 August 1955, 2, NBM, folder 48.

52. Walker, *Ralph Walker, Architect*, 144–48.

53. Pietro Belluschi, "Architecture and Society (Reed College, 1951)," in Joe Stubblebine, ed., *The Northwest Architecture of Pietro Belluschi* (New York, 1953), 11.

54. Goethe quoted in Walter Gropius, *Apollo in the Democracy: The Cultural Obligation of the Architect* (New York, 1968), 71.

55. Walter Gropius quoted in "United States Embassy Office Building, Athens," *Architectural Record* 122 (December 1957): 161.

56. Eero Saarinen, "Function, Structure, and Beauty," *Architectural Association Journal* 73 (July–August 1957): 49.

57. Edward Durell Stone, *The Evolution of an Architect* (New York, 1962), 138–39; "Buildings of the Future as a Noted Architect Sees Them: An Interview with Edward Durell Stone," *U.S. News and World Report*, 15 August 1977, 55–56; Wolf Von Eckhardt, "USA in Steel and Concrete," *Foreign Service Journal* 41 (April 1964): 25–27, 41.

58. On Chandigarh see the comments of William J. R. Curtis, "Modern Architecture, Monumentality, and the Meaning of Institutions: A Reflection on Authenticity," *Harvard Architecture Review* 4 (Spring 1984): 86–97.

59. For a brief summary of Le Corbusier's architectural philosophy—in particular, his concept of monumental building—see H. Allen Brooks, ed., *Le Corbusier* (Princeton, 1987), and Charles Jencks, *Le Corbusier and the Tragic View of Architecture* (London, 1973).

60. For a wonderful exposition of sculptural vernacular architecture in the United States see Robert Venturi, Denise Scott Brown, and Steve Izenour, *Learning from Las Vegas: The Forgotten Symbolism of Architectural Form* (Cambridge, Mass., 1977), and Reyner Banham, *Los Angeles: The Architecture of Four Ecologies* (Harmondsworth, Eng., 1973).

61. Eugene A. Santomasso, "The Design of Reason: Architecture and Planning at the 1939/40 New York World's Fair," in Helen A. Harrison, ed., *Dawn of a New Day: The New York World's Fair, 1939/40* (New York, 1980), 229–42.

62. "Critical Appraisal of the New American Embassy," *South African Architectural Record* 46 (January 1961): 27. This article is a reprint from the London *Times*, 28 October 1960.

63. Saarinen cited in Fello Atkinson, "U.S. Embassy Building, Grosvenor Square, London," *Architectural Review* 129 (April 1961): 257.

64. R. Furneaux Jordan cited in "Controversial Building in London," *Architectural Forum* 114 (March 1961): 84.

65. "Sinewy Drum for Dublin," *Architectural Forum* 121 (August–September 1964): 145–47.
66. Comments of architect John Johansen attached to correspondence between James A. Healy and Secretary of State Christian Herter, 29 September 1959, RG 59, 121.40A5.
67. "For Eire, a New Celtic Tower," *Architectural Forum* 109 (November 1958): 127–31.
68. Comments of John Johansen, RG 59, 121.40A5.
69. "DEMO's Dismal Record," *Architectural Review* 150 (September 1971): 149–51.
70. Ibid.; "Buildings for the Foreign Service," *Architectural Review* 119 (June 1956): 342.
71. On the embassy in Athens see "United States Embassy Office Building, Athens," 159–66; "The U.S. Builds in Greece," *Architectural Forum* 115 (December 1961): 118–23; "Embassy Building of the United States—Athens, Greece," *Arts and Architecture* 79 (May 1962): 12–13. On the embassy in The Hague see "A New Kind of Bearing Wall," *Architectural Record* 120 (December 1956): 171–76; "Recent Works of Marcel Breuer," *Architectural Record* 127 (January 1960): 123–38.
72. Pictures of the American Embassy in Quito, Ecuador, in "Three Buildings for the FBO," *Progressive Architecture* 43 (June 1962), reveal a screen facade that appears to follow exactly the pattern of the screens in the embassy in Baghdad.
73. Melvin Gurtov, *The United States Against the Third World: Antinationalism and Intervention* (New York, 1974).
74. U.S. Congress, *Foreign Service Buildings Act Amendments, 1959*, 209; U.S. Congress, *Foreign Service Buildings Act Amendments, 1962*, 12.
75. "USA Abroad," *Architectural Forum* 107 (December 1957): 114–23.
76. "U.S. Embassy: Accra, Ghana," *Architectural Record* 121 (June 1957): 197–202; "Eyeful in Africa," *Architectural Forum* 111 (September 1959): 134–35.
77. "U.S. Legation for Tangier," *Architectural Forum* 103 (July 1955): 156–58.
78. "L'ambasciata degli Stati Uniti a Karachi," *Domus* 391 (June 1962): 8. On Richard Neutra's problems with the design of the Karachi complex see Thomas Hines, *Richard Neutra and the Search for Modern Architecture* (New York, 1982), 233–34, 244.
79. Edward Larrabee Barnes, "Indigenous Architecture: Modern Technology and Native Tradition, U.S. Consulate for Tabriz," *Perspecta* 8 (1963): 55.
80. Edward Said, *Orientalism* (New York, 1978), 72.
81. "A Cornerstone at Baghdad," *Foreign Service Journal* 36 (February 1959): inside front cover.
82. Comptroller General of the United States, *Review of the Construction of the Embassy Office Building and Ambassador's Residence: Rabat, Morocco* (Washington, D.C., 1963).
83. Ibid.; *New York Times*, 25 July 1964, 18.
84. "Open Diplomacy," *Time*, 12 April 1963, 60–61.

85. Ibid.
86. "A Cure for Anti-American Violence," *U.S. News and World Report*, 30 March 1964.
87. Octavio Paz, "Eroticism and Gastrosophy," *Daedalus* 101 (Fall 1972): 119. This entire issue is devoted to "How Others See the United States."
88. *New York Times*, 16 June 1962, 22.
89. Ibid.
90. U.S. Congress, *Foreign Service Buildings Act Amendments, 1962*, 2–3, 10–11.

Chapter Seven
Epilogue: Retreat

1. Colonel John C. Kook, "Graves Registration in the Korean Conflict," *Quartermaster Review* 32 (March–April 1953): 18, 131–44.
2. For a comprehensive analysis of the Korean conflict as a civil war see John Halliday and Bruce Cumings, *Korea: The Unknown War* (London, 1988), and Bruce Cumings, *The Origins of the Korean War*, vol. 2 (Princeton, N.J., 1990).
3. I am indebted to Walter LaFeber for his comments on the symbolic significance of the Honolulu memorial.
4. The ABMC is currently attempting to gather funds for a national monument to the Korean conflict, a campaign that has been marred by acrimonious debate and yet-to-be-solved questions of appropriate symbolism.
5. George Mosse, *Fallen Soldiers: Reshaping the Memory of the World Wars* (New York, 1990), 224.
6. Spiro Kostof, *America by Design* (New York, 1987), 273.
7. John Carl Warnecke, "The United States Embassy in Bangkok: The Story of Its Design," *AIA Journal* 30 (November 1958): 36–40.
8. Comments of Dean Rusk in minutes of AAP meeting, 9–10 May 1963, 12, NBM, folder 44.
9. Ibid.
10. "Designed Diplomacy," *Industrial Design* 17 (June 1970): 38–41.
11. Paulsson cited in "In Search of a New Monumentality," 123.
12. Minutes of FSBC meeting, July 1929, NBM, folder 33.
13. Ibid.

Bibliographical Essay

THE FOLLOWING description of sources and historical literature covers the framework of this study only. For additional details please consult the notes.

Primary Sources

This study of American government architecture abroad began at the National Archives, where the great majority of documents pertaining to these projects are deposited in various record groups. The activities of the American Battle Monuments Commission (ABMC) in the aftermath of the two World Wars are recorded in Record Group 117, at the Suitland, Maryland, division of the National Archives. Correspondence surrounding diplomatic architecture is scattered throughout Record Group 59, the Files of the Department of State. In addition to examining the outgoing material of the Office of Foreign Buildings Operations (FBO) in this record group, I sought incoming correspondence from key diplomatic outposts, where significant diplomatic construction was under way. The Files of the Commission of Fine Arts, in Record Group 66, Project Files 1910–1952, have material on embassy construction and overseas military cemeteries as well as general information on concepts of government political architecture at home and abroad. Record Group 353, the files of interdepartmental government correspondence, contains the minutes of the Foreign Service Buildings Commission (FSBC) meetings from the late 1920s through the 1940s.

The National Building Museum in Washington, D.C., holds an extensive collection of material on diplomatic architecture abroad, in particular from the 1950s and 1960s. In addition to many recorded interviews with some of the architects of the period, the museum has obtained a selection of minutes of the State Department's Architectural Advisory Panel (AAP) from the 1950s and 1960s. Numerous appeals to both the office of the historian of the Department of State and the FBO for additional material have been quite frustrating. Both offices claim to have no records of embassy construction abroad other than the FBO's picture collection. By contrast, the ABMC in Washington, D.C., publishes a series of booklets on military cemeteries abroad, one for each cemetery.

Additional primary material is scattered throughout the professional architectural journals. As most projects were executed by private architects, eager to display their accomplishments, these trade journals have extensive pictorial essays and technical analyses of both cemeteries and diplomatic structures. The *American Foreign Service Journal* contains numerous pictures and brief descriptions of diplomatic projects. Of particular interest is the supplement to volume 13, number 11 (November 1936), which contains pictures of every American diplomatic structure in the world. Additional surveys and information on the state of diplomatic architecture prior to the Great War are included in a publication of the American Embassy Association entitled *American Embassies, Legations, and Consulates Mean Better Foreign Business* (New York, n.d.). This booklet also contains fascinating insights into the lobbying campaign for more symbolic federal architecture abroad prior to the Great War. I have gleaned much information and important insight into the ideology behind the construction of American monuments abroad from the *Congressional Record*, to which both the ABMC and the State Department submitted detailed reports on their architectural projects.

Architecture, National Symbolism, and American Culture

Wilbur Zelinsky, *Nation Into State: The Shifting Symbolic Foundations of American Nationalism* (Chapel Hill, N.C., 1988), and David Lowenthal, *The Past Is a Foreign Country* (Cambridge, Mass., 1985) are comprehensive surveys of the iconography of nationalism. Charles Alexander, *Here the Country Lies: Nationalism and the Arts in Twentieth Century America* (Bloomington, Ind., 1980), Neil Harris, *The Artist in American Society: The Formative Years, 1790–1860* (New York, 1966), and Lillian B. Miller, *Patrons and Patriotism: The Encouragement of the Fine Arts in the United States, 1790–1860* (Chicago, 1966) discuss the developing symbiotic relationship between institutional art and government in the young American republic. As this book goes to print I have come across a citation for a new book by Karal Ann Marling and John Wetenhall, *Iwo Jima: Monuments, Memories and the American Hero* (Cambridge, Mass., 1991), which presumably deals with the issue of national symbolism. Unfortunately, I have not been able to consult the book to date.

The architects involved in these projects were members of a privileged elite of institutional architects, with lucrative ties to government. As such, their own architectural tastes as well as previous relationships with institutional clients are important features of this study. I have sought an understanding of the institutional client-architect relationship by examining the planning and execution of large monumental international expositions both at home and abroad. The symbolism of international expositions is discussed in a wide variety of books, such as Robert W. Rydell, *All the World's a Fair: Visions of Empire at American International Expositions, 1876–1916* (Chicago, 1984), as well as in collections of essays, including Burton Benedict, ed., *The Anthropology of World's Fairs: San Francisco's Panama Pacific International Exposition of 1915* (Berkeley, Calif., 1983), and Helen A. Harrison, ed., *Dawn of a New Day: The New York World's Fair, 1939/40* (New York, 1980). Large government projects of the New Deal provide additional opportunities for investigating the complex relationship between architect, artist, and federal client. For the political significance of New Deal art and architecture see Belisario R. Contreras, *Tradition and Innovation in New Deal Art* (London, 1983), Phoebe Cutler, *The Public Landscape of the New Deal* (New Haven, Conn., 1985), Karal Ann Marling, *Wall-to-Wall America: A Cultural History of Post-Office Murals in the Great Depression* (Minneapolis, 1982), and Marlene Park and Gerald E. Markowitz, *Democratic Vistas: Post Offices and Public Art in the New Deal* (Philadelphia, 1984).

Two journal issues, both dedicated to monumentality and architecture, proved extremely useful: *Harvard Architecture Review* 4 (Spring 1984), and *Oppositions* 25 (1983). Paul Zucker, ed., *New Architecture and City Planning* (New York, 1944), contains articles by Sigfried Giedion, George Nelson, Louis Kahn, Philip Goodwin, and Ernest Fiene on "The Problem of New Monumentality." Of equal importance is the debate concerning democracy and monumentality, "In Search of a New Monumentality," in *Architectural Review* 104 (September 1948).

American Culture and Foreign Policy

On the nexus of American culture and foreign policy see Emily Rosenberg, *Spreading the American Dream: American Economic and Cultural Expansion, 1890–1945* (New York, 1982). Walter LaFeber's *The American Age: United States Foreign Policy at Home and Abroad since 1750* (New York, 1989) incorporates much of his earlier work on the impact of internal cultural developments on the nation's foreign policy. On the concept of cultural diplomacy—the mobilization of American arts, architecture, and culture in the service of the nation—see Frank Ninkovich, *The Diplomacy of Ideas: U.S. Foreign Policy and Cultural Relations, 1938–1950* (New York, 1981), and Frank Costigliola, *Awkward Dominion: American Political, Economic and Cultural Relations with Europe, 1919–1933* (Ithaca, N.Y., 1984). Morrell Heald and Lawrence S. Kaplan, *Culture and Diplomacy: The American Experience* (Westport, Conn., 1977), and Edward H. Berman, *The Ideology of Philanthropy:*

The Influence of the Carnegie, Ford, and Rockefeller Foundations on American Foreign Policy (Albany, N.Y. 1983), are helpful too. David Kennedy, *Over There: The First World War and American Society* (New York, 1980), Richard Polenberg, *War and Society: The United States, 1941–1945* (Philadelphia, 1972), and John Blum, *V Was for Victory: Politics and American Culture During WWII* (New York, 1976), furnish multifaceted views on the impact of world wars on American culture and society.

Political Architecture

The scholarly investigation of American political architecture is extremely sparse. There are only two significant works on American political architecture abroad. Both are articles, and both are written from the perspective of the architect and architectural historian: Jane C. Loeffler, "The Architecture of Diplomacy: Heyday of the United States Embassy-Building Program, 1954–1960," *Journal of the Society of Architectural Historians* 49 (September 1990): 251–78, and Elizabeth Grossman, "Architecture for a Public Client: The Monuments and Chapels of the American Battle Monuments Commission," *Journal of the Society of Architectural Historians* 43 (May 1984): 119–34.

For more general surveys of political architecture, a good point of departure is Lois Craig, *The Federal Presence: Architecture, Politics, and National Design* (Cambridge, Mass., 1984), a discussion of federal architecture both at home and abroad. Charles T. Goodsell, *The Social Meaning of Civic Space: Studying Political Authority Through Architecture* (Lawrence, Kans., 1988), focuses mainly on city halls and changes in design as signs of shifts in the country's political culture. James Mayo, *War Memorials as Political Landscapes: The American Experience and Beyond* (New York, 1988), looks at the architecture of military monuments from the perspective of the environmental designer. Henry-Russell Hitchcock and William Seale, *Temples of Democracy: The State Capitols of the USA* (New York, 1976) is an architectural survey of state legislative edifices. Lee Friedlander, *The American Monument* (New York, 1976), is a pictorial essay of American monuments and memorials.

I have gained important insight from the literature of European colonial architecture—in particular, the architecture of the British Raj. Among the many fascinating books on this subject are Thomas Metcalf, *An Imperial Vision: Indian Architecture and Britain's Raj* (Berkeley, Calif., 1989), and Jan Morris and Simon Winchester, *Stones of Empire: The Buildings of the Raj* (New York, 1983). Paul Rabinow, *French Modern: Norms and Forms of the Social Environment* (Cambridge, Mass.,

1989), discusses the French context of colonial architecture. Diane Ghirardo, *Building New Communities: New Deal America and Fascist Italy* (Princeton, N.J., 1989), is an important comparison of American and Italian approaches to political architecture during the 1930s and 1940s. I have found many provocative insights in George L. Mosse, *The Nationalization of the Masses: Political Symbolism and Mass Movements in Germany from the Napoleonic Wars Through the Third Reich* (New York, 1975), and, of course, Carl E. Schorske, *Fin-de-Siècle Vienna: Politics and Culture* (New York, 1980). Classic studies on totalitarian architecture in the twentieth century, such as Barbara M. Lane, *Architecture and Politics in Germany, 1918–1945* (Cambridge, Mass., 1968), Hellmut Lehmann-Haupt, *Art Under a Dictatorship: Using Architecture as a Triumphant Symbol of Conquest* (New York, 1973), and the essays in Henry A. Millon and Linda Nochlin, eds., *Art and Architecture in the Service of Politics* (Cambridge, Mass., 1978), have helped me identify the uniqueness of the American experiment with political architecture.

The literature on military cemeteries as political architecture is once again much richer outside of the American context. George Mosse, *Fallen Soldiers: Reshaping the Memory of the World Wars* (New York, 1990), and the many books on the British military cemetery system—in particular, Gavin Stamp, *Silent Cities: An Exhibition of the Memorial and Cemetery Architecture of the Great War* (London, 1977), Sidney Hurst, *The Silent Cities: An Illustrated Guide to the War Cemeteries and Memorials to the "Missing" in France and Flanders, 1914–1918* (London, 1929), and Rose Coombs, *Before Endeavours Fade* (London, 1983)—suggest many different strategies for analyzing these cultural manifestations of global warfare. In the American context, the cultural significance of cemeteries is discussed in James J. Farrell, *Inventing the American Way of Death* (Philadelphia, 1980), and Kenneth T. Jackson and Camilo José Vergara, *Silent Cities: The Evolution of the American Cemetery* (Princeton, N.J., 1989). The Civil War experience is, of course, the obvious place to begin an analysis of military cemeteries, but, to date, the literature is quite poor. One particularly lucid and concise work is John Patterson, "A Patriotic Landscape: Gettysburg, 1863–1913," *Prospects: The Annual of American Cultural Studies* 7 (1982): 315–33. Michael Wilson Panhorst, "Lest We Forget: Monuments and Memorial Sculpture in National Military Parks on Civil War Battlefields, 1861–1917" (Ph.D. diss., University of Delaware, 1988), is useful as well.

Index

Note: Page numbers in italic refer to illustrations.

Acropolis, 157
Aden, 82. *See also* Yemen
Africa, 94, 96, 139, 158, 160, 161
Amateis, Edmund, 122, *123*
Aldrich and Chase, *81*
American Armed Forces, 29, 35, 36, 167
American Battle Monuments Commission (ABMC), 3, 4, 8, 39, 40, 42–45, 49, 55, 58, 61, 91, 92, 104, *105*, 107–11, 116, 117, 120–23, 127, 133, 134, 168, 169, 173, 196
American Embassy Association, 20, 21
American Expeditionary Forces (AEF), 30, 50, 111
American Foreign Service Journal, 65
American Historic and Scenic Society, 34
American Institute of Architects (AIA), 4, 41, 55
American legion, 61
American Moderne, 114. *See also* Depression Modern; Machine-Age Design
anti-Americanism, 61, 80, 136–37
Architectural Advisory Panel (AAP), 148–52, 153, 157, 164, 172
Architectural Forum, 104, 105, 107
Architectural Review, 113, 116, 156
Argentina, 84
Arkansas, 61
Asia, 79, 83, 86, 158
Athens, 151, 157

Baguio, 24, 25, 26, 28, 29
Baker, Herbert, 176
Baldwin, Stanley, 46
Baltimore, 94
Bancroft, Edgar, 86
Battle of Chatanooga, 31
Bauhaus, 115, 147, 157
Beijing, 22, 70, 72
Boxer Revolt, 34, 35
Buchanan, James, 17
Burnham, Daniel, 24–28, 41

CBS building, 153
cemeteries and memorials, American military: Aisne-Marne, 56; Ardennes, 117, *119*, 128, *131*; Arlington, 31, 35, 45, 48; Battery Park, 168; Battleground, 31; Brittany, 122, 127; Brookwood, 49; Chateau-Thierry, 53, *53*; Epinal, 112, 122; Flanders Field, 49; Florence, 126; Honolulu, 168, 169; Lorraine, 124, *125*; Luxembourg, 111, 113, 120, *121*, 130, 133, 149; Manila, 113, 117, *118*; Margraten, 113, 124, *125*, 134; Meuse-Argonne, 49, 57; Mexico City, 35; Montfaucon, 50, *51*; Montsec, 50; National Memorial Cemetery of the Pacific, 168; Nettuno, 128, *130*; Normandy, 111, 128, *129*; Oise-Asne, 49, *59*; Presidio, 35, 168; Pyonyong, 167; Rhone, 122; Sivry-sur-Meuse, 30; Somme, 49, 57, *58*; St. Mihiel, 50, *52*, 57; Suchon, 167; Tongyok, 167; Vietnam Memorial, 169
cemeteries, British military, 45–47, 116, 184n.51
cemetery design, 58–60, 118, 122, *123*, 124–27, 128; British influence, 46, 48, 58; Civil War influence, 57, 61, 169; classical influence, 31, 32, 36, 38, 50, 54–55, 66, 112, 120, 126; medieval influence, 55, 56; modernism, 110, 120; New Deal influence, 107, 118; Scrapped Classicism, 116, 117, 127, 133, 142, 168
ceremonial architecture, 127
Chandigarh, 152
Charleston, South Carolina, 79
Chicago, 24, 41
Chile, 67
China, 34, 70, 72, 80, *81*, 98, 99
Choate, Joseph H., 15
"City Beautiful" movement, 24, 25, 29, 174
Civil Service Act of 1871, 19
civil service reform act of 1883, 18
Civil War, 29, 31, 32, 33, 35, 45, 49, 54
Clansmen, The, 78
Cleveland, 24

Cleveland, Grover, 18, 19
Columbian Exposition of 1893, 24, 41
Commission of Fine Arts (CFA), 4, 8, 41, 42, 66, 91, 113, 122, 148
Congressional Record, 138
Constantinople, 22
Consulates, American: Amoy, 22, *82*; Fukuoka, 158, *159*; Jerusalem, 92; Seoul, 22; Tabriz, 162; Tahiti, 22; Yokohama, 22, 86, *87*. *See also* Embassies; Legations
Coolidge, Calvin, 63, 65, 70
Costa, Lucio, 114
Côte Dame Marie, 57
Country Life, 76
Cret, Paul, 41, 42, 43, 44, 53, 54, *55*, 112, 116, *117*, 127, 176
Crusades, 55
Cuba, 34, 37, 80
Cuba-China Battlefield Commission, 34
Curl, James, 31
Curti, Merle, 18
Cyprus, 165

Dailey, Gardner, 117, *118*
Davidson, Donald, 78
Dawes, Rufus B., 17
DeLue, Donald, 122, *129*
Department of the Environment (Britain), 157
depression (1890s), 19
Depression Modern, 114, *115*. *See also* American Moderne; Machine-Age Design
Directorate of Estate Management Overseas (DEMO), 157
Dixon, Thomas, 78
Dondero, George, 121
Dulles, John Foster, 139, 148
Dulles International Airport, 153
Dutch Colonial, 92

Early, James, 55
Embassies, American: Accra, 160, *161*; Athens, 151, 157, *158*; Baghdad, 96, 158, *159*, 162; Bangkok, 22, 170, *171*; Beijing, 22, 70, 72; Canberra, 101; Chungking, 96, *98*; Ciudad Trujillo, 99, 101; Constantinople, 22; Copenhagen, 143; Dublin, 155, *156*, 161; Guatemala City, 99; The Hague, 157; Havana, 143; Helsinki, 101; Karachi, 162; Lima, 83, 99, *100*, 142; London, 3, 21, 101, 152, 153–55, *154*, 161; Madrid, 143; Managua, 99, 103; Manila, 25, 26, *27*; Mexico City, 69; Monrovia, 94, *95*, *96*; Moscow, 93; New Delhi, 152, *164*; Ottawa, 101, 177; Paris, 101; Rabat, 162, *163*; Rio de Janeiro, 67, *68*, 143, *144*; Tokyo, 22, 84, 86, *87*, 88. *See also* Consulates; Legations
Embassies, British, 76–77, 156
Embassies, Soviet, 143
embassy and consulate design: British influence, 76–77; classical and Beaux Arts, 41, 68, 73, 79, 106, 116, 117, 154, 157; colonial design, 74, 80, 84, 85; early national style, 93, 94, 173; eclecticism, 86; expressionism, 152, 170; Georgian style, 101; historicism vs. modernism, 73; International Style, 142, 143, 145–48, 151; landscaping, 83–84, 100–101; little White Houses, 26, 75, 86, 96, 98, 99, 101; palatial design, 9, 67, 69, 75, 84, 173; post office style, 70; plantation style, 6, 7, 9, 76–88, 93, 94, 99, 100, 173; pseudo-Moslem style, 158, 161, 162; pseudo-traditional style, 158; Spanish colonial style, 25, 99, 100, 143
Enduring Memory, 122

Fairbank, John King, 98
Faulkner, William, 85
Federal Reserve Building, 117
Federal Triangle, 66, 71
Finland, 101
Fitch, James Marston, 115
Folger Shakespeare Library, 117
Foreign Policy Association, 85
Foreign Service Buildings Act, 166
Foreign Service Buildings Commission (FSBC), 6, 65, 70, 75, 79, 84–86, 93, 140, 177
Foreign Service Buildings Office, 65
Forgie, George B., 15
France, 28, 30, 36–38, 40, 42, 44, 48, 50, 53, 61, 67, 74, 79, 80, 91, 98, 100, 109, 112, 124, 130
Fried, Albert, 94

Gabriel, Ralph, 93
Galbraith, John Kenneth, 163
Gallman, Waldemar J., 149

INDEX

Germany, 67, 113, 134
Gestalt, 143
Gettysburg, 31, 32, 39, 45, 48
Ghana, 136, 137, 160, *161*
Giedion, Sigfried, 113, 116
Gilbert, Cass, 177
Goethe, 151
Gold Star Fathers' Association, 38
Gold Star Mothers, 40
Gone with the Wind, 85
Good Neighbor policy, *99*
Greece, 32, *158*
Griffith, D. W., 78
Gropius, Walter, 113, 114, 147, 151, 157, *158*, 176
Gurtov, Melvin, 160

Hamlin, Talbot, 113
Harbeson, John, 112, 113, 120, 124, 126
Harding, Warren, 40, 63
Harrison and Abramovitz, 143, *144*, 152
Hart, Frederick, *169*, *170*
Havana, 143
Hawaii, 168
Hays, Wayne, 165
Hazzard, Elliot, *82*
Herter, Christian, 148
Hindenberg Line, 57
Hitchcock, Henry-Russell, 113
Hitler, Adolf, 133
Hoffman, Malvina, 122, *123*
Holford, William, 113
Hoover, Herbert, 33, 64
House Appropriations Committee, 69
House Armed Services Committee, 109
House Committee on Public Works, 121
House Foreign Affairs Committee, 66, 70, 71, 165
Howe, George, *58*
Hudnut, Joseph, 106
Hughes, Charles Evans, 63
Huntington Mausoleum, 106
Huxtable, Ada Louise, 137

Iliad, 32
India, 80, 152, 163, *164*
Indonesia, 137
Industrial Design, 172
International Style exhibition, 103, 104
International Style, The, 113
Iran, 16, 162. *See also* Persia
Iraq, 97, 158, *159*

Ireland, 155, *156*
Italy, 28, 175

Japan, 80, 86, 88, 158, *159*, 165
Jaquet, Franz, *100*
Jefferson, Thomas, 3, 92–94, 98
Jefferson Memorial, 106
Jennewein, C. Paul, 118
Jennings, Allyn R., *125*
Jerusalem, 92
Johansen, John M., *155*, *156*
Jones, E. Clarence, 21
Jones, Roger W., 166

Kearny, Stephen, 35
Kellogg, Frank, 63, 70, 80, 86
Kennan, George, 96
Kennedy, David, 54
Ketchum, Gina, and Sharp, *163*
Khartoum, 137
King, Leland W., 99, *100*, 142, 146, 148
Kinkaid, Thomas, 120
Korea, 167, 168, 169
Korean War, 167, 168n.4, 196
Kostof, Spiro, 11, 169

Larkin, Frederick, 142
Latin America, 17–18, 66–68, 79–83, 99, 100, 158, 172
Lawrie, Lee, 122, *123*
Le Corbusier, 152, 153
Legations, American: Baghdad, 97; Managua, 103; Mexico City, 68, 69; Monrovia, *95*, 96; Teheran, 17. *See also* Consulates; Embassies
Leopard's Spots, The, 78
Leuchtenberg, William, 33, 63
Lewis, Peirce, 10
Liberia, 94, *95*, 96
Life, 139
Lima, 80, 82, 100, 142
Lin, Maya Ying, 169
Lincoln, Abraham, 32, 44
Lindeberg, Harrie T., 79, 93, 102, *103*
Linthicum, J. Charles, 71, 75, 176
Lippmann, Walter, 61
Lisbon, 91
London, 15
Lowden Act, 22, 23, 64
Ludington, Marshall I., 35
Lutyens, Edwin, 76, 77, 176

Maastricht, 134
Machine-Age Design, 114. *See also* American Moderne; Depression Modern
MacLeish, Archibald, 104, 105
Madden, Martin B., 69
Magonigle, Harold Van Buren, 86, *87*
Managua, 80–82, 85, 103
Manila, 24–29
Manship, Paul, *130*
Marathon, 38–39, 112, 126
Marshall, George C., 111–13
Massachusetts Institute of Technology, 149
Matanzas, 80
May, Henry, 54
McBride, Harry, 149
McCrae, John, 49
McDonald, James, 85
McKim, Mead, and White, 50
McKinley, William, 18
Mechanization Takes Command, 113
Meigs, Russell, 31
memorial architecture, debates about, 42–44, 105–8, 175
Mepkin plantation, 79
Mestrovic, Ivan, 122
Mexico, 34–36, 67
Mexico City, 35, 68, 69
Middle East, 158, 184n.51
Ministry of Public Works (Britain), 157
Mitchell, Margaret, 85
Monticello, 93
Moore, John Bassett, 23
Morgan, Jay, 86, 87
Morgan, J. P., 21
Morocco, *163*
Morris, Richard B., 3
Moscow, 93, 102
Mott, T. Bently, 91
Mukden, 82
Mumford, Lewis, 106, 114
Museum of Modern Art, 103
Mussolini, Benito, 133

Natchez, Mississippi, 83
National Archives, 65, 138
National Gallery of Art, 149
National Geographic, 112
National Sculpture Society, 5, 121, 122
Netherlands, The, 113, 124
Neue Sachlichkeit, 143
Neutra, Richard, 162

New Deal, 107
New Delhi, 26, 76, 152
New Jersey, 45
"New Objectivity," 143
New Orleans, 94
Newport, Kentucky, 70, *73*
Newton, Isaac, 55
New York, 79, 86, 103, 117, 143, 149, 153, 168
New York Times, 75, 106, 112
New York World's Fair (1939), 153
Nicaragua, 80, *81*, 82, 103
Niebhur, Reinhold, 63
Nkrumah, Kwame, 136
North, Thomas, 111, 113

Observer, 154–55
Office of Foreign Buildings Operations (FBO), 4, 6, 8, 96, 99, 101, 102, 140–43, 146–50, 158, 162, 164–66, 172
Office of Information and Culture (OIC), 101–2
Olmsted, Frederick Law, 42
Orwell, George, xi

Packard, Frank, 67, *68*
Palestine, 47, 92
Panama City, 80
Panofsky, Erwin, 57
Paris, 61, 101, 176
Parsons, William, 25
Patterson, John, 31
Patton, George C., 111
Paulsson, Gregor, 113, 175
Paz, Octavio, 165
Peace Corps, 23
Pennsylvania, 71
Pericles, 32, 112, 126
Pershing, John J., 30, 34, 40, 111
Persia, 16–17. *See also* Iran
Peru, 80, 82–83, 99–100
Philippines, 23, 26–29, 37, 41, 174; American colonial policy in, 23–24
Player, Emerson, 136
Polenberg, Richard, 127
political architecture: definition of, 9–10; Soviet, 143
Pope, John Russell, 50, *51*, 66, 106
Porter, Stephen G., 71, 75, 85, 176
Porter Act, 65, 70
Presidio (San Francisco), 35, 168
Price, Xenophon H., 40, 44

INDEX

Propylea, 50, 52, 120
Prown, Jules, 10

Quartermaster General Corps, 40, 110, 111

Rapuano, M., *125*
Reed, David A., 40
Reed College, 151
Reinhard, Hofmeister, and Walquist, 117, *119*
Remembrance and Victory, 104
Rio de Janeiro, 67, *68*, 143, *144*
Rivers, Mendel L., 109, 110
Rockefeller Museum (Jerusalem), 92
Rogers Act, 64
Rome, 26, 28
Roosevelt, Alice, 111, 120
Roosevelt, Franklin D., 85, 92–94, 98, 99, 101, 102, 104
Roosevelt, Kermit, 111
Roosevelt, Quentin, 111
Roosevelt, Theodore, 19, 44, 71
Roosevelt, Theodore, Jr., 111
Roth, Alfred, 114, 152
Rusk, Dean, 171, 172

Saarinen, Eero, 3, 153, *154*
Said, Edward, 162
Sanctuary, 85
San Francisco, 24, 35, 37, 168, 176
Santa Cruz, Bolivia, 137
Satterthwaite, Joseph C., 149
Scholl, Sharon, 32
Scott, Winfield, 35
Segre, Roberto, *99*, *100*
Sert, José Luis, 159, 162
Shepley, Henry R., 149
Simla, 25, 26
Sivry-sur-Meuse, 30
Smith, Henry Nash, 16
Sound and the Fury, The, 85
Soviet Union, 93
Space, Time, and Architecture, 113
Spain, 21, 67
Spanish-American War, 21, 34, 35, 37
Steere, Edward, 35
Stimson, Henry, 71, 176
St. Louis Arch, 153
Stone, Edward Durell, 79, 152, 163, *164*
supervising architect of the Treasury Department, 22, 70, 72, 73, 95

Sussman, Warren, 74
Swartwout, Egerton, 43, 44, 50, 52, 66

Taft, William Howard, 24, 41
Tardie, André, 30
Tarnsey Act, 22
Taylor, William, 78
Taylor, Zachary, 35
Teague, Walter Darwin, 115
Temko, Allan, 145
Thailand, *171*
Thermopylae, 31
Thomas, George H., 31
Tokyo, 22, 86
Torre Tagle, 99
Treasury Standardization Act of 1915, 22
Truman, Harry, 99
Tunisia, 113

United Nations, 143, 152
United States Information Service (USIS), 139
University of Pennsylvania, 112
University of Virginia, 93
U.S. News and World Report, 165

vandalism, 61, 136
Van Der Rohe, Ludwig Mies, 143, 147
Vanity Fair, 108
Venezuela earthquake, 16
Versailles, 26, 28
Veterans Administration, 168
Vichy, 91
Vietnam, 172
Vietnam War, 168, 169
Voice of America, 102

Walker, Ralph T., 120, *121*, 122, 133, 149, 151
Wall Street, 41
War Department, 33, 35, 40
Warnecke, John Carl, 170–72
Washington, D.C., 24, 28, 31, 32, 38, 41, 42, 66, 76, 96, 106–8, 153, 169
Washington Monument, 44
Weber, Kem, 73
Weese, Harry, 160, *161*
Werking, Richard, 18
West Point, 50
Wheatley, Paul, 25
Wiebe, Robert, 22

Wilson, Woodrow, 61
Wisconsin, 45
World's Fair of 1924, 67
Wren, Christopher, 76
Wright, Frank Lloyd, 106, 147

Wurster, William, 172

Yale University, 169
Yemen, 80. *See also* Aden
Yokohama, 86

Printed by Libri Plureos GmbH in Hamburg, Germany